The Scottish Soldiers of Fortune

"HE RESCUED A CHILD."

The Scottish Soldiers of Fortune

Mercenaries in Foreign Service from the 14th to 19th Centuries

James Grant

LEONAUR

The Scottish Soldiers of Fortune
Mercenaries in Foreign Service from the 14th to 19th Centuries
by James Grant

First published under the title
The Scottish Soldiers of Fortune

Leonaur is an imprint of Oakpast Ltd

ISBN: 978-0-85706-816-3 (hardcover)
ISBN: 978-0-85706-817-0 (softcover)

http://www.leonaur.com

Publisher's Notes

The views expressed in this book are not necessarily
those of the publisher.

Contents

Introduction

It is intended to give, in this work, as far as possible, a faithful record of the worth and valour of those military adventurers, the "Quentin Durwards" and "Dugald Dalgettys" of other days, who carried the name of Scotland with honour under every European banner, from the earliest period; but more particularly of those who, in the seventeenth century, by the force of circumstances—such, for instance, as the union of the Crowns, which brought temporary peace at home— were enabled to offer their swords and services to the monarchs of other countries.

The number of these Scottish Soldiers of Fortune was very great, and in detailing their adventures and achievements during the sixteenth and seventeenth centuries, not only individuals, but in some instances entire regiments, almost armies of them, will have to be dealt with as there were fully 13,000 under Gustavus Adolphus, "the Lion of the North" (as Dugald Dalgetty has it). About the same number went at various times to Denmark, 3,000 were in Russia, some 6,000 in Holland, 3,000 in France at least, and others in Prussia, Spain, and Italy, making more than 40,000 Scottish soldiers on the Continent, exclusive of 3,000 sent to the Isle Rhé under the Earl of Morton.

Their achievements will form, it is hoped, a stirring addition to our military annals, omitted in Scottish history, and will further show how our people, in whatever land they are cast, rise above those by whom they are surrounded, as surely as oil rises above water, to quote a writer who certainly was no friend to Scotland or her fame; and how many of them won the highest honours, civil and military— honours which many of their lineal descendants hold in the lands of their adoption.

It will be shown how Scotsmen trained the armies and founded the fleets of Russia; how for generations the old Scots Brigade of immortal memory was the boasted "Bulwark of Holland"; while second to none in war and glory were the Scottish Guard of the French Kings—that Guard of which only four were left alive when Frances I gave up his sword on the field of Pavia.

Moreover, in this new mine of Scottish history, many, it is hoped, may discover the names of ancestors, relatives, and clansmen hitherto unknown to them.

CHAPTER 1

The Scots in Russia

Among the earliest Scottish adventurers in Russia was John Carmichael, son of the Laird of Howgate, and grandson of James Carmichael of Hyndford and that ilk, who took service under the Czar Ivan Basilowitz, a prince who did much to promote the civilisation of his subjects, by inviting artisans from Lübeck and elsewhere, and who first formed a standing army—the *Strelitz*, or Body Guard of Archers—at the head of which he conquered Kazan in 1552, and two years subsequently Astrakan.

John Carmichael, at the head of 5,000 men, greatly distinguished himself at the siege of Pleskov, in the district of Kiev, then invested by Stephen, King of Poland, when its garrison was said to consist of 70,000 foot and 7,000 horse (which seems barely probable); and of this city, then the only walled one in Muscovy (*Atlas Geo.*, 1711), John Carmichael was made Governor.

Feodor, the successor of Ivan, in 1595 gave up to Sweden the province of Esthonia, where at some early period the Douglases must have acquired lands, as there is a place there still named the Douglasberg; but the last heiress of that line (says Murray, in his letters from the Baltic, 1841), the Countess of Douglas, was married to Count Ingelstrom. According to *Relations of the most Famous Kingdomes*, published in 1630, the number of Scotch and Dutch in the *Czar's* service is given at only 150 "all in one band."

General Baron Manstein, in his *Memoirs of Russia* (1773), tells us that during the war with Poland the Czar Alexis Michailowitz, grandson of Feodor, who succeeded to the throne in 1645, formed his regiments of infantry on the European plan, and gave the command of them to foreign officers. "The Regiment of Boutinsky had subsisted ever since 1642; one Dalziel commanded it," he records; "this regiment was composed of fifty-two companies, each of a hundred men. There are also to be seen ancient lists of the regiment of the First Moskowsky of the year 1648: a General Drummond was the commander."

The name of the former is pretty familiar to the Scots as that of the terrible old "Persecutor," Sir Thomas Dalziel of the Binns, whose spirit is yet averred to haunt the fields where he slew the children of the Covenant, who was supposed to be shot-proof, and whose spectre, with a voluminous white "vow-beard," still haunts the house in which he was born and the tomb in which he was laid at Binns, in 1685.

After serving as colonel in the Scottish contingent of eight battalions sent in 1641 to protect our Ulster colonists, being Governor of Carrickfergus, and fighting at Benburb and leading a brigade at Worcester, he was committed to the Tower of London; but escaped to reach Russia, where a letter from Charles II, then at Cologne, at once procured him rank in the Russian service when in his 53rd year; but some obscurity involves his movements in that country, as the wars in which he was engaged but little interested the rest of Europe.

The other officer. Lieutenant-General Drummond, was afterwards Governor of Smolensko, a city even then of great strength; and was the same officer who brought into Scotland the use of the thumbscrew as an instrument of torture.

Finding them skilful and brave, Alexis invited other Scots to join his army; and erelong, says General Manstein, three thousand of them arrived in Russia "after the defeat and imprisonment of Charles I. These were very well received; they had a place assigned them contiguous to the town of Moscow, where they built good houses and formed that part of this great city which is distinguished to this day by the name of *Inostranaya Sloboda*, or the habitation of strangers."

One of these adventurers was very probably Christopher Galloway, the Scottish horologer, who constructed the great clock in the ancient tower of the *Spaski* at Moscow, stated to have been done about this time.

Among these was certainly James Bruce, who became a general, attained the highest honours, and whose successor was afterwards the plenipotentiary of the *Czar* at the Treaty of Neistadt. Two of this name won distinction on the Continent. In the German memoirs of Henry James Bruce (whom we shall ere long meet in the Prussian service) he begins thus:—

James Bruce and John Bruce, cousins, and descendants of the family of Airth, in the county of Stirling, a branch of the family of Clackmannan), formed a resolution, during the troubles by Oliver Cromwell, to leave their native country and push their fortunes abroad; and as there were some ships in the port of Leith ready to sail for the Baltic, they agreed to go to that part of the world; but as there happened to be two of these ships' masters of the same name, by an odd mistake the cousins embarked in different vessels—one bound to Prussia, the other to Russia—by which accident they never again saw each other. John Bruce, my grandfather, landed at Köningsberg, went to Berlin, and entered the service of the Elector of Brandenburg.

His brother James, in the Russian service, was the first officer to render the artillery of that country efficient, and this was perfected by his grandson, under Peter, by whom the latter was made Master-General of the Ordnance. "Artillery was known in Russia," says Baron Manstein, "so long ago as the reign of Ivan Basilowitz II; but the pieces were of enormous size, and quite unserviceable."

Under the Master-General Bruce it was soon made equal to any artillery in Europe, and by 1714 it numbered 13,000 pieces. Bruce had foundries at Moscow, St. Petersburg, Woronitz, Catharinenburg, and other places, and to each regiment of horse and foot two 8-lb. field-pieces were attached. Bruce invited his kinsman, Henry James (whose memoirs we have quoted), to join him in Russia, which he did about 1710 with the rank of Captain of Engineers and Artillery. Manstein also records that the elder Bruce "took care to form a body of engineers. He instituted schools at Moscow and St. Petersburg, where youth were taught practical geometry, engineering, and gunnery." And this at a time when the Muscovites despised all science, looked upon a mathematician as a sorcerer, and nearly slew a Dutch surgeon for having a skeleton in his study. (*Earl of Carlisle*, etc.)

The Scots had much to do in developing discipline among the half-barbarous hordes of the Russian army. The *Atlas Geographus*, an old topographical work published at the Savoy in London in 1711, says that the Russians, in endeavouring to bring their soldiers under better discipline, "make use of a great many Scots and German officers, who instruct them in all the warlike exercises that are practised by other European nations."

For a long period, says Manstein, Russia had no other troops than the Strelitus, ill-disciplined, ill-clothed, and armed with whatever came to hand; few had firearms, but many had a battle-axe called a *berdash*; the rest had only wooden clubs.

In the early part of the eighteenth century their infantry were armed with a musket, sword, and hatchet, the latter slung behind. Their cavalry wore steel caps and corselets, and were armed with bows, sabres, spears, mauls, and round targets; and during the epoch of Dalziel, Drummond, Bruce, and the Gordons the army had a monster battle-drum, braced on the backs of four horses abreast, with four drummers at each end to beat it.

The scene of their first active service was against the Poles, with whom Alexis Michailowitz had gone to war in 1653, and from whom he captured Smolensko, the government of which was given to General Drummond, and dreadful devastations followed in Livonia at the storming of Dorpt, Kokenhousen, and many other places.

Dalziel, now raised to the rank of full general, commanded against the Tartars and the Turkish armies of Mohammed IV (1654-5), and in these contests, waged at the head of barbarous hordes against hordes equally barbarous, the wanderer must have acquired much of that unyielding sternness, if not ferocity, which characterised his future proceedings in his own country. In these campaigns quarter was never asked nor given; prisoners were shot, beheaded, impaled, or put to death by slow fires, and by every species of torture that Muscovite brutality or the most refined cruelty the Orental mind could suggest; and in this terrible arena of foreign service was schooled the future Colonel of the Scots Greys and commander of the Scottish troops—the scourge of the Covenanters.

After eleven years of this wild work. Sir Thomas Dalziel and General Drummond were invited home by Charles II, whose restoration was accomplished. The first-named officer requested from the *Czar* a certificate of his faithful service in Russia. It was given under the great seal of the Empire, and a part of it states:

"That he formerly came hither to serve our Great Czarish Majesty: whilst with us, he stood against our enemies and fought valiantly. The military men under his command he regulated and disciplined, and himself led them to battle, and he did and performed everything faithfully as a noble commander."

From Russia he was accompanied by his comrade, General William Drummond of Cromlix, who had also fought at Worcester, and who in 1686 was created Lord Drummond and Viscount Strathallan, and was ultimately Lord of the Treasury, and on the death of Dalziel became commander-in-chief of the Scottish army. He died in 1688. There can be little doubt that these two officers, who, Burnett says, were "not without difficulty sent back by the *Czar*," returned to Scotland with hearts boiling with rancour against the party which had sold the king and driven themselves into long exile.

After the defeat of Montrose at the Battle of Philiphaugh there came into the service of Russia Colonel Walter Whiteford—son of Walter Whiteford, Bishop of Brechin in 1634, and previously Rector of Moffitt, but who was deposed by the General Assembly of 1638—an officer who figured in a very dark and terrible episode.

While he was at The Hague with Montrose there came thither a Dr. Dorislaus, a D.G.L., a native of Delft, but who had been a Professor in Gresham College, was Judge-Advocate to the Army of Essex, and as such had assisted at the trial of Charles I. While he was at dinner in an inn, Colonel Whiteford, with eleven English cavaliers, entered the room with their swords drawn, and telling all who were present "not to be alarmed," added sternly "that their only object was the agent of the rebel Cromwell"; and crying, "Thus dies one of our king's judges," they stabbed Dorislaus to death. "The first thrust was given by Whiteford, who thereafter clave his skull by one blow of his broadsword."

From The Hague, Whiteford joined the Russian army, with which he served for several years, and with which he remained until the accession of James VII, when he returned to Edinburgh, where he was resident in 1691. (Dodd's *Hist.*, fol., Brussels; Echard, Tindal's *Rapin*, etc.) His father, the bishop, was a daring prelate, who never ascended the pulpit without a brace of pistols under his cassock.

The Russia to which the Scots of those days went was a barbarous land indeed. In Geijer's *History of the Swedes* a state of Russia was drawn up for Gustavus Adolphus—

> There are two causes of weakness in Russia, one, corruption of the clergy, whence the education of the people was wretched, so that gluttony and bloodshed were not vices, but matters of boast; the other was the foreign (Scots and German) soldiery. For the Muscovites, though hating everything outlandish (or foreign), could effect nothing without foreign aid. All they accomplished was done by treachery and force of numbers. The indigenous soldier received no pay, therefore he robbed. . . . With respect to taxes there was no law, but the lieutenants ex-

torted what they could, and took bribes for remissness. The condition of the lower class of the Russians was miserable from four causes—slavery; from the multiplicity of races; through the weight of imposts; the number of festival days, which are consumed in debauchery. Laws are unknown, and the peasants, who must labour five days of the week for their lords, have only the sixth and seventh to themselves.

CHAPTER 2

The Scots in Russia—(Continued)

The arrival in Russia of the two Generals Gordon, of Marshal Ogilvie and others, tended still farther to develop in the army the seeds of good discipline sown by their Scottish predecessors.

The principal of these, General Alexander Gordon of Auchintoul, wrote a life of the Czar Peter the Great, to which he prefixed a memoir of himself. It was published at Aberdeen in 1755, and (according to the *Nouvelle Biographie Générale*) in German at Leipzig ten years subsequently.

This officer was the son of Lewis Gordon of Auchintoul, Lord of Session in 1688 (whose predecessor was Lord Edmondston), by his wife Isobel Gray of Braik. He was born in 1669, and in 1688 entered, as a cadet, one of the ill-fated Scottish companies raised by desire of James VII to assist the French in the war in Catalonia.

In these companies were Major Buchan of Auchmacoy, Irvine of Cults, Colonel Wauchop of Niddry, Graham of Braco (afterwards a Capuchin friar), and many other Scottish gentlemen of good family.

In that service young Gordon carried a musket for two severe campaigns, and eventually was made a captain by Louis XIV.

In 1693 he went to Russia to push his fortune, and there met—already high in position and rank—his clansman, General Patrick Gordon of Auchleuchries, in Aberdeenshire, the general-in-chief of the whole Russian army, through whom he obtained his first commission therein as captain, we believe from the subsequent incident.

He had been invited to a festive gathering, where several young Russian nobles were present, and as these were rather prone to insult all strangers (but more especially Scots), "when in liquor," he states, he soon heard disrespectful language applied to foreigners, and particularly to his own countrymen. Gordon's blood took fire at once.

Patrick Gordon, tutor to Peter the Great

The sword was not much used in Russian quarrels. With one blow of his clenched fist he levelled the most impertinent of these lords on the floor, and, in the general row that ensued, severely wounded five others. The affair reached the ears of Peter I, who sent for Captain Gordon, who went into his presence with vague fears of the knout or Siberia; but his bearing so won the favour of the prince that the latter said:

> Well, sir, your accusers have done you justice in admitting that you soundly beat *six* of them, so I will also do you justice.

A few minutes after he put in Gordon's hand his commission as major—a rank speedily followed by that of lieutenant-colonel.

In 1696, when in his twenty-seventh year, he was despatched to *Azak*, or Azofif, as it is now named, a city on the left bank of the Don, to relieve the first siege of that place by the Turks. He had under his orders 4,000 horse, 20,000 infantry, and a strong body of Cossacks and Calmacks. He fulfilled his instructions; levelled the fortifications, and marched back to Moscow, (*Life of Peter I.*)

In 1697 he married the daughter of General Patrick Gordon, the widow of Colonel Strasburg, a German. The general, who was a cadet of the Haddo family (now Lords of Aberdeen), had first entered the Swedish service in his eighteenth year« and was taken prisoner at the great battle and capture of Warsaw in 1655, and at the peace entered the Russian service. On the 30th of November, 1699, he died in his 66th year, as his son-in-law records, "much regretted by the *Czar* and the whole nation. His Majesty visited him five times during his illness, was present at the moment he expired, and shut his eyes with his own hand; he was buried in great state."

Marshal Baron Ogilvie now began to take a prominent part in military matters, and to him, says Baron Manstein, "the Russians are indebted for the first establishment of order and discipline in their army, especially in the infantry. As to the dragoons, it was General Ronne, a Courlander, who had charge of them.

Ogilvie's grandfather had been in the Austrian service, under the Emperor Ferdinand, by whom he was created, for his bravery, a Baron of the Empire. From his youth he had served on the Rhine and in Hungary against the Turks. He was in his sixtieth year when he entered the service of Peter the Great, and commanded at Narva; "but," says Gordon, "he never could hit it off with Prince Mentschikoff, nor bear his insolence."

PETER THE GREAT

On having 1,000 men added to his regiment, Alexander Gordon was sent to Tevere, 160 miles from Moscow, to have them disciplined, which he achieved personally and perfectly. He was then despatched—in the course of the war against Charles XII—on the expedition to Narva, which Ogilvie besieged on the 24th of May, 1700, and took by a remarkable ruse. Having taken prisoners a number of Swedes, he stripped them of their uniforms, which were dark blue faced with bright yellow. In these he clad 2,000 of his Russian troops, and drew the Swedes thereby into an ambush where the river of Narva is broad and deep, and has a fall of eighteen feet over a ledge of rocks. There he cut to pieces 1,200 horse and foot, after which the city fell into his hands, and many more were put *hors de combat*, Gordon was detached to Piahagie with orders to build and garrison a fort there.

Ogilvie next captured Ivanogorod, on the right bank of the Narva, 90 miles from St. Petersburg, and commanded the whole army in the Grodno, a province forming part of Lithuania; he sent a detachment to capture the King of Sweden's baggage at Haza, *en route* to Wilna, and did so, killing 100 of the convoy and taking 40 prisoners; but in November, 1700, near Narva, Charles XII, at the head of only 9,000 Swedes, obtained a victory over 39,000 Russians, led, as some wrongly state, by Peter in person.

Alexander Gordon was taken prisoner, but was exchanged for the Swedish Colonel, Einshild; after which he was made Brigadier-General, and despatched upon all hazardous exploits.

In January, 1708, he forced the Pass of Zeipts without the loss of a man, and blocked up the strong castle there. He then attacked the Swedes near Kysmark, routed them, and on the 13th June "marched into Royal Prussia, there to take orders from King Augustus."

When Charles XII was about to cross the Disna, which issues from a lake in the district of Wilna, to form a junction with the troops of the Hetmann Mazeppa (whose name has been made so familiar to us by Byron), Peter the Great sent Brigadier Gordon with a battalion of Grenadiers, four columns of dragoons, and eight pieces of cannon to oppose the passage on the 21st October, 1708.

At six o'clock, in the gloom of the evening, the Swedes made an attempt to cross the river on floats or rafts constructed of freshly felled trees; but Gordon's guns opened upon them, flashing redly out of the gloom of the dark pine forest, and they were repulsed, their exultant shouts of triumph giving place to shrieks of drowning and despair. The firing lasted till eleven p.m., when the ammunition of the

Russians became expended, and Gordon reluctantly had to retire, in obedience to an order from Marshal Schermatoff; with the loss of 800 killed and 900 wounded—a strange disproportion; but 2,000 Swedes were slain or drowned in the river. The passage of the latter was nevertheless effected, leaving Mazeppa free to pursue his march, "with a remnant of 6,000 Cossacks, being all that had escaped the swords of the Muscovites." Bad ammunition had been purposely and scantily sent to Gordon by his private enemy, Prince Mentschikoff.

Gordon's next service was his expedition to oppose the Swedes under General Crassow, and the Poles and Lithuanians in the interest of King Stanislaus.

The Battle of Pultowa soon followed—

> Dread Pultowa's day,
> When fortune left the royal Swede,
> Around a slaughtered army lay,
> No more to combat or to bleed.
> The power and glory of the war,
> Faithless as their vain votaries, men,
> Had passed to the triumphant Czar,
> And Moscow's walls were safe again!

By that defeat, Charles, so long the terror of Europe, became a fugitive in Turkey, while the *Czar* restored Augustus to the throne of Poland, deposed Stanislaus, expelled the Swedes, and made himself master of Livonia, Ingria, and Carelia. (Voltaire, *History of Russia*,)

Old Marshal Ogilvie now took service under Augustus, and, dying "in harness," in 1712, was solemnly interred at Dresden.

But, prior to that event, Gordon tells us that the Russians, 10,000 strong, came up with the Poles at Podkamian, in Black Prussia, defeated and pursued them to Limberg. He led the infantry on this occasion, and sent home to Scotland several Polish standards and other trophies.

Next we find him in Transylvania with a powerful Russian column, assisting Prince Ragotzky against the Austrians, from whom he tells us he captured several tons of *tokay*, which he also sent to Scotland— we presume to his old ancestral house of Auchintoul, in the parish of Aberchirder, where it still stands.

In 1711 he heard of his father's death, and returned home *via* Dantzig, Holland, and England, where he landed at Harwich. In the September of the same year he made additions to the house of Auchintoul, and purchased the barony of Laithers in the same country.

In 1715 (according to Smollett's *Hist.*) he joined the Earl of Mar at Sheriffmuir, where he led the Western clans in battle, and, escaping with him after the conflict, was offered the rank of Lieutenant-General in the Spanish army; but he declined, and, returning to Scotland, died in 1751, in the eighty-second year of his age, and was buried near Marnock Kirk, where "no memorial marks the spot." (*New Stat. Acct.*)

The portrait prefixed to his history shows him a long-faced yet handsome man, with a high wig, the ends of which curl down on his breast-plate and coat, which is worn open.

The most distinguished engineer officer in the army of the Czar Peter was Captain Bruce of Buzion, a native of Fifeshire, who had been trained in the Prussian service. He served under Peter till 1724, and was with him on his memorable Prussian expedition, and was at the Battle of the Pruth. He died at his seat near Cupar (after having served in the campaign of 1745-6) in 1768. (*Scots Mag,*)

Peter the Great died on the 8th February, 1727, and was succeeded by Peter II, son of Prince Alexis, his grandson by his first wife.

It was in the year 1728 that James Francis Edward Keith, the future field-marshal, and ill-fated hero of Hochkirchen, entered the Russian service. The younger son of William, ninth Earl Marischal, he was born in 1696 in the now ruined Castle of Inverugie, a once splendid edifice at St. Fergus in Aberdeenshire, Destined for the law, he preferred the profession of arms, and in the rising for King James in 1715 he was wounded at Sheriffmuir in his nineteenth year and had to fly to France, before which he had made great progress in the classics under the tutelage of the famous Bishop Keith.

After joining in a futile attempt for the Stuarts in 1718, with other Scottish Cavaliers he entered the Spanish service, in which he remained till 1728, with a regiment of the Irish Brigade, commanded by the Duke of Ormond, in which he had been placed by the Duke of Leria, when, seeing advancement hopeless unless he tamed Catholic, he came with a letter to the king, and in attendance upon Leria, the Ambassador to the *Czarina*, by whom he was appointed Lieutenant-Colonel of a newly raised corps of three battalions, called the Regiment of Ishmaëlow (from a palace near Moscow, says Manstein), and was invested at the same time with the Order of the Black Eagle.

Of this regiment Count Lowenwalde was colonel, and Gustavus Biron, major. It was in augmentation of the Foot Guards; and the author of *Letters from Scandinavia* says that in Keith's battalion "the illustrious Romonzow served as a private soldier," to acquire a knowledge of his military duties. "The greatest part of the officers," adds Manstein, "were chosen among foreigners and the Livonian nobility. These regiments of Guards were raised as checks upon the old ones, and to overawe the people from sedition or insurrection."

During all the twenty years of his service in Russia, James Keith was uniformly distinguished by his valour, good conduct, and humanity—the latter being one of the most striking features of his character.

Other Scotsmen came prominently forward about the same time—among them Admiral Thomas Gordon and the Count de Balmaine.

In 1738, when the Russian and Saxon armies invested Dantzig, in hope of securing the person of King Stanislaus, the town was strong, the garrison numerous, and, inspired by the presence of the French and Poles, made an obstinate defence; and on the arrival of the Russian fleet under Admiral Gordon the siege was pressed with greater fury. Under its fire the city submitted to Augustus III as King of Poland; Stanislaus fled to Prussia in the disguise of a peasant; an amnesty was proclaimed, and the French prisoners of war were taken away in Gordon's ships. (Smollet's *History*.)

In 1735 Colonel Ramsay was one of those officers who, with the Count de Bounival in the Turkish service, had been disciplining the OsmanIn troops, thus causing much uneasiness in St. Petersburg. Catharine gave Ramsay and others such assurances of promotion in Russia that they joined her army, by the way of Holland, and Ramsay was commissioned as major. "He took the name of Count de Balmaine," says Manstein, "and distinguished himself on many occasions, insomuch that he rose to the rank of Colonel, and was lolled in the action of Wilmanstrand." This was in 1741.

A writer in the *Times*, in 1857, stated that "he was a son of Viscount Balmaine, whose adherence to the Stuarts compelled him to quit Scotland"; but gave no authority for this.

In 1735, when the empress sent 10,000 men to the Rhine to succour the Emperor Charles VI, Keith commanded as lieutenant-general under the Irish veteran Marshal Lacy. They crossed Bohemia and reached the great river in June, and Europe generally was astonished at the good order and discipline these Muscovites exhibited.

War was now resolved upon with the Turks, and in the army which began and accomplished the conquest of the Crimea were Generals Count Douglas, Leslie, Forman, Bruce, Stuart, Colonel Ramsay, Count

JAMES KEITH

de Balmaine, Johnston, and Lieutenant Junes (who distinguished himself at the capture of Otchakow), all Scotsmen—of whom in their places.

It was agreed that a Russian army, under Lacy, should march against the city of Azoff to punish the Tartars of the Crimea for their outrages, while another, under the Count de Munich, should penetrate to the Ukraine, and Seckendorf with the Austrians should enter Servia.

In those days the Crimean *khan*, a powerful prince, paid tribute to the *sultan*, and his territory, besides the noble monuments of the Genoese, contained many great cities.

Lacy came in sight of Azoff on the 16th May, 1736. Situated on an eminence, it is in a district of dangerous swamps, bleak and barren; but had a castle of great strength. In the attack Lacy was nobly seconded by the column of Count Douglas, particularly on the 14th June, when a frightful encounter took place at the palisades, which the Tartars and Turks defended by bullets, arrows, dart's, and stones for twelve consecutive days, after which the town was taken, and the Bashaw marched out with 3,400 men and 2,233 women, surrendering 167 pieces of cannon and 291 Christian slaves.

Lacy next forced the Lines of Perecop, till then deemed impregnable, and Count Balmaine stormed Kaffa, where the beautiful mosques and minarets were converted into magazines or torn down, and the stately fountains and aqueducts destroyed for the sake of their leaden pipes.

Bakhtchissari, within 22 miles of Sebastopol, next fell, and Ockzakow, where Innes led the stormers, and where 11,000 Russian regulars and 3,000 Cossacks were killed, and Keith was highly complimented for his valour by Count Munich (Manstein), but received a dreadful wound in the thigh. It was by his valour chiefly that the place was captured, and then his humanity was grandly conspicuous, for while the furious Muscovites were sanguinary in their ferocity, he sought to check it. He rescued a child, six years of age, from the hands of one whose sabre was uplifted to cleave the helpless creature as she endeavoured to creep out from the rubbish and dead that had fallen over her. Her father, a Turkish *pasha* of high position, had fallen in the siege, and she was now an orphan.

Unable to protect her himself, Keith sent her to his brother, the loyal, yet attainted, Earl Marischal, who brought her up as a Christian, treated her as a daughter of his own, "and, as she grew up," says Lord de Ros, "gave her charge of his household, where she did the honours of the table, and behaved herself with great propriety and discretion."

CHAPTER 3

The Scots in Russia—(Continued)

Before referring again to Keith we may state that during its stay in the Crimea the Russian army ravaged the whole country. During the winters of 1736 and 1737 the Tartars, thirsting for vengeance, burst into the Ukraine, despite all the precautions of Munich, giving towns to the flames, and carrying off above 1,000 Christian slaves.

The defence of the Ukraine was assigned to General Keith, with the column of troops that had served with him on the Rhine. It had recrossed Bohemia and Poland, and in September, 1736, was in winter quarters in Kiow.

In the February of the next year, on the 24th, some thousand Tartars crossed the Dnieper on the ice, near the small town of Kilberdna, where a brigade of Keith's, under Major-General Leslie, was posted. Finding that the Tartars had passed his outposts, he gathered 200 bayonets to attack them. The Tartars, supposing this was the advanced guard of a large body, fell back, but on learning their mistake they returned; a conflict ensued, and Leslie, with nearly his whole detachment, perished. No prisoners were taken but his son, Captain Leslie, who served as his *aide-de-camp*, and twenty men. Penetrating farther now, the Tartars gave all to fire and sword for forty-eight hours, till overtaken by a column of 2,000 cavalry sent by Keith, who cut down 300 and retook all their booty.

On the 25th of July, 1737, in the engagement near Karasu-Bazaar, in a valley 36 miles from Kaffa—now the great mart of the Crimea for fruit and wine—Lieutenant- General Count Douglas, who led the advanced guard, consisting of 6,000 dragoons and infantry, had orders to seize the town, while Marshal Lacy followed with the main body. Douglas was repulsed by 15,000 Turks, who held an entrenched camp above the town; but, on being reinforced by only two regiments of

25

cavalry, he returned to the attack again and captured it, *sabre à la main*, after an hour's conflict, and won a vast amount of plunder.

In the army which opened the campaign of April, 1788, against the Turks, the quartermaster general, Fermor, a Scotsman, led the vanguard, consisting of seven regiments of infantry, one of hussars, and 2,000 Cossacks, which he marched in hollow square to examine the position of the enemy in the neighbourhood of the Dniester, where the OsmanIn troops were defeated; and now everywhere the rapid successes of the Russian arms roused the Court of Vienna, which was bound by treaty to assist the Porte. But the Russians still pressed on towards the shores of the Black Sea, and prophecies were as usual propagated that the period fatal to the Crescent had arrived. (*Mém. de Brandenburg,*)

In 1788 Major William M'Kenzie of Conansby entered the Russian army as colonel under the Empress Anne, but returned to the British service on the war breaking out with Spain, and died in 1770.

In the year 1739 occurred what was termed "the affair of Prince Cantemier," in which Keith was concerned.

The Count de Munich having formed a regiment of Wallachians when the new campaign opened, gave command of it to Prince Cantemier, a near relation of one of the same name, who had joined Peter I in 1711. The prince, *en route* to Russia, passed by the way of Brody, a town of Galicia, the residence of Count Potosky, Crown-General of Poland, and consequently averse to Russian interests. He threw the prince into a loathsome vault, and offered to deliver him up to the Porte—tidings of which the prince contrived to send to Kiow, where Keith commanded. The latter instantly sent an officer to demand the release of the prince; but Potosky denied all knowledge of the matter.

Keith threatened to enforce his demands with the sword, on which he was set at liberty and escorted to the frontier of the Ukraine: and soon after took vengeance upon his enemy, whose possessions he ravaged with fire and sword at the head of his Wallachian regiment. "He committed the most horrid cruelties," says Manstein, "and could he have got "hold of Count Potosky, there is no doubt but that he would have made him undergo the same punishment to which the count had meant to expose him."

The general progress of these wars lies apart from our narrative, and before the end of 1709, by the pacific disposition of their Christian allies, the Turks, so recently devoted to destruction, obtained an advantageous peace.

The following year saw General Keith made Governor of the Ukraine—that vast region which lies south-east of Russian Poland. Says Manstein:

He had just returned from France, where he had been for the cure of his wounds. He had orders to repair to Glogan as governor, where he did not reside one year; but in that time he despatched more business than his predecessors had done in ten. The Ukraine received great benefit from the mildness of his government and the order which he established in the administration of affairs. He began to introduce, even among the Cossacks, a sort of discipline, which till then had been unknown; but he had not time to complete that work, for, the war coming on with Sweden, he was recalled. When he quitted Glogan the whole country regretted him.

In April, 1741, there died at Cronstadt, Thomas Gordon, Admiral of all Russia. (*Scots Magazine*, 1741.)

In 1741, when the preparations for war began, the Grand Duchess Anne removed Lacy and Keith to St. Petersburg, and it was in Finland they were to act offensively, as soon as the field was taken.

The second column, to be commanded by the Prince of Hesse-Homburg, was to remain in Ingria. Others were to be formed in Livonia and Esthonia, to cover the coasts under Count Lowendal, as the Russian fleet had been in a different condition since Gordon sailed from Dantzig.

Under General Keith the first camp was formed on the 22nd July, 1741, four miles from St. Petersburg. It consisted of five regiments of infantry, three of dragoons, and several independent companies of grenadiers, all of which were reviewed four days after by Marshal Lacy. During this ceremony the sound of cannon was heard in St. Petersburg, announcing the birth of a princess, who was named Catherine. Keith, accompanied by the Count de Balmaine, now began his march, and on the 24th August declared the war against Sweden was then inaugurated, as it was the birthday of the emperor. At the head of each great battalion he made a harangue, exhorting the soldiers to do their duty and uphold the glory of the Russian arms.

Sweden was at that time rent by political schism. One party, called the *Hats*, was ever for war, but remained at peace when Russia was pressed by other Powers; and now, when the latter was at peace and

Sweden had but few troops in Finland, that power was ready and ripe for war, and scorned the pacific advice of what was named the "Nightcap party."

The day after war was declared, Keith again marched through Wybourg and encamped near the bridge of Abo. All the troops had fifteen days' rations, and, on a junction being formed with the column of General Uxkul, three regiments were left to hold Abo, an important town in Finland, and the advance began again, Lacy commanding the whole, towards Wilmanstrand, a fortified village on the south bank of Lake Saima, where Majors General Wrangel was in position at the head of 4,000 Swedes, while 4,000 more, under General Buddenbrog, were six miles distant.

The march lay through thick woods, deep marshes, and rocky defiles, when a false alarm was given one night that nearly proved disastrous. The Russians fired on each other in the dark, and many officers and men were killed. "The generals, Lacy and Keith, ran a great risk of being slain in this false alarm," says Baron Manstein. "They had small tents pitched for them between the lines which several balls had quite gone through, and about 200 of the dragoon horses, taking fright at the fire, broke loose from the picquets and ran through the highroad to Wilmanstrand."

Buddenbrog's column, on hearing the firing, pushed on to the latter place, believing it was attacked, and by 4 a.m. on the 2nd September the Russians were in front of the position, which was defended by palisades, earthworks, and fascines.

When the conflict began on the 3rd, the Swedish artillery did much execution among the attacking Russian grenadiers, on which Keith ordered two fresh battalions, those of Ingermaland and Astrakan, under General Manheim, to support them, and, on receiving a volley from them at sixty paces, the Swedes gave way. The position was carried by 5 p.m., the Swedes routed, and their own guns turned on them and Wilmanstrand.

Nearly the whole of the Swedes were taken prisoners, with all their cannon and colours. The Russian losses were 529 killed and 1,837 wounded. Among the former there fell, gallantly leading their columns. Colonels Lockman and the Count de Balmaine.

The descendants of the latter are still in Russia, (as at time of first publication). When Napoleon was at St. Helena in 1817, the then Count de Balmaine was there as a Russian commissioner—the descendant of the captor of Kaffa. (See O'Meara's *Napoleon in Exile*, 2 vols.)

The command of Wilmanstrand was assigned to General Fermor (or Farmer), with two regiments of infantry, till the place was razed to the ground, and its inhabitants were marched into Russia.

The army now returned into Russian Finland, and Lacy returned to St. Petersburg, leaving Keith in full command, and he carried on the close of the campaign by skirmishes, in which his troops were always victorious, till the 8th November, when he went into winter quarters.

Intelligence, however, was soon sent to him that the Swedes were about to invade Russian Finland, and after repairing to St. Petersburg for special orders and to attend a Council of War, he left it on the 4th December to have his troops in readiness, and on the night of the 5th the great revolution took place which placed on the throne the Princess Elizabeth, youngest daughter of Peter the Great.

In the execution of the plot which brought that startling event to pass, Manstein states that the first step of the conspirators was to seize the officer commanding the grenadiers in the imperial barracks, adding that "his name was Grews, a Scotsman, after which they took an oath of fidelity to the Princess." The name given is perhaps "Grieve," misspelt.

In 1742, when hostilities began again with Sweden, in the army assembled at Wybourg in the end of May, consisting of 36,000 men of all arms (including 10,000 in the galleys), two brigades were led by Scotsmen—Count Bruce and Major-General Brown. A dangerous mutiny broke out in the Guards, and a cry was set up that they would massacre all foreign officers and be led by none but Russians.

Finding that no officer would venture near them, Keith, without a moment's hesitation, drew his sword and flung himself among the mutineers, and, seizing a leader with his left hand, ordered a priest to confess him, that he might shoot him on the spot at the time, commanding his *aide-de-camp* and some officers to seize or cut down others. On this, the mob of soldiery dispersed and rushed to their tents. "Keith," we are told, "ordered a call of the rolls at the head of the camp, that the absent should be taken into custody and information issued against all who were present at the meeting. As neither the Horse Guards nor the country regiments were concerned in this rising, they had taken arms to repel the insolence of the two regiments of Foot Guards, if they could not be otherwise appeased. If it had not been for the spirited resolution of General Keith this revolt would have spread far, as no Russian officer would have undertaken to oppose the rage of the soldiery."

The complaints of the latter were not without justice, and their hatred of foreigners rose from the fact that all the best posts were given to Scots, Germans, and other strangers; but now the knout, mutilation, and Siberia were the doom of all that were brought before the court-martial of General Romanzow.

After the final reduction of Finland, General Keith was appointed governor, and held Abo, the capital, with a strong force, while twenty-one galleys and two *prahms* guarded the coast.

In the war that broke out in 1743, in connection with the Duke of Holstein's succession to the crown of Sweden, Major-General Stuart had a brigade under Lacy on board the sea squadron. It consisted of three regiments of infantry and three companies of grenadiers, and Stuart's vessels carried a red ensign.

The Swedes continued to burn all the timber which Keith had amassed on the Isle of Aland to build war-galleys, and, after many operations, Marshal Lacy effected a junction with the former, after he had beaten the Swedish galleys in a sea-fight in July.

Keith, in his new *rôle* of a naval commander, had left Hangow on the 18th of May, his galleys towed by *prahms*, as the wind was light, and on the 22nd came in sight of the Swedish squadron in Yungfern Sound, but could not give orders for engaging till the 29th, owing to the contrary winds that set in. Then the Swedes bore away, and Keith's galleys took up the station they had quitted.

Several minor engagements between Keith's galleys and those of the Swedes and the land batteries of the latter took place till the 1st of June, when the Swedes, whom he had always worsted, bore away and vanished in the night.

Peace followed in 1743, and Keith resumed his command at Abo, and to bring off the Russian troops under Stuart, Lapouchin, and others.

CHAPTER 4

The Scots in Russia—(Continued)

A quarrel having ensued with the Dalecarlians, and when Keith, on duty at Stockholm, had one of his *aide-de-camps* insulted (as a Danish officer) because he wore a scarlet uniform, Keith received orders to repair to Sweden, at the head of 11,000 men, to support the interests of the Prince of Holstein and act as ambassador.

"He suffered much in his passage with the troops under his orders from the cold and storms he had to undergo before he reached the coast of Sweden," says his comrade Manstein; "and the Russian galleys, which never used to keep the sea later than the beginning of September, were obliged to remain on it till the latter end of November." Any other man than Keith would hardly have been able to execute this expedition. He had not only to struggle with the violence of the storms and the piercing cold, but with the officers of the marine, who were often representing the impossibility of proceeding in so severe a season. But Keith, who had served a long time in Spain, where he had seen the galleys keep the sea in all weathers, and who, besides, knew better than any of the officers that served in the squadron how much could be done with this part of the fleet in any climate with a good will, continued to be single in his opinion for proceeding.

He remained with his column in Sweden until 1744, when, matters being amicably adjusted, he returned with the fleet and troops to Revel on the 13th of August.

Keith served the Russian Crown in many important embassies, and a pretty well-known anecdote in connection with one of his last, on the termination of a war between the Russians and the Turks, is recorded in the *Memoirs and Papers of Sir Andrew Mitchell.*

The commissioners to treat of a peace were General Keith and the Turkish grand *vizier.* These two personages, he relates, met with the interpreters of the Russ and Turkish between them. When all was concluded, they arose to separate. The general made his bow, hat in hand, and the turbaned *vizier* his *salaam*; but the latter, when the ceremonies were over, turned suddenly, and coming up to Keith, took him warmly by the hand, and with a broad Scottish accent, declared that "it made him unco happy, noo that they were sae far frae hame, to meet wi' a countryman in his exalted station."

Keith stared with astonishment, and, in answer to his exclamation of surprise, the grand *vizier* gave this explanation:

"My faither was the bellman o' Kirkcaldy, in Fife, and I remember to have seen you and your brother the earl occasionally passing."

But, with all the honours he had won in Russia, Keith began to deem service then only a species of splendid slavery, and, leaving the Muscovite court in 1747, he entered the army of Frederick the Great of Prussia, where we shall meet him again.

Such was the career of one of the many brilliant soldiers of whose services loyalty to their native kings and the mal-influence of England deprived their mother country.

In 1748 we read of a Scottish artisan named Scott being more peacefully employed in repairing the famous globe of Gottorp after it was burnt in that year. He made the skeleton of another, on which he was seven years at work. It was deemed the largest globe in the world, and had been first made for the Duke of Holstein in 1664. The Castle of Gottorp, though in Denmark, belonged to Duke Carl-Peter, Emperor of Russia in 1762, and when bestowed on Russia, the enormous globe was conveyed on sledges to St. Petersburg through the woods of Esthonia and Finland, where trees were felled to facilitate its passage. (Stœhlin's *Monuments of Peter the Great*.)

During the war in Silesia, in 1758, the Russian army was commanded by General Fermor, who was wounded at the battle of Zorndorf, fought with the Prussians, and sent to General Dohna a trumpeter asking a three days' armistice to bury the dead and take care of the wounded, "presenting to his Prussian Majesty," says Smollett, "the humble request of General Brown, who was much weakened with loss of blood, that he might have a passport to a place where he could find such accommodation as his situation required."

In answer to this Count Dohna gave General Fermor to understand that, as the King of Prussia remained master of the field, he would bury the dead and protect the wounded; but granted the request of General Brown. "Fermor was of Scottish extraction," adds

Smollett, "but General Brown was actually a native of North Britain." (*Hist, Eng.*, vol. vi.)

In the preceding June General Fermor had been created a prince of the Holy Roman Empire.

In the *Caledonian Mercury* of the same year, under date of Versailles, 6th March, we read that "the Sieur M'Kenzie-Douglas, to whom we owe the restoration of a good understanding between our court and that of Russia, has obtained a warrant for 60,000 *livres* and a pension of 4,000 more."

And, as the Scots were not behind in the arts of peace in Russia, we find in 1764 that when the Empress Catherine II invited several foreigners of skill and talent to prepare plans for the improvement of St. Petersburg, those received most favourably by her were presented by "Mr. Gilchrist, a Scotsman, in consequence of which a valuable present has been ordered him by the Empress; and several wharves, docks, storehouses, and public streets approved of in his plans are to be carried out under the aforesaid gentleman's direction." (*Edinburgh Advert,*, vol. ii.)

In the same year we find that John Ochterlony (a name familiar in recent Russian annals), a native of Montrose, was an eminent merchant at Rigi.

In 1764, Sir Samuel Greig, who was Governor of Cronstadt, Admiral of all the Russias, and became known as the father and founder of the Russian navy, entered the service of the Empress Catherine II with many other Scotsmen, among whom was one from the same native place, Iverkeithing, the famous old Commodore Roxburgh. In Russia he bore the name of Samuel Carlovitch Greig, as his father Charles Greig was skipper of a small ship, the *Thistle*, of Inverkeithing, trading with St. Petersburg. (*Edinburgh Courant*, 1761.)

In that ancient Fifeshire seaport Samuel Greig was born in 1735, and was educated by the parish dominie, who was alive in 1794. Entering the British navy, he was a lieutenant in the fleet of Hawke, when blockading Brest in 1759; and, subaltern though his rank, he distinguished himself in the great battle off Cape Quiberon, and in that war, during which we took or destroyed 64 sail of French ships, including 27 of the line.

He next served at the capture of several of the West India Islands, but the provincial prejudices of the English rendered the time unfavourable for Scotsmen or Irishmen rising in the British service. Thus, when, during Lord Bute's administration, the court of St. Petersburg requested that a few of our naval officers, who were distinguished for ability, might be sent to improve the Russian fleet, Greig, with several others, gladly volunteered, and had his rank as lieutenant confirmed, his only stipulation being that he might return as such to the British service when he chose; and we are told that he rapidly raised the Russian naval service to a degree of respectability it had never attained before.

In the same year he joined Captain Douglas was appointed commodore of the Russian fleet and senior rear-admiral; and in 1768 we note the death at Cronstadt, in his 23rd year only, of Captain William Gordon of Cowbairdie, Aberdeenshire, commodore of a ship in the Russian navy.

When war broke out between the empress and the *sultan*, the partial breaking up of the ice in the Baltic enabled a Russian fleet to put to sea for the Mediterranean. Of that fleet Greig was commodore, under Alexis, Count Orloff, and his zeal soon led to his promotion to the rank of flag-officer. In 1770, Mr. Gordon was Director-General of the Imperial dockyard at Rigi and Knight of St. Alexander Newsoki. In 1776 he was presented with 1,000 Livonian peasants and 30,000 *roubles*. On the 14th January, 1770, one squadron of the armament under the admiral, John Elphinstone, consisting of a 70-gun ship, two of 60 guns each, and 70 others arrived at Spithead on its way to the Archipelago. This officer, a cadet of the Scottish house of Elphinstone, was then a captain of the British navy. He had a claim to the attainted title of Balmerino, which was also advanced by his grandson. Captain Alexander Elphinstone, R.N., and noble of Livonia. (*Burke.*)

The other squadron, consisting of 22 sail of the line, had reached Minorca so early as the 4th January, and before the end of July the Russian fleet had twice defeated the Turkish—on one occasion Elphinstone encountering thrice his force, sinking eight ships; on the other, with nineteen, overcoming Giafar Bey with twenty-three.

A curious, gossipy anecdote is connected with this war. Dr. Lauchlan Taylor, minister of Larbert, who in those days enjoyed the reputation of being a prophet, published in 1770 a book, in which he stated the strife then waging would end in the total destruction of Turkey; and the empress, under whose notice the work was brought by some of the many Scots in her service, had the prophecy translated, freely circulated among her troops, and great bets were laid on the fulfilment of it.

In the great battle of the 6th July, Greig, Admiral Mackenzie, and other Scottish officers in the fleet rendered good and gallant service; and in the *Scots Magazine* for that year the carnage of the scene is well depicted by the pen of a Lieutenant Mackenzie, then serving on board Her Imperial Majesty's ship *Switostoff*, Orloff was not much of a sailor, so the mauling of the Turks fell chiefly to the share of Admiral Elphinstone and Commodore Greig, who compelled them to slip their cables and run under their batteries between Scio and the coast of Anadoli.

Under the care of the two Scottish commanders two fire-ships were prepared to enter the harbour, covered by a part of the squadron; but leaders were required for this perilous service, and at once three officers, all Scotsmen—Commander Greig, Lieutenant Mackenzie, and Captain-Lieutenant Drysdale (sometimes called Dugdale)—volunteered. Though the latter was abandoned by his crew at the supreme crisis, the service was achieved. The fire-ships were exploded with dreadful effect, and the whole Turkish fleet, including twelve ships of the line, armed with 566 guns, was destroyed by Grieg, while 6,000 Turks were shot, burned, or drowned.

By his boats he towed out *La Barbarocine*, of 64 guns, bombarded the town, and rescued 400 Christian slaves. For these services he was promoted to the rank of rear-admiral, with 2,160 *roubles per annum*, and his two brother officers were made captains. His ship was named the *Three Primates*.

The Sieur Rutherford, another Scottish adventurer, who was commissary of the Russian court, sold at Leghorn all the prizes which were taken by the fleet. (*Scots Mag.*)

From the volume quoted we learn that a dispute took place between Count Orloff, the nominal commander-in-chief, and Admiral Elphinstone, whom he ordered to go on a secret expedition, "which the latter thought proper to decline; in consequence of this a great altercation ensued between them. Count Orloff put him under arrest, and sent an express to inform the empress of what he had done." She recalled him, and he left the Russian service in disgust, taking a farewell of Catherine, clad in his uniform as a captain of the British navy.

The fleet meanwhile was sweeping the shores of the Archipelago, under Greig, Mackenzie, Drysdale, Brodie, and others, led by Admiral Spiritoff. Sinope, Giurgevo, and other places on the Turkish coast were bombarded or taken; and in a conflict at the latter on 31st October, 1771, among the slain appears the name of David Gordon, a landed proprietor of Galloway and lieutenant of our 67th Foot, a volunteer on board the fleet.

Greig destroyed the magazines formed for the supply of Constantinople, bombarded Negroponte, swept the coast of Macedonia, beat down Cavallo in Roumelia, and destroyed all the stores at Salonica; and in a ten hours' fight off Scio, 10th October, 1778, he routed or took a whole Turkish squadron, but had a narrow escape, as a ball struck one of the points from St. George's cross on his left breast. His sailors were repulsed, however, at Cyprus, and four sacks of their *scalps*, salted, were sent to the *sultan* from Stanchio, the ancient Cos.

"In the preceding month Rear-Admiral Mackenzie commanded the Russian fleet in the Black Sea (*Edinburgh Advt.*, vol. xl.), and from him the place in the Crimea called Khouter Mackenzie takes its name, as it was a plantation of timber he formed to furnish the dockyards at Actiare, now Sebastopol, which he first fortified. The place then "consisted of two houses, a wooden barrack, a military storehouse," says Slade, in his *Travels in Turkey , etc.* "Our countrymen," he adds, "Admirals Mackenzie, Priestman, Mason, Mercer, and three Greigs have all hoisted their flags in the Black Sea."

There were also Admiral Tait and four captains—Denniston, whose head was shot off; Marshall, drowned when leading his boarders; Miller and Aikin, who each lost a leg in action. It lies on the highroad from Simpheropol, and our troops passed through it on their march to Balaclava after the battle on the Alma.

From the scarce memoirs of a military adventurer of dubious character, a native of Dumbarton, named Major Semple Lisle, who once served in our 15th Foot—was wounded at Rhode Island—and joined the Russian service under Catherine, we may make two extracts with reference to 1784.

At Moscow I met several cartloads of English midshipmen, who, being thrown out of employment by the conclusion of the American war, had entered the Russian service. They were under the care of a sergeant and two marines, and were going to join Admiral Mackenzie on the Black Sea.

From Karasu-bazaar I was sent on military duty to Actiare, where I met my old friend Admiral Mackenzie with his fleet. While I was at Actiare, Mackenzie and myself received the compliments of some of the Tartar chiefs of that country, together with the present each of a horse. Mine was richly caparisoned, but his was almost covered with silver. The saddle was of purple cloth, studded over with silver nails; from each side depended a stirrup of the same metal made in the fashion of the country, the size and shape of the sole of the foot.

In this year, 1784, another Captain Mackenzie joined the Russian service—the laird of Redcastle, in Forfarshire. He had been tried at the Old Bailey for illegally executing a convict at Black Town; and, after serving for some time in Russia, was killed in a duel near Constantinople. (Kay's *Portraits*.)

Other Scots of higher position came to Russia about this period. Among them John Robison, LL.D., the distinguished mechanical philosopher, a native of Stirlingshire (Nimmo's *Hist.*), recommended as a fit person to superintend the navy, in 1770 was appointed Inspector-General of the Marine Cadet Corps of Nobles at Cronstadt, with the rank of colonel, an office which he relinquished in 1778 on becoming Professor of Natural Philosophy in the University of Edinburgh; Dr. Rogerson, who was appointed counsellor of state and court physician in 1776, with a pension of 4,000 *roubles* yearly, and returned in 1815 to his native district, where he purchased property to the value of £130,000; and Dr. Guthrie, a cadet, of the family of Halkerton, in Fifeshire (and nephew of William Guthrie, a well-known miscellaneous writer employed by Cave), who was appointed personal physician to the empress.

Dr. Rogerson's father was tenant of the half of Lochbroom, Dumfriesshire, and there he was born. The other half was rented by William Haliday, whose son Matthew was also one of her Imperial Majesty's physicians. (*Old Stat, Account Scot.*)

CHAPTER 5

The Scots in Russia—(Continued)

To Major Semple Lisle, who was A. D. C. to Prince Potemkin, and who, when in Russia, was mixed up in a disreputable way with the famous Duchess of Kingston, was assigned at this time the training and command of a Corsican corps, 250 strong, with which he went to the Crimea in 1783; and in his memoirs he gives himself the credit of inaugurating useful changes in the Russian uniform, which he describes as being green, lined and faced with red; the coat long and reaching to the calf of the leg, with long boots and small hats, to which the soldiers added flannel ear-covers in cold weather. He suggested also the cropping of the hair, and the fixing of the bayonet only when about to charge.

In the winter of 1773 Admiral Greig returned to St. Petersburg, and made every exertion to fit out a more efficient squadron for the Dardanelles; and, sailing with it from Cronstadt, took with him his wife on board his ship, the *Issidorum*, of 74 guns. In the spring of 1774 the rendezvous of the squadrons of Greig and Spiritoff was at Port Naussa, in the channel between Paros and the rocky coast of Naxos; but now Catherine made peace with the Turks, stipulating that the Crimea was to be ceded forever to the rule of its own *khans* or *sultans*.

Greig returned to Russia with the fleet, and spent all the last years of his life in remodelling its discipline, training cadets, and earning for himself the endearing *sobriquet* of the "Father of the Russian Navy." For these and his other services he was made Governor of Cronstadt, Admiral of the whole Empire, with the orders of St. Andrew, St. George, and, in 1782, St. Anne of Holstein, with 7,000 *roubles per annum*. His great assistant was his countryman Gordon, Director-General of the Dockyards, who at that time was constructing two 100-gunships, three of 90, six of 70, and ten 40-gun frigates—all of a form and beauty hitherto unknown in Russia. The chief engineer and naval architect was then another Scotsman, Andrew Watson, who died in 1799.

The empress dined with Grieg on board his ship in July, 1786, accompanied by Counts Bruce and Galitzin; and when he hoisted the Imperial standard *nine hundred* guns thundered at once from the ramparts of Cronstadt.

He once more prepared a great fleet to sail for the Black Sea, against the Crimea, but its *khau*—the last descendant of Gengiz— submitted, and his territories became an integral portion of Russia.

In 1788 Grieg put to sea against the Swedes, after great discontent and threatened resignation had occurred among the Scottish officers of his fleet, owing to a false rumour that Paul Jones was to be taken into the Imperial service; and he fought his great battle with the fleet of the Duke of Sudermania and Count Wachdmeister on the 17th of July in the Narrows of Kalkboder. He had thirty-three sail in all, while the enemy had fifteen of the line carrying from sixty to seventy guns, eight frigates armed with twenty-four pounders, and eight others. The Swedes were defeated; Grieg's loss was 319 killed and 666 wounded. "I must say, on this occasion," contains his despatch to the empress, "that I never saw a battle maintained with more spirit and courage on both sides." He signed it "Sam. Carlovitch Grieg."

On Count Wachdmeister yielding up his sword, Grieg returned it, saying:

"I will never be the man to deprive so brave and worthy an officer of his sword, I beseech you to receive it."

He next blockaded the Duke of Sudermania in Sveaborg; but his health became impaired now, and on the 15th of October, 1788, he expired on board the ship *Rotislaw*, which had lost 200 men in the late battle.

His funeral was conducted with a pomp and splendour never before seen in Russia; every officer attending it received a gold ring from the empress, and his monument records, with truth, that "he was a man no less illustrious for courage and naval skill than for piety, benevolence, and every private virtue."

The estate in Livonia bestowed upon him by the Emperor of Germany is still in the possession of his descendants, whose names have often appeared in the public prints.

His son John died in China in 1793. Another son became Sir Alexis Grieg, admiral of the Russian fleet, privy councillor, and Knight of all the Imperial Orders. He studied at the High School of Edinburgh under the Rector Adam from 1783 to 1785, and then served as a volunteer on board H.M.S. *Culloden,* under Admiral Trowbridge.

When a captain, he and another Scotsman, Captain Brown, were involved in some trouble by the wreck of the Imperial frigate *Archangel,* commanded by the latter in 1797. In the following year, in the squadron off the Texel, he commanded the *Ratisvan,* 64 guns; and Captain Robert Crown, said to be a Scot, had the *Utislaw,* 74. (*Edinburgh Herald.*) In 1801 he was banished to Siberia for a time, in consequence of boldly remonstrating with the Emperor Paul for his severity to some British naval prisoners; but in 1828 he was in fall command of the Russian fleet at the sieges of Varna and Anapa, whither he had sailed from Sebastopol with forty vessels—eight being of the line— acting in conjunction with the troops under Prince Mentschicoff for three months by sea and land.

During these operations the emperor was his guest on board the *Ville de Paris,* which had the Diplomatic Chancery and 1,300 persons under her flag. (Slade's *Travels,*) He founded the great astronomical observatory at Nicolaeff, where Captain Samuel Moffat, of the Imperial navy, died in 1821. In 1837 (according to Spencer's *Travels*), on being made a privy councillor, he was requested for state reasons to reside at St. Petersburg.

His son, Woronzow Grieg, also educated at the High School of Edinburgh, was A.D.C. to Prince Mentschicoff during the Crimean war in 1854; and, when sent to our lines with a flag of truce, the purity of his English excited surprise. He was killed by a mortal wound on the desperate field of Inkermann.

Two other members of the same family figured prominently in 1877, when Adjutant-General Greig was sent from St. Petersburg to the Danube in August, to investigate the alleged frauds in the commissariat department; and Admiral Greig, comptroller-general of the Russian Empire, arrived at Bucharest in October to inspect the accounts of the army contractors.

Since then he, or another of the same name, has commanded (1886) the first squadron of the fleet in the Black Sea.

Among the prominent Scots in the Russian army towards the end of the last century were Lieutenant-General Robert Fullarton, Knight of St. Catherine, who died at his house of Dudwick, near Edinburgh, in 1786; and Sir Alexander Hay, Bart., Knight of St. George, who died in 1792, as colonel at the head of his regiment. His family is now extinct.

In 1790, Sir James Wylie, a native of Kincardineshire, entered the Russian service as a physician, and eight years after was appointed surgeon-in-ordinary to the Emperor Paul and heir-apparent. In 1812 he was director of the medical department of the Minister of Marine, Inspector-General of the Board of Health for the Russian army, and privy councillor. He was knighted by George IV at Ascot Races in 1814—an honour conferred by the sword of the Hetman Count Platoff—and was made a Baronet of Great Britain in the same year, on his return to Russia, where he died in 1854, bequeathing a vast fortune to the *Czar*, greatly to the astonishment of his Scottish relations.

Says a local print of that year:

Many years ago, during the reign of the Emperor Alexander, a shrewd Scotswoman of the old school, without either rank or education to recommend her, left the shores of the Forth for those of the Baltic on a visit to her son. She was received by the Russian government with all the pomp accorded by one monarch to another. The cannon fired a salute, and the emperor touched the hand of the old Scottish matron and bade her welcome to the coast of Russia. This good lady was the mother of Sir James Wylie; and while her heart would doubtless beat with gratitude for the gift of a son who was so much respected by the emperor, such a welcome to his mother would strengthen the affection of Sir James for his master, and make him anxious to show his appreciation of such delicate kindness by every means in his power.

The Scots colony in the Caucasus, so prominently referred to in Mackenzie Wallace's recent work on Russia, is first mentioned in the *Scots Magazine* for November, 1807, thus:—

His Imperial Majesty has been pleased to grant a very remarkable charter to the colony of Scotsmen who have been settled for the last four years in the mountains of the Caucasus. The rights and privileges accorded to these Scotsmen, who form a detached settlement in a district so thinly populated, and bordering on the territories of so many uncivilised tribes of Mahometans and heathens, are intended to increase their activity in extending trade and manufactures, and to place them in respect to their immunities on the same footing with the Evangelical Society of Sarepta.

To this colony the Tartars, whose lands they occupied, were long hostile, and the Russian government, suspicions of these Scots, had previously, we are told, put opposition in their way. One way in which these Scots sought to extend Christianity was by the purchase of Tartar children, whom they educated, and at a certain age set free. One of them, named John Abercrombie, became of some note; and a Dr. Glen was author of three forgotten pamphlets on this colony. It was, no doubt, some of these people that Spencer referred to in his *Travels* in 1837, when he says that among the bravest of Circassian warriors were the Marrs, sons of Mr. Marr, a Scottish merchant of Redoubt-Kalch, and subject of Prince Dabion of Mingrelia. After returning from Scotland, where he had sent them for education, "these young Scots may now (1837) be reckoned among the most daring hunters in the wilds of Mingrelia."

Mr. Wallace, in his work published in 1877, says that when travelling on the great plain that lies between the Sea of Azoff and the Caspian he was surprised to see on his map a place indicated as the *Schotlandskaya Koloneya*, or Scottish Colony; and in pursuing his inquiries about it at Stavropol he found a venerable man, "with fine regular features of the Circassian type, coal-black, sparkling eyes, and a long beard that would have done honour to a patriarch," who asked him in turn what he wanted to know about the colony.

'Because I am myself a Scotsman,' said Wallace, 'and hoped to find fellow-countrymen here.' Let the reader imagine my astonishment when he answered, in genuine broad Scots:
'Oh, man, I am a Scotsman tae— my name, my name is John Abercrombie. Did ye ever hear tell o' John Abercrombie, the famous Edinburgh doctor?'

Mr. Wallace, who is a native of Paisley, continues:

In the first years of the present century, a band of Scottish missionaries came to Russia, for the purpose of converting the Circassian tribes, and received from the Emperor Alexander I a large grant of land in this place, then on the frontier of the empire. Here they founded a mission and began the work, but soon discovered that the population were not idolaters but Mussulmans, and consequently impervious to Christianity. In this difficulty they fell on the idea of buying Circassian children from their parents and bringing them up as Christians. One of these children, purchased about the year 1806, was a little boy named

Teoona. As he had been purchased with money subscribed by Dr. Abercrombie, he had received in baptism that gentleman's name, and considered himself the foster-son of his benefactor. Here was the explanation of the mystery. Teoona, *alias* Mr. Abercrombie, was a man of more than average intelligence.

Besides his native language, he spoke English, German, and Russian fluently; and he assured me that he knew several other languages equally well. His life had been devoted to missionary work, especially to translating and printing the Scriptures. The Scottish mission was suppressed by the Emperor Nicholas in 1885, and all the missionaries except two returned home. The son of one of these two (Galloway) is the only genuine Scotsman remaining. Of the 'Circassian Scotsmen' there are several, most of whom have married Germans. The other inhabitants are German colonists from the province of Saratof; and German is the language now spoken in the village of the Scottish colony.

The present eminent Russian explorer and *savant*, Baron and Dr. Miclucho Macleay, is of Scottish descent, and his scientific researches in New Guinea from 1870 to 1883 were published at St. Petersburg in 1886.

His father, Colonel Duncan Macleay, of the Russian army, died in 1828, at Colpina, near St. Petersburg, and, according to the *Edinburgh Weekly Journal* for that year, was the nearest heir to Lord Balmerino, who was attainted in 1746. (See also *Blackwood's Magazine*, 1828.)

Concerning Baron M. von Macleay, *Nature*, in 1874 (Macmillan and Co.) states:

Contrary to the advice of every one, this intrepid traveller and true devotee of science is determined again upon visiting the east coast of Papna. When his researches here are complete he intends to visit the islands of Polynesia and certain parts of the coast of Australia. This he calculates will take up five or six years. The Governor of the Dutch East Indies, like a true man of science, had given to Dr. Macleay for the last six months roomy and comfortable quarters in his palace at Buitonrovg. It would be well if all in high position would imitate this kind of 'patronage.'

CHAPTER 6

The Scots in Russia—(Concluded)

One of the most distinguished Scotsmen who took service in Russia towards the end of the last century was Sir Archibald William Crichton, a native of Edinburgh, where he was born in 1763, and who became physician to the Emperor Alexander and to the Imperial Guard. Descended from the Crichtons of Woodhouse and Newington, his father was Patrick Crichton, long well known in Edinburgh as a coach-builder, and colonel of the 2nd Local Militia, though originally a captain in. the 57th Regiment

Archibald became a member of the Imperial Academy of St. Petersburg, and that of Natural History at Moscow. He was K.G.C. of the Orders of St Anne and St.Vladimir, and of the Red Eagle of Prussia. He was a member of the Royal Institute of Paris, and author of various valuable works. He accompanied the Grand Duke Nicholas and Count Kutusof to Edinburgh in 1817, and was knighted, and became F.R.S., F.L.S., and F.G.S. He died in Russia in his 93rd year, on the 4th June, 1856.

In September, 1820, there was celebrated in Edinburgh a marriage which made some noise at the time, that of "Alexander Ivanovitch, Sultan Katte Ghery Krim Ghery, to Anne, daughter of James Neilson, Esq., of Millbank," a secluded house near the Grange Loan.

A writer in *Notes and Queries* in 1855 states that this personage, the lawful *sultan* of the Crimea, had fled from that province in consequence of his religion, and was educated in Edinburgh at the expense of the Emperor Alexander of Russia, with a view to his becoming a Christian, "and that his wife was hardly ever known by any other appellation than that of *sultana*."

Spencer, in his *Travels*, in 1837, says the "*sultana*, Miss Neilson, of Edinburgh, whose excellent conduct I found the theme of universal praise," had a husband who embraced the Russian interest, secured himself a handsome pension, and after residing several years in Scotland, preached Christianity to the Tartars, who despised a paradise without *houris*, and to that year had not made a single convert. His residence in Scotland must have been short, as Dr. Lyall visited him and his *sultana* in the Crimea in 1822, and Clarke, in his *Travels*, mentions visiting him at Simpheropol. He was dead before 1855, when his mother was living near the field of Alma. He had a son in the Russian army, and a daughter who was maid-of-honour to the wife of the Grand Duke Constantine. In the obituaries for 1855 we find the following:—

> At Simpheropol in the Crimea, in June, H.H. the Sultana Anne Katte Ghery Krim Ghery, daughter of the late J. Neilson, Esq., of Millbank; and at Simpheropol, in the nine month, Alexandrina Baroness Gersdorf, her eldest daughter; and at Ekatermoslav, the following week, her younger daughter, Margaret Anne, wife of Thomas Upton, an Englishman in the Russian service.

In the Crimea in those days, James Sinclair, a Scottish gardener, resided for thirteen years on the estate of Prince Woronzoff, laying out the gardens; and Hunt, a Scottish architect, prepared plans for the unfinished Imperial Palace at Great Orlanda.

Besides those of the Greigs, several Scottish names came prominently forward in the Russian service about the time of the Crimean war. Among these we may note the names of Generals Stuart, Ochterlony, Ramsay, Wilson, Bead, the Armstrongs, and Nicholas Baird.

General Stuart, a very aged officer, shortly before his death was at Inverness in 1853, making the last of his periodical pilgrimages to the scenes of the "Forty-five," and, according to the *Courier*, "was connected with the Royal family of Stuart through Prince Charles' daughter, the Duchess of Albany." He was probably a relation of Baron Stuart, Russian agent-general at Bucharest in May, 1877.

General Ochterlony was a son of John Ochterlony, Esq., of Montrose, and of the line, we believe, of Guynde. His father settled in Russia about 80 years before the Crimean war. An Alexander Ochterlony, merchant, late of Narva, died in 1805 at Novo Mirgorod in the Ukraine.

The general's great-grandfather was Laird of Kintrochat, and his great-grandmother was Miss Young of Auldbar.

He commanded a Russian brigade at the Battle of Oltenitza, in

November, 1853, and fell, mortally wounded, on the field of Inkerman, according to Prince Mentshicoff's despatch.

In 1854, General Ramsay (probably of the Balmaine line) was appointed governor of Finland.

General Wilson, a Scottish engineer officer, who, on the 1st August, 1856, "completed his half century of military service under the double-headed eagle," stipulated that he should not be called upon to fight with British troops. When the fiftieth year of his service was concluded, he held his jubilee at Alexanderoffski, twelve miles from St. Petersburg, which became a scene of boisterous merry-making. The village ran with *vodka*, and was ablaze with fireworks. Next day the emperor sent the veteran a splendid diamond cross, with the highest Order to which he was eligible.

He was in his 80th year when the war broke out, and he was still at the head of millwright and other engineering establishments at Colpina. By his mediation passports were given to all British citizens desirous of returning home.

General Read, who fought at the Battle of Tchernaia, was the son of a civil engineer, a native of Montrose, who settled in Russia early in life. The general rose to be Imperial lieutenant of the Caucasian provinces in absence of Prince Woronzow.

He was slain at the head of the Russian column, and on his body was found the orders signed by Prince Gortchakoff for fighting the battle. From them it would appear that a most determined attempt was to be made to raise the siege of Sebastopol. Had he succeeded. Balaclava was to be attacked and the heights stormed, while a sortie was to have been made from the city.

The gallant Marshal Pelissier sent in some relics of the general, and ordered a search to be made for his body till found. On this, Prince Gortchakoff wrote him thus:—

Sebastopol, August 19th.—M. le Commandant-in-Chief,—I have the honour to receive your communication of 16th inst., as well as the portfolios, containing property and a letter of General Read. I acknowledge gladly all the worth of so noble an act, as well as the generous solicitude which has led your Excellency to order a search for the body of this gallant general. Accept the sincere expression of my feelings on this subject, and the assurance of my highest esteem.—Michael Gortchakoff.

General Armstrong we only know to have been originally from

Jedburgh, where his son, Colonel Armstrong, also of the Russian army, had possession in 1867 of what is known as Queen Mary's House, in that ancient Border burgh.

In 1854, Nicholas Baird, a Scotsman born, but naturalised Russian subject, was, and had been since 1820, a naval and mechanical engineer of the highest class at Cronstadt (*Journal de St, Pétersbourg*, May, 1854); and he was vigorously assailed in all the English newspapers as "a disgrace to his country."

In the mobilisation of the Russian army in November 1876, Prince Barclay de Towie (or Tolly) Weiman appeared as commander of the 7th Corps, representative of that "Sir Valter Barclay of Tollie, *miles*," who founded in 1210 the old castle bearing that inscription on the Banff Road near Turriff, and was progenitor of the great Russian field-marshal, Prince Barclay de Tolly, whose name is imperishable as one of the heroes that shook the power of Napoleon.

CHAPTER 7

The Scots in Prussia

So far back as the year 1380 we find a train of Scottish knights and men-at-arms fighting under Waldenrodt, Grand Master of the Teutonic Order, in defence of Dantzig, or *Danesvick*, as it was then named, when besieged by the Pagans of Prussia under Udislaus Jagello during that fifty years' war which ended in nearly extirpating the ancient inhabitants, who seemed incapable of receiving the Christian faith.

The Scots were led by William Douglas, Lord of Nithsdale, known as the "Black Douglas" from his swarthy complexion, who made such havoc on the English borders—where his name became so terrible that nurses, as Godscroft tells us, scared their children "when they would not be quiet, by saying, 'The Black Douglas comes! The Black Douglas will get thee!'" (fol. ed., 1643). He married a daughter of Robert II before setting out for Dantzig, in making a furious sally from which he and his Scottish knights cut the besiegers to pieces and cleared the district.

For this he was created Prince of Danesvick, Duke of Spruce, and Admiral of the Fleet, while all Scots were forever made free men of the town; and in token thereof the Royal arms of Scotland, with those of Douglas, were placed over the great gate, where they remained "until it was lately rebuilt," says the *Atlas Geographicus* for 1711. A part of the suburbs is still called *Little Scotland*, and near it was the ancient bridge on which Douglas was foully murdered by a band of English assassins employed by Lord Clifford, who had insulted him, and yet dreaded to meet him in mortal combat. By his wife he left a daughter, known in the encomiastic language of the age as "The Fair Maid of Nithsdale."

In 1639-40 "Colonels William Cunninghame, Drummond, and Mill, who had commanded Scottish regiments in Prussia, Lusatia, and

Silesia, introduced great improvements into the army of the Covenant." (*Memoirs of Montrose*, London, 1858.)

We have elsewhere referred to John Bruce, of the Airth family, who about 1650 landed by mistake at Kônigsberg in Prussia, and entered the service of the Elector of Brandenburg, as that province comprising the ancestral domains of the reigning family is still named, and was very soon appointed to the command of a regiment, which was the highest rank he ever obtained, though he stood well in the regards of the Elector, as the following anecdote, related in the same memoir of his grandson, proves:—

My grandfather one day was hunting with the Elector, when his Highness, in eager pursuit of the chase, entered a large wood, and was separated from all his attendants except my grandfather (Colonel Bruce), who kept up with him. Night overtaking them in the wood, they were obliged to dismount and lead their horses, when, after groping their way for a considerable time in the dark, they perceived a light in the distance, and found themselves at the miserable hut of a poor tar-burner (*sic*), who lived a great way into the forest. Being informed that they were a long way from any village or habitation, the prince, being tired and hungry, asked what they could get to eat, upon which the poor man produced a loaf of coarse black bread, of which the Elector ate heartily, with a draught of pure water, declaring that he had never eaten with so good an appetite before.

On asking how large the forest was, he was told that it was of vast extent, and bordered on Mecklenburg-Strelitz. My grandfather observed that it was a pity such a tract should lie useless, and asked a grant of it, offering to build a village on the spot where they then stood. To this the Elector agreed, confirmed the gift by charter, with a great privilege annexed; so my grandfather built the village in the middle of the forest, which he called *Brucewald*, or 'Bruce Wood,' and another at the peasant's hut, which he called Jetzkendorf, its ancient name from some ruins there visible. The Elector slept upon some straw till daybreak, when he was awakened by his attendants, who had been searching for him all night, and with whom he returned to Berlin. (*Memoirs of P. H. Bruce, Esq.*)

Colonel John Bruce married then a lady of the Arensdorf family, with whom he got several estates, and by whom he had two sons and three daughters. One of the latter was married to the governor of Pomerania; the second became Abbess of a Protestant convent, but afterwards married Colonel Rebeur, who got Bruce Wood with her. Colonel Bruce's eldest son Charles was killed, a lieutenant of infantry, at the siege of Namur; his youngest son James married Catherina Detring, of a noble family in Westphalia, when lieutenant of a Scottish regiment, commanded by David Earl of Leven, who, according to Douglas, brought that regiment over with him to Britain in 1688, and was made governor of Edinburgh Castle after the great siege in 1689. H. P. Bruce was born in the castle of Detring in 1692. Bruce says:

> This regiment was ordered to Flanders, and my father carried my mother with him, where he remained till 1698, when the regiment returned to Scotland, whither we accompanied him. The regiment was then put in garrison at Fort William.

After being educated at Cupar-Fife, young Henry P. Bruce joined his uncle, Colonel Rebeur's Prussian regiment, as a volunteer, carrying a firelock, and served four campaigns under the Duke of Marlborough, the first being in 1707. In the winter of 1710 he was quartered at Tournay, and while there received an invitation—as elsewhere recorded—to join his cousin, the master of the ordnance in Russia, with the rank of captain, which he accepted.

After serving in various parts of the Russian empire, in 1716 he was ordered to discipline thirty grenadiers, men of enormous stature, for the King of Prussia, who had a craze for tall soldiers. Some of these men, one of whom was an Indian, one a Turk, two Persians, and two Tartars, the rest being Muscovites, were six feet nine inches in height, without shoes; and to the king they were sent as a present from the *Czar*. By marching and sledging he conveyed these to Prussia, halting at Riga on the 12th April, and there they were "regaled" by seeing twelve men broken alive on the wheel for a robbery and murder, which he details at great length. He arrived at Berlin and received a purse of 200 *ducats* for "his giants, who were all in good health and spirits," and whom the king declared to be "the handsomest men he had ever seen."

In 1721 he received intelligence that by the death of his grandfather certain Scotch estates had devolved on him; but he failed to get leave from the *Czar*, with whom he went on the Persian expedition in 1723, and, after making a survey of the Caspian coasts and performing other services, he ultimately returned to Scotland, was employed in the fortification of Berwick in 1745, and died in his ancestral house in the year 1767.

In 1724 (according to the *Evening Courant* of 9th April) the people of Edinburgh had the spectacle of "a band of drums beating through the city, by permission of King George," for recruits for the King of Prussia's tall Grenadier Regiment; and again a levy in Edinburgh was made for the same corps in 1728—each recruit getting two guineas as *arles*.

In 1747, General James Keith, leaving the Russian service, entered that of Frederick the Great,[1] who, aware of his high attainments in war and diplomacy, at once made him a field-marshal of the Prussian armies, and so far distinguished him by his confidence as to travel in disguise with him over a great part of Poland, Hungary, and Germany. In public business Frederick made him his chief counsellor, and in diversions his chief companion.

He was greatly delighted with a war game which Keith invented—something suggested by chess. The latter ordered some thousand tiny statuettes of men in armour to be cast by a founder, and these were massed opposite each other in battle array; then parties would be ordered from the wings or centre to show the advantages of such movements; and in this way the king and the marshal would amuse themselves for hours together, to the improvement of their military knowledge.

It is recorded of Keith that when he went to Paris to be treated for the terrible wound he received at Ochachof, Folard was writing his *Polybius*. As a military author was rare then, the marshal's chief desire was to make his acquaintance, and Folard readily showed him some of his writings—among others, his remarks on the Battle of Telemone, where the Gauls, when attacked by two double Roman armies, had to present a double front. Keith told him there was a similar case in the Bible: when David in the same order fought the Amorites and Syrians. Folard, on making good the discovery, embraced Keith, and said: "My dear sir, could you not procure that book for me? it is not to be found in Paris!"

When Keith expressed his astonishment at this remark, the chevalier excused himself by saying "he knew the book only by the name of the Holy Writings, and not by that of the Bible; and that, as he never believed it contained such excellent things, he had never taken the

---

1. *Frederick the Great & the Seven Years' War* by F. W. Longman also published by Leonaur.

51

trouble to read it."

In 1750, we find (*Scots Mag.*, 1750) that there was married, at Berlin, the *chevalier* Keith, eldest son of Sir William Keith of Ludquharne, Aberdeenshire, deceased, and nephew of Marshal Keith, to the only daughter of M. de Suhm, one of the King of Prussia's privy councillors. He was previously a captain in the Russian service, but left it with his kinsman, and was made lieutenant-colonel and A.D.C. to the King of Prussia.

In 1751 the King of Prussia sent the marshal's brother, George, the attainted earl marshal, as his ambassador to the court of France, and three years after he was appointed governor of Neufchatel

Frederick, in his history of the Seven Years' War, refers to a famous political *intriguante*, "Madame Ogilvie," who in 1766-7 was first lady-in-waiting to the queen, and had extensive estates near Leutzneritz, and to whom letters of great importance were sent from Balumia containing secret intelligence, concealed in boxes supposed to contain puddings—a discovery "which rendered the court more circumspect in its correspondence."

Other Scotch names crop up about the same time in Prussia.

The *London Gazette* of 31st January, 1768, records that Major John Grant, of the Prussian Regiment of Guards, and A.D.C. to the King Frederick, returned to Berlin from London, and passed on to Silesia "to give his Majesty an account of the commission he has executed at the Court of England. This officer has received several handsome presents from the King of Great Britain."

The *Caledonian Mercury* of the following year mentions the death of Patrick Grant of Dunlugus, in Banffshire; adding that he died a bachelor. He is succeeded in his estate by his brother, Major John Grant, A.D.C. to the King of Prussia, and that he had been twice on missions "to the court of Britain since the present war." He was major-general in 1759. He had formerly been in the Russian service, and, like Ludquharne, accompanied Marshal Keith to Prussia, where he died in 1764, Baron Le Grant and governor of Neisse, in Prussian Siberia. (*Edinburgh Advert.*, vol. iii.)

In 1758, when Frederick the Great inaugurated a new campaign by entering Moravia, he invested Olmutz, and after the siege was raised the Prussian army, led by Marshal Keith, then governor of Berlin, had several skirmishes with the Austrians, whom he either defeated or foiled by the skill of his movements, till at length he found means to effect a junction with the column of the king, who was impatient to engage the Austrians under Count Daun.

With coolness and ability the latter affected to decline an engagement, and seemed even to retire before the king; but he never halted two days in the same place till the 10th of October, when he took post in a strongly entrenched camp in front of the well-trained Prussian army, which was full of ardour to engage. A courier was then despatched to Marshal Keith, who was scouring the country with a body of cavalry, which encountered a column of the enemy on the 12th and dispersed it, taking the leader prisoner.

At five in the afternoon of the 13th the marshal marched into camp, when he found the whole army in order of battle opposite to the Austrians. With his friend the king he concerted a plan of operations, and had assigned to him the command of the right wing.

"But take a little rest," said Frederick; "you will need all your vigour for the morrow."

This was at Hochkirken, a village of Saxony, in the Lusatian circle, and situated, as the name implies, on a height.

Count Daun, however, precluded the execution of this purpose by surprising the Prussian trenches at four a.m. on the 14th October. In order to draw the king, he sent a detachment into an adjacent wood, with orders to fell the timber as noisily as possible, and meanwhile got his main body in motion, leaving all their tents standing. The Saxons in his army were clothed in the Prussian uniform, and some of these he seat forward to reconnoitre the outposts of Frederick. Unluckily for this artful scheme, two sentinels who were advanced at the extremity of the Prussian lines had gone beyond the limits of their post, and were made prisoners, thereby causing some alarm at the very time when the Austrians were extending their front.

The Prussian uniform, the darkness of the morning, and the prevalence of a thick fog, deceived the army of Frederick; thus, when the other sentinels, who were next the two who had been seized, said, "Is all well?" the answer came, "All's well."

This was exactly at 4 a.m., when the Austrian grenadiers, after pouring in a volley, slung their muskets and assailed the trenches sword in hand. In the camp of Frederick the most dreadful confusion now ensued; the officers rushed to their posts. Marshal Keith sprang up in his tent, and was in the act of stooping to draw on a boot when a ball passed through his heart and he fell dead without uttering a word.

The right wing, deprived thus of a leader, was nearly cut to pieces by the Austrians, though the king, when informed that Keith had fallen, assumed the command in that quarter, and got as many regiments as possible to close up and present a front to the enemy, while he began to retire with the rest, unfollowed by Count Daun, who was too wary to pursue.

One account has it that Marshal Keith's body was disgracefully stripped by the retreating Prussians. Another (in the *Gentleman's Magazine*) states that the king sent to Count Daun, earnestly recommending the wounded to his care, and the interment of the dead in accordance with their rank. The count went immediately to the tent of Marshal Keith, "when he found the corpse not yet stripped, and lying on the spot where he fell. Orders were immediately given for carrying him to a church within two miles of Hochkirken, where his lordship surveyed the body, but, unable to stand unmoved in view of such a spectacle, he embraced him and kissed him amid a flood of tears. Everyone in the army pressed forward to gaze on him; all the general officers lamented his misfortune and joined in high encomiums on his valour and virtues."

And of the many who stood by few were more deeply moved than the gallant Irish exile. Count Joseph Lacy, under whose father, the conqueror of the Crimea, Keith had served, and who burst into tears when he saw the old wound won at the storming of Okzokof. On the day of his temporary funeral at Hochkirken, the general officers of the Austrian army offered to carry the coffin on their shoulders, and, as it was lowered down, three rounds were fired from twelve field-pieces, with three rounds of musketry. Wrote one at the time:

> Such was the end of the great Scottish field-marshal, James Keith, in whose person were united the virtues of a man, a hero, and a Christian. He was a friend to merit, a benefactor to the indigent, and a well-wisher to mankind in general. He was so amiable in his temper and agreeable in his conversation that he won the love and admiration of all who knew him with any degree of intimacy. . . . Such uncommon desert could not fail to procure him the esteem and confidence of the Prussian monarch, who is so sagacious in discovering and so generous in rewarding merit.

By order of Frederick, the body was removed to Berlin, and interred with great pomp in a vault of the garrison church. All the bells in the city tolled while the vast funeral *cortège*, the Hussars, the battalions of Leuderitz and Langen, with arms reversed and craped colours, the marshal's helmet, sword, gloves, and *bâton*, and a mourning coach containing his nephew, Mr. Keith, and Marshal Kulstein, passed through Boss Street, King Street, and over the great bridge to the grand-parade.

In this year a pardon was most grudgingly granted by George II to his brother, the Earl Marshal, and he was permitted to succeed to the estates of Kintore, and to return home. It was then the King of Prussia wrote that letter which we find in Cordiner's *Antiquities, etc., of the North of Scotland*:—

> I cannot allow the Scots the happiness of possessing you altogether. Had I a fleet I would make a descent on their coast and carry you off. I must therefore have recourse to your friendship to bring you to him who esteems and loves you. I loved your brother (James Keith) with all my heart and soul; I was indebted to him for great obligations! This is my right to you—this is my title! I spend my time as formerly, only at night I read Virgil's *Georgics*, and go to my garden in the morning to make my gardener reduce them to practice. He laughs at Virgil and me, and thinks us both fools.
>
> Come to ease, to friendship, and philosophy; these are what, after the bustle of life, we must all have recourse to.
>
> Frederick.

Thus urged, the Earl Marshal again returned to his government of Neufchatel, after which he entered the Spanish service.

To the memory of Marshal Keith a monument was erected in the Wilhelm Platz, near the Potsdam gate of Berlin, and, on the recommendation of Prince Bismarck, a copy thereof was sent to Peterhead, and erected in front of the town-house there, as the Emperor of Germany in 1868. With it he sent a Cabinet order, of which the following is a translation:—

> I have received with particular satisfaction the representation of the provost, magistrates, and town-council of the worthy town of Peterhead, that the memory of Field-Marshal J. F. E. Keith and his heroic career in Prussia still live in his native place. I therefore willingly grant the town of Peterhead the wished-for statue of the Field-Marshal, after the model of the monument which my great ancestor ordered to be placed to his deserving general in Berlin, and hope that this statue may contribute to maintain a lasting connection between the birthland of the

Field-Marshal and his adopted home, Prussia.

With the execution of this present order I commission you, the Minister of Foreign Affairs.

Coblenz, 23rd August, 1868.

(Signed)   Wilhelm.

For the Minister of Foreign Affairs,

Gr. Eulenburg.

CHAPTER 8

The Scots in Prussia—(Concluded)

During the siege of Dantzig by the French in 1807, Alexander Gibson, a Scottish merchant there, distinguished himself on the walls and batteries so greatly as to obtain personal letters of thanks from the King of Prussia and the officer commanding. General Kalkrenth. This gentleman was a fourth son of William Gibson, a merchant of Edinburgh, and a brother of the well-known Sir James Gibson-Craig of Riccarton; but during the Franco-Prussian war of 1869-70 many Scottish names came prominently forward in the service of the King of Prussia.

A Major Douglas, commanding a regiment in garrison at Pillau, asserted his claim to the dukedom of Douglas, in right of a seventh son of that house (whose name is not to be found in the *Douglas Peerage*), born to William, ninth Earl of Angus, who died in 1691, but the claim was not pressed; and concerning the Scotsmen "who have served with distinction in the Prussian army," the *North German Correspondent* of October, 1869, stated that the families of most of these had left Scotland "in 1657 to escape from the power of General Monk. Many noblemen then thought it advisable to seek a refuge on the Continent, or at least to send their children to a place of safety.

"Among the names of the refugees we find many who occupy a high place in Scottish history, as, for example, Douglas, Bothwell (of the Holyrood House family?), Gordon, Hamilton, Keith, Morton, Crichton, and Abernethy. Prussia was then rising into importance under the rule of the Great Elector, 'and,' as one of them wrote, 'this country being fertile and well situated for trade, made us stay here.' They long continued to maintain friendly and intimate relations with the country of their birth and the branches of their families who had remained at home; but the losses which the Scottish nobility suffered by the Civil War prevented their return.

"Thus, even before the Huguenot emigration, Prussia formed an asylum for the exiled Scots, who, as we have lately showed, have nobly repaid her hospitality. Among those who are still serving in her army we may specially mention Lieutenant-General Hellmuth von Gordon, who fought at the head of the Magdeburg brigade with great bravery at Königgratz."

In 1870, Lord Charles Hamilton, son of the eleventh Duke of Hamilton, served in the German army, particularly at the siege of Strasbourg; he underwent such hardship from exposure, and his constitution suffered so severely, that he died of it in after years; and in the summer of 1880 the German navy in the Baltic was commanded by Rear-Admiral MacLean, "the descendant of a noble Scottish emigrant, who accompanied Keith to Berlin in the time of Frederick the Great," according to the *Globe*, "and was the first Prussian naval cadet. He early distinguished himself, took an active part in the improvement of the German navy, and commanded the *Prinz Aldabert* on her late voyage round the world. His resignation is generally deplored, as it will deprive the Imperial service of one of its most experienced and valuable officers."

In 1871, when the Campbell clan presented a magnificent necklace to the Princess Louise on the occasion of her marriage with the Marquis of Lorne, among the subscribers appeared the name of Lieutenant Ronald Campbell, of the 7th or Magdeburg Cuirassiers, who had won the Iron Cross for saving his colonel's life at Vionville; and further attention was drawn to him when, as Captain, as Baron Craignish and A.D.C. to the Duke of Saxe-Coburg and Gotha, he was in London in 1884 in charge of the band of that regiment, clad in white tunics and bright steel helmets.

The 7th, or, as it is more often called, Bismarck's Cuirassiers, played a very important part in the desperate Battle of Mars-la-Tour, on 14th August, 1870, when Prince Frederick Charles sacrificed his cavalry to save his infantry. On that memorable day the Brandenburg division was thrown forward to overlap the advance quad of Marshal Bazaine's army on the Verdun road. For a long time it was as much as the division could do to hold its own. Suddenly on its right flank a French battery galloped into position, and began to decimate its ranks. Then, from under cover of the little hamlet called La Ferme, the Bismarck Cuirassiers, in column of squadrons, and led by Count Schmetto, charged up the slope and rushed on the battery sword in hand.

"IN THE *MÉLÉE* THAT ENSUED A FRENCH INFANTRY
OFFICER SEIZED THE STAFF."

Says the *Army and Navy Gazette:*

> Beside the count rode a young Scotch lieutenant named Campbell, who had entered the German army and won his commission on the field of Sadowa. The squadrons reached the guns and captured them, cutting down the gunners and striking the horses as the guns were being limbered up. At that moment the *cuirassiers* received a most galling fire from the regiments of French infantry, until then invisible, but formed in square on the Verdun Road, and without a moment's hesitation Count Schmetto led his squadrons at these squares.

The French cast away their arms and flung themselves prone on the earth crying for mercy! Then appeared on either flanks of the *cuirassiers* bodies of French cavalry, but, wheeling to the right and left in splendid style, the Germans drove both the 7th French Cuirassiers and 4th Chasseurs d'Afrique into some woods, after which they re-formed at leisure, though volleys were poured on them. Says the writer before quoted:

> At the infantry went Count Schmetto again, this time punishing both battalions fearfully," " Lieutenant Campbell was carrying at this time the colours of the French *cuirassiers*, which he had captured. In the *mêlée* that ensued a French infantry officer seized the staff, and, placing a revolver to Lieutenant Campbell's hand, sent a bullet clean through it, thus forcing him to drop his prize. The Frenchman did not live long to tell the tale! The Bismarck Cuirassiers went into this action 800 strong, and came out of it numbering some 250 officers and men. Lieutenant Campbell received the Iron Cross from the hands of the Crown Prince of Germany, the Order of Saxe-Coburg Gotha, and was further made Baron von Craignish in recognition of his gallant conduct throughout the war, and was subsequently promoted.

A writer in *Notes and Queries* stated that this officer's great-grandfather, Farquhar Campbell, married Margaret, daughter of Dougald Campbell of Craignish, and though removed from being the head of the old family, is sprung from it in more than one line of descent, and that he is "simply a cadet of the Clan Dougal Craignish."

His brother officer. Count William Douglas, captain of the Garde du Corps of the German army, was presented at the Prince of Wales's *levée* in June, 1886.

A few Scotsmen have found their way into the service of Hanover, that petty electorate (kingdom it could scarcely be called) which is now an integral portion of the Prussian empire—fortunately for Great Britain, that was so often called on to defend it.

There, some time about the year 1640, Major-General Sir James Lumsden of Invergellie was commandant of Osnaburg. He had been third colonel of the Green Brigade of Scots in Sweden, and was afterwards Scottish governor of Newcastle. (Turner's *Memoirs, etc.*)

Major Drummond Graham of Inchbraikie, son of Captain Graham, of the 72nd Highlanders, who was wounded at Gibraltar, and grandson of the Laird of Inchbraikie, who was a captain in the Dutch service, served in the Hanoverian Guards, and at Waterloo was severely wounded in the defence of La Haye Sainte, falling under a charge of French *cuirassiers*. He died at Tours in April, 1855.

Two other cadets of the Pitfirran family were in the same service, sons of General Sir Hugh Halkett, C.B., and G.C.H., a Peninsula and Waterloo officer of the German Legion, who also served in North Germany, and at the siege of Stralsund in 1807.

These were Colonel James Halkett (once of the Coldstream Guards), who died at Largs in 1870, a baron of the kingdom of Hanover; and Baron Colin Halkett, who died at Celle (or Zell) in 1879.

A few Scots also are to be traced in Poland, or Polish Prussia, and of these a curious collection of "Birth Brieves" will be found in the fifth volume of the *Spalding Club Miscellany*.

In 1568 (according to the *Atlas Geographicus*, vol. i), George, fifth Earl of Huntly, when under forfeiture, probably for his father's share at the Battle of Corrichie in 1562, "was made a Marquis of Poland, and is the only one there."

According to *Letters of the Reign of James VI*, in 1624, Poland is described as being literally "swarming with Scots pedlars"; but in Dantzig many of these so-called pedlars were very opulent merchants, who had a rule of government among themselves, and lived in such a way as to secure the respect and esteem of the people there. A great tide of emigration seems to have gone on, "exorbitant numbers of young boys and maids unfit for service," till, in the summer of the year named, an expulsion of the Scots was threatened, and seemingly was only obviated by the influence of Patrick Gordon, agent for James VI in the city of Dantzig.

About 1648 we find two of the Huntly family in Poland.

Lord Henry Gordon and his sister. Lady Catherine, were son and daughter of George, the second marquis. The former, during the usurpation of Cromwell, took military service in Poland under John Casimir, and won high distinction by his bravery; and the latter, who accompanied him, by her marriage with Count Morstain, high treasurer of Poland, became the ancestress of Prince Czartorinski, who during the middle of the last century was one of the candidates for the Polish crown, and of several other families of distinction (Sir Robert Douglas, etc.)

In 1656 Lord Cranston levied a Scottish regiment for the King of Poland's service; "the Royalists," says *Fraser of Kirkhill,* "choosing rather to go abroad, though in a mean condition, than live at home in slavery." This corps would seem to have been chiefly enlisted at Inverness, where forty-three Frasers joined it, including Lovat's son as captain, young Clanvacky as a lieutenant, young Phopachy as an ensign, and young Foyers as a corporal. The rest came from Stratherrick, Strathglass, etc., and marched out of Inverness in the face of Monk's garrison. This levy proved unfortunate. Most of them were cut off in Poland, and we shall meet with the survivors elsewhere fourteen years after.

In a Scottish newspaper called *The North Briton,* long since defunct, there occurs the following paragraph:—

> It is a circumstance not unworthy of remark that a great number of persons of Scottish lineage are now to be found in Poland. Among the Polish nobility are several names very common in this country, as belonging to our oldest and best families—such as Johnston, Lindsay, Gordon, and Middleton. These individuals are in general descended from Scottish adventurers who sought employment in Russian armies in the 17th century. (*North Briton,* January 6, 1831.)

There died in October, 1886, at Munich, a Scottish lady, the Countess of Usedom (in Pomerania), whose husband was deliverer of the famous "Stab in the Heart" despatch. She was the daughter of Sir John Malcolm of Burnfoot (the distinguished soldier and Persian diplomat), and his wife Charlotte, daughter of Sir Alexander Campbell, Bart., and was born in 1818.

CHAPTER 9

The Scots in Austria

Curiously enough, an ancient Scottish pilgrim, called St. Colman in the Roman Breviary, is the apostle of Austria. When proceeding on a pilgrimage to Jerusalem, he reached Stockheraw, on the Danube, six miles from Vienna, where the inhabitants, believing him to be a spy, tortured him to death on the 13th October, 1012. He was canonised by Gregory IX, became honoured in Austria as the tutelary saint of the country, where several churches were founded in his honour, and—according to the *Atlas Geographicus*—in Vienna there was still (in 1711) a Scottish house or convent, "founded for the reception of Scotsmen in their pilgrimages to the Holy Land"—a fashion surely past at that period.

The Princess Eleanor Stuart, second daughter of the illustrious James I, was married to Sigismund, Duke of Austria, who came again to Scotland with Mary of Gueldres, in 1449. She had all her father's love of literature, and translated the romance of *Ponthus et Sidoyne* into German for the amusement of her husband.

In May, 1620, the drums of Sir Andrew Gray (designed sometimes of Broxmouth) were beating up for recruits to follow him to the Bohemian wars against the Emperor of Germany, and he formed a camp on the Monkrig in Haddingtonshire, where he was joined by Sir John Hepburn of Athelstaneford and other gallant soldiers of fortune. Sir Andrew Gray figures frequently in history during the reign of James VI. Being a Catholic, he was obnoxious to the Church, and in 1694, as "Captain Andrew Gray," was classed among "Papists and traitors" in the *Book of the Universal Kirk*; and at the battle of Glenlivet, as "colonel," he commanded the Earl of Huntly's artillery. (*Wodrow.*) A letter of Lady Margaret Setoun's, dated 19th May, 1620, states that "Coronell Gray, his captains and their men of weir, are all going to Bohemia the

xx. of this instant." (*Eglinton Memorials.*)

On being recruited by 150 moss-troopers, captured by the Warden of the Middle Marches, for turbulence on the Border, Sir Andrew Gray, on finding that his force amounted to 1,500 men, embarked at Leith and sailed for Holland, *en route* for Bohemia, in the Protestant cause, which was also the cause of the son-in-law of the King of Scotland, the cowardly Elector Palatine, and they were conducted, by way of Frankfort, with the aid of Henry Frederick, Prince of Nassau, to escape the Marquis of Spinola, who was hovering on another route to cut them off.

Though aware that the Spaniards and Germans, under the Archduke, under Spinola, and others, were about to invade the Palatinate, James VI remained strangely apathetic. Thus the Protestants of Scotland and England were indignant— of the former kingdom all the more so as the people considered the good and gentle Princess Elizabeth one of themselves. Thus Sir Andrew Gray, though "a ranke Papist," as he is called by Calderwood, drew his sword in her cause.

Under Sir Horace Vere, who had served with distinction in that desperate affair at Sluys, when under Count Wilhelm, "the old Scots Regiment led the van of battle," some 200 English volunteers sailed from Gravesend two months after the Scots had led the way, and these combined British auxiliaries joined a part of the Bohemian army, consisting of 10,000 men, the Margrave of Anspach not having mustered his entire force.

In September the Duke of Bavaria and Spinola took the field to enforce the Imperial authority; and, in the campaigns which ensued, young Hepburn, by his own valour, when in his twentieth year, became captain of a company of pikes in Sir Andrew Gray's band, and, prior to the fatal battle of Prague, had the special duty of guarding the King of Bohemia.

Among his comrades was one named Edmonds, son of a baker in Stirling, who on one occasion, with his sword in his teeth, swam the Danube, where it was both deep and rapid, stole past the Austrian lines, and, favoured by the gloom of a dark night, penetrated into the heart of the Imperial camp. There, by equal strategy and personal strength, he gagged and brought off as prisoner Charles de Longueville, the great Count de Benguoi, recrossed the stream, and presented him as a prisoner to the Prince of Orange, then an ally of the Elector-King of Bohemia. For this deed he was at once made colonel.

He amassed great wealth in these wars, and in the decline of life returned to die in his native town, where he built a handsome manse for the parish minister, and, in memory of his father, placed in the eastern gable thereof the bakers' arms in stone—three *piels*—which remained there till 1710; and to his daughter, who married Sir Thomas Livingstone, Bart, of Westquarter, he left a magnificent fortune. (*Douglas Peerage,*)

This was, no doubt, the same Colonel Edmonds who is referred to as serving at the defence of Ostende, eighteen years before. We are told that when the States-General reviewed the garrison the commands were assigned to "Colonel Dorp, a Dutchman; Colonel Edmunds, a Scotsman; and Hertoin, a Frenchman; while Sir Francis Vere, with the former garrison, joined the army under Prince Maurice." (Russell's *Modern Europe*, vol. iii.)

Three Haigs—Robert, George, and James—sons of John Haig of Beimerside, served in these wars. Their mother, Elizabeth Macdougall of Stodrig, had been nurse to the Princess Elizabeth in Falkland; and all died in their armour fighting for her on the plains of Bohemia.

By this time the Battle of Prague had been fought on the 8th November, 1620. There Gray's Scots guarded the King of Bohemia; there the latter, in one day, by his kinsman Maximilian of Bavaria, was stripped of the Bohemian crown and Electoral hat, and 4,000 Bohemians were slain. Then, in grim earnest, began the terrible Thirty Years' War; while the timid Elector fled to Silesia, and finally to France—in his flight and terror leaving behind his queen, the Scottish princess, who was protected and carried off on his own horse by Ensign Hopkin, a young officer of pikes, in the band of Sir Horace Vere. She was conveyed by him to Breslau. (*Memoirs of the Queen of Bohemia*, 2 vols.)

In 1622, under Colonels Sir Andrew Gray, Henderson, younger of Fordel, Captains Hepburn and Hume, the Scottish bands transferred the scene of their services to Bergen-op-Zoom, the great fortress which bars the way to Spanish Brabant, and which they defended with heroic valour In the summer of that year it was invested by Spinola, who left 30,000 men to keep the conquered Palatinate in awe. Borgia attacked the fortress on the north, Baglioni on the south, but the Scottish pikemen hurled them from the breaches. There, Colonel Henderson was slain, and then "one Morgan with his English brigade gave them their hands full, for it is a great disadvantage for living bodies to fight against dead walls." (*Atlas Ge .,* 1711.) After firing above 200,000 cannon-shot, Spinola, on the approach of Prince Maurice, abandoned a siege which had cost him 12,000 men.

The Protestant religion was now crushed in Bohemia. The Scottish bands had joined Count Mansfeldt, to keep whose army out of Flanders Spinola met it in battle at Fleura, in Hainault, in August, 1622; and though the Scots, under Gray, Hepburn, Hume, and Sir James Ramsay, evinced the greatest bravery, the Spaniards remained masters of the field. Mansfeldt's army fell to pieces in the following year, and the remnant of his Scots who had survived the war in Bohemia turned to seek another banner under Hepburn and others. The veteran Sir Andrew returned to Scotland.

In 1624 he was seeking military employment in London from King James VI. He usually wore buff and armour, even in time of peace; and the timid monarch never saw the grim veteran without emotions of uneasiness, for, in addition to his long sword and formidable dagger, he always wore a pair of iron pistols in his girdle. On one occasion the king, seeing him thus accoutred, "told him merrily he was now so well fortified that if he were but well victualled he would be impregnable."

The year 1684 saw some Scots taking a prominent part in the fall of the great Wallenstein. When the daring ambition of the latter led him to think of dismembering the great Empire, it was crushed when he was spending his Christmas holidays in the old Castle of Egra, in Bohemia—a place then fortified by a treble wall. The garrison was commanded by John Gordon, a Presbyterian, a native of Aberdeenshire, who, from being a private soldier, had risen to the colonelcy of Tzertzski's regiment; while Wallenstein's private escort consisted of 250 men of James Butler's Irish Regiment, commanded by that officer in person.

The latter, with Colonel Gordon and Major Walter Leslie, son of the laird of Balquhain, in the Garioch, on receiving secret orders from Vienna, resolved to put the ambitious general to death. The Scots were both Presbyterians, but Butler, a Catholic, made some remarks expressive of admiration of Wallenstein.

"You may do as you please," said Gordon, grimly; "but death itself can alone alienate me from the duty and affection I bear his Majesty the Emperor."

Various modes of removing Wallenstein were suggested, and the last adopted was a resolution to slay him and his friends at a banquet to which they were invited. All the avenues were blocked up by troops. The feast was protracted to half-past ten at night, and Wallenstein had retired, when Colonel Gordon filled a goblet with wine, and proposed the health of the cunning Elector of Saxony, the chief enemy of the emperor.

Butler affected astonishment, pretended high words ensued, and while the friends of the fated Wallenstein looked about them in perplexity the hall doors were dashed in, and two Irishmen, Geraldine and Deveron, with their armed soldiers, rushed in with shouts of "Long live Ferdinand the Second!" Then Butler, Gordon, and Leslie seized up each a candle and drew their swords.

Wallenstein and his friends snatched their weapons, the tables were thrown over, and a deadly combat began. Defending himself in a corner, Colonel Tzertzski slew three.

"Leave me for a moment," he cried; "leave me to deal with Leslie and Gordon hand-to-hand, and then kill me; but oh, Gordon, what a supper is this for your friends!"

He was hewn to pieces, together with the young Duke of Lerida and others; while Deveron and thirty soldiers rushed to the bedchamber of Wallenstein, Duke of Friedland and Prince of the Vandal Isles, who, finding escape by the lofty window impossible, turned to face his destroyers—in his shirt, pale, defenceless, for Schiller asserts that he was disturbed in the study of astrology.

By one thrust of his partisan into his heart the Irishman slew him, though his soldiers shrunk back appalled; and then his naked body, with those of Colonels Kinkski, Illo Niemann, and Tzertzski, were carried through the streets of Egra and flung into a ditch. So perished the great dictator of Germany!

Butler was made a count, Deveron a colonel, Gordon was created a Marquis of the Empire, colonel-general of the Imperial army and high chamberlain of Austria.; while Leslie, who was then a captain of the Bodyguard, was created Count Leslie and Lord of Neustadt, an estate worth 200,000 florins. He died at Vienna, Field-Marshal, Governor of Sclavonia, and Knight of the Golden Fleece, in 1667-8. There is an engraving of him by Kilion, dated 1637, which states that he was ambassador from Austria to the Sultan Mahomet IV. This embassy was so magnificent that Father Taffernier, a Jesuit, wrote a particular account of it.

Butler bequeathed £3,300 to the Scottish and Irish colleges in Prague.

The famous Marquis of Montrose was in Austria in 1647, after his defeat at Philiphaugh. In summer he was in Prague with the Emperor

Ferdinand, who offered him a commission as marshal, and appointed him colonel of a regiment, with power to appoint all the officers; but he seems to have declined this honour, and proceeded to the Netherlands, prior to raising the king's standard once more in Scotland.

The Leslie who figured in the Wallenstein tragedy on his death was succeeded in his titles and estates by a son of Count Patrick Leslie, James, who gave timely succour to Vienna when besieged by the Turks, and gave to the flames the town and wooden bridge of Essek (amid the marshes of Austrian Slavonia) when defended by the Turks, for which he was made a privy councillor and president of the Imperial Council of War.

Patrick, Count Leslie, twelfth of the line of Balquhain, was privy councillor to James VII, and entailed his estate in 1698. (Shaw's *Index*)

Four counts of the Empire sprang from the family of Balquhain, whose old castle of that name, a noble square keep, erected in 1630, to replace a more ancient fortress burned by the Fortresses in 1626, still stands in the Garioch. (*Aberd, Coll.,* 4to.)

Some Scottish adventurers took part in the recapture of Buda from the Turks in 1636—among them, notably, Sir Arthur Forbes, of the Corse family, first Earl Granard, who so zealously espoused the royal cause in Scotland; George Hay, from Scotland, and "Lord Quberry (*sic*), from Scotland," whose name was referred to in the recent Buda bicentenary. The last given is some strange misspelling, as sent by the *chargé d'affaires* to the *Standard*, in August, 1886.

In 1735, John, eighteenth Earl of Crawford, joined the Imperial army at Bruschal on the Salzbach. He had previously been in the Scots Greys, 7th Dragoons, and Scots Guards; but finding there was no chance of distinction, when the provincial prejudices of the English and the enmity of the court were so high against Scotsmen, he resigned in disgust, and was received with every mark of honour by Prince Eugene of Savoy, under whom Hugh, Viscount Primrose (of Rosebery), and Captain Dalrymple were also serving as volunteers. The three served in that expedition in October, in which their force was assailed by thrice its numbers, and when the Count of Nassau was slain and Primrose was severely wounded in the head. The same afternoon was fought the Battle of Claussen, in which Lord Crawford greatly distinguished himself, and the French were driven across the Moselle.

After taking a term of service with the Russian army, under Count

Munich, and shining on more than one occasion in single combat with the Tartar horsemen, he rejoined the Austrians at Belgrade, and went to winter quarters with Prince Eugene's regiment at Comorra, where he employed himself till 1739 in drawing military plans.

Under Marshal Wallace he was at the Battle of Krotzka, near Belgrade, where, when leading a charge of Count Palfi's *cuirassiers*, on the 22nd July, 1739, his favourite black charger was shot under him, and his left thigh was shattered by a musket-ball. General Count Luchesie now ordered some grenadiers to place him on horseback, but they were compelled to leave him, and the gallant earl was found next morning by his own grooms in a deplorable condition, his face pale as death, but his hands still grasping the mane of his dead charger.

They bore him to Belgrade, but he never fully recovered from the effect of his wound, though the bullet was extracted at Comorra on the Danube, to which place he sailed. This was in February, 1740. Proceeding up the river, he was conveyed to Vienna, where he arrived on the 7th May, still in a recumbent position, for pieces of fractured bone were continually coming away.

He was able to walk on crutches for the first time in September, and removed to the baths at Baden, where he remained till August, 1741. *Via*, Vienna and Hanover he reached the fortified town of Hameln on the Weser, where he chanced to have an interview with George II, who was struck with his military enthusiasm, and prevailed upon him to resume his duties in the British army, in which, in the July of 1739, he had been gazetted colonel and captain of the Scots Horse Grenadier Guards, and afterwards to the Fourth or Scots Troop of Life Guards all of which he commanded in brigade at Dettingen and Fontenoy. But he never recovered from his wounds received at Krotzka, and died in 1749, first colonel of the Black Watch.

CHAPTER 10

The Scots in Austria—(Continued)

In 1742 the famous Baron London joined the Austrian service, from in 1716 at Tootzen, in Livonia, he was descended from the Loudons of that ilk, an important old Ayrshire family, a member of whom settled in the vicinity of Riga, where his bravery and achievements won him fiefs and honours, of which his successors were dispossessed by Charles XII of Sweden, after the peace of Oliva. During the reign of Charles XII the forfeited Loudons betook them again to the sword; one became a captain in the Royal Swedish Guards, and his nephew, Gideon Ernest Loudon, joined first, in his fifteenth year, the Russian infantry as a cadet, and made his first essay in arms when the war of the Double Election caused such a stir in Northern Europe. He served with the blockading force at Dantzig, and in 1734 his regiment formed part of the army sent by the Empress Anne to spread terror in Germany, till the peace of Vienna enabled Count Munich, with Lacy and others, to engage in barbarous wars elsewhere, and in the conquest of the Crimea as already detailed.

On the reduction of the army, Lieutenant Loudon offered his services to Maria Theresa, the empress-queen, and in passing through Berlin met several Scots with whom he had served under Munich, who urged him to join the King of Prussia. The latter affronted him by some slighting remark, so Loudon took service in Austria, and became in future wars the most formidable enemy Prussia had met in the field, and to attempt to detail his achievements would far exceed our limits.

He obtained a command in Baron Trenck's corps of Free Pandours, and was at the storming of Rheinmark, when they put the garrison to the sword, and the invasion of Lorraine, where terrible deeds were done. Loudon in disgust quitted the regiment of Trenck and was ten years on garrison duly in Croatia, where he became colonel of Croats in 1757, and distinguished himself at Hirschfeld, on the frontiers of Bohemia.

When in Croatia he spent much of his time in the study of geography and fortification. Having once obtained a great map of Germany, he spread it on the floor, and was found poring over it by his wife, Clara de Hagen, a Hungarian lady.

"My dear Major," said she, " still, as ever, busy with these horrid plans and maps."

"They will be of service to me, my dear Clara, when I obtain the *bâton* of a field-marshal of Austria."

Then she laughed, for Loudon was then only in his thirty-eighth year, and the *bâton* he referred to seemed remote indeed.

He served at the Battle of Rosbach, and in all the operations of what was known as the "combined army" of French and Austrians, to clear Saxony of the Prussians. Though daily exposed to danger for years, a bullet-wound received at Zalern was the only one suffered by Loudon in his long and arduous career.

In May, Frederick invested Olmutz, which was defended by General Marshal, a Scotsman, while Loudon with Count Daun cut off the Prussian supplies. The siege was pressed by Marshal Keith, and Loudon was made lieutenant-field-marshal and Knight of Maria Theresa; but the siege, as we have told elsewhere, was abandoned, and Frederick had to oppose the Russians under Generals Brown and Fermor, two Scotsmen, whom he ultimately drove into Poland.

Loudon, now a baron, proved one of the most famous leaders in the Seven Years' War, and the Count de Wallace was colonel of his special regiment, the Loudon Fusiliers, which they both led at the storming of Schwednitz in 1761. Previous to the attack he promised the stormers 100,000 florins to take the place without pillage.

"No, no!" cried the Walloon grenadiers; "lead on, Father Loudon; we shall follow to glory, but take no money from you."

Then Count Wallace, colonel of the Loudon Fusiliers, after being twice repulsed by two battalions of the regiment of Treskow, said:

"I must win or die! *I promised Loudon—remember our regiment bears his name, and must conquer or perish!*"

He again led them on, and the place was won.

In this war one Austrian column under Loudon was led by a General Grant, another of Prussians under Frederick was led by General Read, also a Scotsman, (see Smollett's *Hist.*, vol. vii, etc.). At Schwednitz there fell Colonel Hume Caldwell (of an old Ayrshire stock) in his 27th year In 1769 he was Aulic Councillor of War and general commanding in Moravia.

In 1778 Loudon was full marshal of the Empire, and ten years after led the armies along the frontiers of Croatia and Bosnia till he captured Belgrade. In the *Edinburgh Advertiser* for September 19, 1788, we have the following:

> On the 16th August the emperor arrived at Panezova with a detachment of 40,000 men from the main army. On reaching Jabuka he ordered the troops to halt, and made a short harangue, exhorting them to persevere to the last in the glorious cause they had undertaken to defend. On this occasion the troops, with shouts of patriotic joy, assured his Majesty they would perish to a man rather than lay down their arms till the House of Austria was restored to its just rights. On the 17th the army marched in three columns for Cubin.
>
> General Loudon took command of the Imperial army from General de Vins on the 18th August, and on the following days the Turks made attempts to force the lines, but were saluted with so heavy a fire as to oblige them to desist, leaving behind them 20 men and 25 horses killed.

In 1790 he died in the midst of his fame—the greatest general of the eighteenth century—and was buried at his estate of Haderdorf in a marble sarcophagus he had brought from Belgrade.

> Therein he now lies in peace, shaded by some stately old trees, in the centre of a green meadow. His funeral monument, which is one of great magnificence, is securely walled round, and among the sculpture with which the Austrian government adorned it can still be traced the shield argent charged with three escutcheons *sable*, the old heraldic cognisance which the Loudons of that ilk bore on their pennons in the wars of the Scottish kings.

In 1746 an Austrian squadron, consisting of eleven sail, under a Scottish Captain Forbes, was active in the operations of the war under Maria Theresa, and when the Irish Count Brown at Nice was waiting with the King of Sardinia in consultation as to their combined operations, Forbes brought over the whole Austrian artillery from Genoa for the bombardment and capture of Mont Albano; and in these wars

Sir William Gordon of Park, in Banffshire, who had escaped after Culloden, and been lieutenant-colonel in Lord Ogilvie's regiment, for his services to the Emperor of Germany, and perhaps influenced by the fact that Sir William's mother was the widow of George, Count Leslie of Balquhain—won for him and his heirs the rank of first-class *nobes* in Hungary. (Burke.) He died at Douay, 1761.

Regarding the count's family, the *Edinburgh Courant* for 1761 records the following:

> The appeal of Charles Cajetan, Count Leslie, and Antonio, Count Leslie, his son, relative to the estate of Balquhain, determined by the House (of Peers) in favour of Mr. Grant, complained of two interlocutors of the Court of Session repelling certain objections on the part of these German counts against the proof led at Vienna by the said Peter Leslie Grant, of the place of their birth and religion, importing that, being aliens and Roman Catholics, they could not succeed by the laws of this country to any heritage, but that the same does, of course, descend to the next Protestant heir.

In the middle of the last century Anthony, Count Hamilton, was lieutenant-general and captain-lieutenant of the noble German Guard of the Empire, grand bailie, minister plenipotentiary, privy-councillor, and receiver of the Order of the Knights of Malta. He died at Vienna, 24th March, 1776.

Twenty-six years afterwards there died an Austrian-Scot of great note in those days, James Lockhart Wishart of Lee and Carnwath, whose monument, erected near Mount Marl, on his estate of Dryden, at Lasswade, records that he was "Lord of the Bedchamber to his Imperial Majesty Joseph II, Emperor of Germany, Knight of the Order of Maria Theresa, Count of the Holy Roman Empire, and General of the Imperial, Royal, and Apostolic Armies. Died at Pisa, 6th February *mdccxc*, in the *lxiv*. year of his age." His uncle. Captain Philip Lockhart, was taken prisoner at Preston in 1715, and barbarously shot in cold blood by the troops of General Willis. Count Lockhart was succeeded by his son Charles, a minor; but Dryden since then has passed to other families.

In 1799, when Vienna was menaced by the French, but saved from impending peril by the Treaty of Leoben, the citadel was garrisoned by two strong battalions of the regiment of Stuart, of whom we know only the name, unless we can connect him with the noble family of

Rohenstart. There died at Dunkeld of the effects of a mail-coach accident, 28th October, 1864, Charles Edward Stuart, Count Rohenstart, a general in the Austrian army, in his ?3rd year.

In 1809 a Scottish officer, General Fowler, who was equerry to the empress, was wounded severely and taken prisoner at the Battle of Wagram by the French on the 6th of July; and in 1826 Baron John Fyfe, a native of Edinburgh, of whom we know only the name, died at Vienna far advanced in years.

There was also Colonel Graham (a brother of Gartmore), who lived—and, we believe, died—in St. Bernard's Crescent, Edinburgh, who in 1854 was a *marshal-de-camp* in the Austrian army, and had a horse shot under him in the war against Kossuth and other Hungarian patriots. He was a Knight of the Order of Maria Theresa.

In 1779 Joseph, Count Murray of Melgum and Bart, of Nova Scotia, was counsellor of state, lieutenant-general of the armies of the emperor, general-commandant and captain-general of the Low Countries.

In that year his daughter Theresa was married at Brussels to James, seventh Earl of Findlater and fourth Earl of Seafield. (Wood's *Douglas*, fol.)

Count Joseph's son, Albert, born in 1774, married the Countess Almeria Esterhazy von Galantha, and the family still exists in Austria, (as at time of first publication).

All these instances serve to show how our people won, by their worth, their probity, and valour, high honours, which, by adverse influence and political events, were denied them in the land of their forefathers.

CHAPTER 11

The Scots in Italy

Differences of religion in latter times doubtless prevented the Scottish Soldier of Fortune from seeking service in Italy as elsewhere; yet in the States thereof a few rose to eminence. The statement made by Sir Robert Douglas in his *Peerage*, on the authority of Fordoun and others, that about the year 800 the King of Scotland sent his brother William, with a William Douglas, to aid the Lombards—that the former was known as William the Scot, and the latter founded the Scoti-Douglassi in Italy; and, further, the statements to the same effect by Godscroft in his folio *History of the Douglasses* that they became the head of the Guelphs in Placentia, and so forth, seem utterly fabulous; and yet the story is strangely endorsed by one or two writers, from whom we give quotations for what they are worth.

Of these Scots are also said to be descended Francesco Scotto or Scotti, an Italian engraver, born at Florence about 1760; Girolamo Scotto or Scotti, also a celebrated engraver, born in 1780; Stephano Scotto, a Milanese painter, who flourished at the end of the fifteenth and beginning of the sixteenth centuries. (See Bryant's *Dict of Painters, etc*)

Citing a work called *Mémoire de Piacenza*, the author of *Italy and the Italian Island* (3 vols., 1841) tells us that:

Piacenza presents nothing that interests us so much as the memoirs of that family of Scotti, who from the position of wealthy citizens rose in the latter half of the thirteenth century to be its absolute lords by a cautions progress which one is almost tempted to consider nationally characteristic. For although we may be allowed to smile at the invented genealogy which claimed for them a descent from an Earl Douglas, brother of the Scottish King Achaius, and companion in arms of Charlemagne, yet the common opinion here is that their founders in Italy were really adventurers belonging to the border clan of Scott.

Another writer, A. F. Drane, writing in 1880, says:—

In Genoa, St. Catherine of Sienna and her party were entertained for a month by a noble lady named Orietta Scotta, one of Scottish origin settled in Italy, *temp.* of Charlemagne, when two brothers, Arnico and Gabriel, sons of William Scott, came to Genoa in 1120, and were given command of the Genoese troops. From Baldwin, son of Arnico, descended Barnabo, the husband of the Saint's hostess. The Scotti afterwards assumed the name and arms of the *Centurioni*. (*Life of St. Catherine*.)

The story of these Italian Scotti is referred to by Godscroft elsewhere, when he states that in 1619 two of them, named Peter and Corneilius, who had settled in Antwerp, sent in that year (when challenged by the burgomaster for putting the Douglas arms on their father's tomb) Alexander Seaton to William, Earl of Angus, "acknowledging their descent from his house, and entreating his testimonial thereupon," with a great deal more to the same purpose, including a long letter in old Italian from Marc Antonio Scoto, Marquis d'Agazono, dated 1622, to the same earl, with his family tree.

Some 30 years before that period a Captain James Scott is recorded to have fought valiantly in the wars of Lombardy, particularly at the Battle of Marignano, fought between the Swiss, the Duke of Milan, and Francis I, in 1515. (*Lives of the Queens of Scotland*,)

To come to more solid ground, we find John Wemyss, second son of Sir John XXI of Weymss and that ilk, went to the wars in Lombardy about 1547, and married a lady of rank and fortune in Brescia, and from him are descended the Counts Wemyss and other families of that surname in Italy (Douglas *Peerage*); and it was in 1583 that James Crichton, younger of Elliock, so well known as "The Admirable Crichton," was basely murdered at Mantua.

Born in Cluny Castle, Perthshire, 1560-1, he was M.A. in his fourteenth year, and rapidly became the first swordsman, tilter, dancer, and, what was then more than all, the first scholar of his age, with a knowledge of twelve languages. His history is too well known to need rehearsal here. Suffice it that, dazzled by his achievements with sword and pen, the Duke of Mantua appointed him tutor to his son, Vincentio di Gonzago, a prince of turbulent and licentious character, for whose amusement he composed a comedy containing fifteen characters, all personated by himself. But one night during the carnival in 1283, while rambling through the streets with his guitar, he was attacked by several masked and armed men.

One of these he disarmed with his characteristic facility; the rest he put to flight. On discovering that their captain, who begged for life, was the prince, his pupil, he knelt and presented him with his sword, which the villain instantly plunged into Crichton's body, inflamed, it is supposed, by rage and jealousy, slaying him upon the spot.

Kipps, an Englishman, was the first, of course, to call in question the many marvellous stories related of him; but his life by Tytler proved the truth of them all; and apart from that, a book printed at Venice in 1580, "for the Brothers Dom. and Gio. Batt Guerra," when Crichton was in his twentieth year (referred to in the *Scottish Journal of Antiquities*), further proves all that has been attributed to him, and adds that, "a soldier at all points, he served two years with distinction in the French wars; unrivalled in the dance and all feats of activity; most dexterous in the use of arms of every description, in horsemanship and tilting at the ring."

In Wishart's translation of Castruccio Bonamici's *Commentaries on the late War in Italy*, an unknown Scottish recluse, about 1640, is thus referred to by the writer, an officer of the regiment of Catalonian Horse. "That part of the Appenines lying between Modena and Lucca goes at present by the name of *Monte di San Pelegrino*, or the Foreigner's Mountain, a Scottish nobleman of the first rank having, according to tradition, lived there a solitary and austere life for many years."

Sir James Scott of Rossie gained, about 1640, a high reputation in the service of the Venetian Republic, when fighting with the Capelliti against the Germans, and was highly esteemed by the Doge Nicola Contarini. In 1644 he was in the army of Montrose, and led the left wing at the Battle of Tippermuir. By 1650 his chief patrimony of Rossie was the property of the laird of Inchture. (*Rentall Book of Perthshire*, 1664.)

He must have been dead before 1653, as Sir Robert Montgomerie, Bart., of Skelmorlie, married in that year Anne his "second daughter and co-heiress by Antonia Willobie his spouse." (Eglinton Memorials.)

He is probably one of the same family, was in the sea service of the same Republic in 1645, and of whom we might have a better account than the brief one given in a MS. in the Advocates' Library. A certain James Scott, it appears, built a vessel in the north of Scotland, described as of "prodigious bigness," and sailed with her to the Straits. He was accompanied by his brother, thus mentioned:—

William Scott was made a colonel at Venice, and his martial achievements in defence of that state against the Turks may well admit him to be ranked amongst our worthies. He became vice-admiral of the Venetian fleet, and the bane and terror of the Mussulman navigators. Whether they had galleons, galleys, *galliasses*, or great warships, it was all one to him. He set upon them all alike, saying the more there were the more he would kill, and the stronger the encounter should be, the greater should be his honour and the richer his prize. He oftentimes so swept the Archipelago of the Mussulmans that the Ottoman Power and the very gates of Constantinople would quake at the report of his victories; and he did so ferret them out of all the creeks in the Adriatic Gulf, that they hardly knew in what part of the Mediterranean they should beat shelter themselves from the fury of his blows. He died in his bed of a fever in the Isle of Candia in 1652. He was truly the glory of his nation and country, and was honoured after his death by a statue of marble, which I saw near the Rialto of Venice in 1659."

Evelyn, in his diary about 1646, gives us an interesting account of a Scottish colonel, who had a high, if not the chief, command in Milan, who, hearing him and a friend speaking English near the cathedral, sent his servant to invite them to dinner next day.

Thither they went, and found the *cavaliero* residing in a noble palace, where he had other guests, "all soldiers, one a Scotsman," to meet them, and said that, discovering they were English, he invited them to his house that they might be free from suspicion by the Inquisition. They had a sumptuous repast and plenty of tempting wine, after which he took them into a hall hung with splendid arms, many of them trophies taken with his own hand from the enemy. He bestowed a pair of fine pistols on Captain Wray, and on the latter's friend, Evelyn, "a Turkish bridle, woven with silk, curiously embossed with other silk trappings, to which hung a halfe-moone finely wrought, which he had taken from a *basshaw* he had slain. With this glorious spoil I rode to Paris, and after brought it to England."

But these English visitors seemed not even to have asked the name of their generous host, who was killed next day, being thrown against a wall by a very spirited horse be was showing off for their amusement, in defiance of the advice of his groom and page. Evelyn adds:

> This sad disaster made us consult about our departure as soon as we could, not knowing how soon we might be inquired after, or engaged, the Inquisition being so cruelly formidable and inevitable on the least suspicion. The next morning, therefore, discharging our lodgings, we agreed for a coach to carry us to the foot of the Alpes, not a little concerned for the death of the colonel who had so courteously entertained us.

Elsewhere he refers to a now unknown Scottish artist named Wright, "esteemed a good painter," and long resident in Rome, and from whose brush came some pieces, afterwards to decorate Whitehall, etc., and whose best portraits were those of Lacy, the comedian, as a cavalier or Presbyterian minister, "and a Scotch Highlander in his plaid."

In 1681 a singularly grave and yet grotesque warrant at considerable length was granted by Charles II in favour of Don Rostaino Cantelmi, Duke of Populn and Prince of Pettorano, a Neapolitan town on a mountain near Sulmona, and his brother, also Duke di Populi, proving their descent from the kings and queens of Scotland "by a continued pedigree of about 330 years *before* the Incarnation of our blessed Lord to this time—given at our Court at Windsor Castle the 25th day of August, 1681, and of our reign the 33rd year. By his Majesty's command—Morray."

This is the signature of Alexander, sixth Earl of Moray, then Secretary of State for Scotland; but no trace can be found of any parliamentary ratification at Edinburgh of this singular document deducing the prince's pedigree from Fergus I, but it is fully referred to by Litta in his *Genealogies of Illustrious Italian Families*, "and is," says a writer, "for its absurdity, quite unique."

In 1767 General Graham, younger of Buchlyvie, in Stirlingshire, died at Venice in command of the forces of the Republic. He was a kinsman of the Duke of Montrose, and brother of James Graham of Buchlyvie, one of the commissaries of Edinburgh. He had been formerly in the Dutch service, but in 1755 entered that of the Venetians. On the day after his death, Sir James Wright, our Resident, and all the British subjects in Venice attended his funeral. The senators sent "a complimentary decree to his family," and ordered a bust of him to be placed in the arsenal. (*Scots Mag., xxix.*)

In that useless and destructive war in which George I involved Britain for the defence of his beloved Hanover, two of the Wauchopes of Niddry-Marshal figured by land and sea in the Sardinian service.

In the fight off Cape Passaro, in Sicily, in 1718, in the Spanish fleet which encountered that of Sir George Byng, the *St, Francis Arves* of 22 guns and 100 men was commanded by one of the family, who, in Lediard's list (*Naval Hist.*, 1735), is simply called "Andrew Wacup, a Scotchman"; but he fought his way through the British fleet, and his ship was one of the very few that escaped an action in which twelve Spanish ships were taken or burnt. (*Schomberg, etc.*)

In the following year there died of fever, in the camp of Randazzo, at the foot of Mount Etna in Sicily, Andrew, son of Sir George Seton of Garleton, a sub-lieutenant in the regiment of Irlanda, late that of Wauchope of Niddry- Marshal. (*Salmon's Chron., etc.*)

The latter, with his brother John, were both generals in the Spanish army, which was then attempting to master the Austrian dominions in Italy, and he was governor of Cagliari, the principal town in Sardinia.

Among the Scotsmen in the army of Charles Emanuel III, King of Sardinia, were General Paterson, who held a high command at Turin, and Henry, Earl of Drumlanrig, eldest son of the Duke of Queensberry, who received £20,000 for his share in achieving the Union.

After serving two campaigns under the Earl of Stair, he entered the Sardinian army, with which he served in three campaigns under Charles Emanuel III, who was enlarging his territories by alliances with France, Spain, and Austria. The earl gave proofs of a high military genius, particularly at the siege of Coni, a fortified city in Piedmont, in consequence of which his Sardinian Majesty desired his ambassador at the British court to wait upon the Duke of Queensberry, and return him thanks for the services of his son in course of that protracted war.

He left the Sardinian army in 1747 for that of the States of Holland, for whom he raised a Scottish regiment; and seventeen years afterwards—in 1764—General Paterson quitted his command at Turin and came home to die in Edinburgh.

Here it may not be without interest to remark that, when Cardinal York died in 1807, the representation of the royal line of Stuart became vested in the King of Sardinia, eldest son of Victor Amadeus III, grandson of Victor Amadeus, King of Sardinia, by Anne his wife, daughter of Henrietta, Duchess of Orleans, daughter of Charles I, King of Scotland and England, as the nearest heir of line to the British throne.

CHAPTER 12

The Scots in the Land of the Turban

In that scarce and quaint topographical work, the *Atlas Geographicus*, we are told that there was to be seen in 1712, in a tower of the city wall of Damascus, near the gate of St. Paul, two *fleurs-de-ljs* and two lions carved in stone, "and near each of them a great thistle. This was probably in honour of some Scottish princes who went with the French to the Holy Land. From hence some think the French built the tower, but we rather believe that the Turks brought the stones from some other place once possessed by the French."

We give this story for what it is worth. The thistle may have been a relic of the Scottish crusaders (of whom we may be tempted to take note at another time), though Bowring and other travellers do not mention it; but a more interesting anecdote, Scoto-Syrian, is one connected with the city of Jerusalem, and related by Richard Verstegan, in his *Restitution of Decayed Intelligence*, Antwerp, 1678, 12mo, in the chapter on the "Surnames of Ancient Families," and which we give in his own words:—

So it fell out of late years that an English gentleman travelling in Palestine, not far from Jerusalem, as he passed through a country town heard by chance a woman sitting at the door dandling her child to sing,

O Bothwell Bank, thou bloomest fair.

The gentleman hereat exceedingly wondered, and forthwith in English saluted the woman, who joyfully answered him, and said she was right glad to see a gentleman of our isle; and told him she was a Scotchwoman, and came first from Scotland to Venice, and from Venice thither, where her fortune was to be the wife of an officer under the Turk, who being at that instant absent, and might soon return, she entreated the gentleman to stay, the which he did; and she, for country's sake, to show herself more kind and bountiful to him, told her husband at his homecoming that the gentleman was her kinsman, whereupon her husband entertained him, and at his departure gave him divers things of good value.

From the *Exchequer Rolls* of Scotland we learn that the heart of James I, in 1437, was removed from his body, like that of Robert I, and taken on a pilgrimage to the East—a journey of which no details are given beyond the payment of £90 "to a certain knight of the Order of St. John of Jerusalem for bringing (back) the heart of the illustrious prince of blessed memory, James, the late King of Scotland, from Rhodes to the Carthusian monastery near the burgh of Perth, where the body of the said prince is buried." Although the return of the king's heart is thus chronicled, we are left in ignorance of the nature and composition of the expedition with which it was sent from Scotland to Palestine.

From this date to the last year of the nineteenth century seems somewhat of a leap; but we read that in 1900, when the government sent an army under Abercrombie to expel the French from Egypt, in the last days of December, when, with other troops, the 92nd Highlanders at Marmorice Bay were waiting reinforcements from the Turks, among the latter who came particularly to see the former was an Osmanli officer of stately and dignified appearance.

He proved to be a gentleman named Campbell, from Kintyre, who, early in life, had been so affected by the death of a friend whom he had killed in a sudden quarrel near Fort William, that he had wandered abroad, and ultimately joined the Turkish army, in which he had risen to be a general of artillery under the Sultan Selim. Says the *Caledonian Mercury:*

When he saw our men in the dress to which he had been accustomed in his youth, and heard the bagpipes playing, the remembrance of former years, and of his country, so affected him that he burst into tears. The astonishment of the soldiers may be imagined when they were addressed in their own language— the Gaelic, which he had not forgotten—by a turbaned Turk in full costume, with a white beard flowing down to his middle.

He sent off several boat-loads of fruit to the Gordon Highlanders, of whose colonel, the gallant John Cameron of Fassifern, he made several inquiries about relations who were then living at Campbelton. Says the Rev. Mr. Clerk in his privately printed memoir of Cameron:

> They entered into correspondence with him, but we have not learned what was the close of his career, whether he revisited his native land or died in his adopted country.

We now come to the story of one whose adventures, if related at length, would surpass any romance ever written, that of Thomas Keith, who became the last Aga of the Mamelukes and governor of Medina—*Medinet-el-Nabi*—(or the city of the prophet), yet whose name is utterly unknown in his own country!

Thomas Keith, a record of whose service was furnished to us by the War Office, was a native of Edinburgh, where he served his apprenticeship to a gunsmith before he enlisted, on the 4th of August, 1804, in the 2nd battalion of the 78th Highlanders, commanded by Major-General Mackenzie Frazer of Castle Frazer; and soon after he went with the corps, under Lieutenant-Colonel MacLeod of Gienis, to join the army in Sicily under Sir John Stuart, the Count of Maida, where he took part in the victorious battle of that name, and the subsequent capture of Crotona on the Gulf of Taranto.

Keith, proving a smart, intelligent, and well-educated soldier, was appointed armourer to the Ross-shire Buffs, now ordered to form a part of the expedition fitted out in Sicily in 1807 to occupy Alexandria, to compel the Turks to defend their own territories, and relieve our allies, the Russians, of the pressure they put upon them.

Like most British expeditions, this one under Mackenzie Fraser proved too slender; it consisted only of the 20th Light Dragoons, a regiment then clad in blue with orange facings; the 31st, 35th, and 78th Regiments, with that of De Rolle and *Les Chasseurs Brittaniques*, a mixed corps, formed of deserters from all countries.

On the 18th of March General Eraser disembarked this force near the Arabs' Tower, westward of Alexandria, and began his march for the latter, with the view of attaching it and keeping open a communication with the naval squadron; but he was either ignorant of the actual strength of the Turkish forces in and about the city, or that the Mameluke Beys, though in arms apparently against the new viceroy, Mehemet Ali, now were ready to follow him against the British troops.

Alexandria was captured, but then, followed our defeat at Rosetta (or *Raschid*) on the Bolbiton branch of the Nile, where General Patrick Wauchope of Edmonston fell, with 185 officers and men of the 31st Regiment alone, and next day the heads of these were displayed on stakes along the road that leads towards Tantah.

Another disastrous affair—when Keith fell into the hands of the enemy—followed at the village of El Hamet, four miles south-west of Rosetta, on the banks of the canal that unites the Nile with Lake Etko. There Colonel Macleod, with five companies of his Highlanders and two of the 35th, with a few of the 20th Dragoons, took post on the embankment, when in the mist, on the morning of the 21st April, they were furiously attacked by an overwhelming force of Albanian cavalry and infantry, that came down the Nile in 70 large river-boats. MacLeod formed a square, but the rush of the foe proved too great for him, with their lances, matchlocks, and *yataghans*.

A company of the 35th and another of the Ross-shire Buffs were cut down though making a desperate resistance, and every officer and man of both companies perished, save some 22 who escaped, and Keith and a Highland drummer who were taken prisoners. Seven Albanians were slain in succession be the claymore of Sergeant John MacRae of the 78th ere his head was cloven from behind by a *yataghan*; and, ere Lieutenant MacRae fell, six men of his surname, all from Kintail, perished by his side. MacLeod also fell, and the Albanians were seen caracoling their horses on all sides, each with a soldier's head on the point of a lance. (*General Stewart.*)

Keith with a few survivors was dragged to Cairo, where 450 heads, hewn from MacLeod's men, were exposed in the market-place, with every mark of barbarous contempt; and there he became the property of Ahmed Aga, who purchased him for a few coins from an Albanian lancer. Ahmed, fortunately for Keith, conceived a strong fancy for him, and finding all chance of escape utterly hopeless, according to the means of locomotion in those days, he and the drummer adopted the turban—Keith taking the name of Ibrahim Aga and the latter that of Osman, under which we shall have to refer to him again when in old age.

Keith had soon to quit the service of his new friend Ahmed. A Mameluke of the latter, a renegade Sicilian, having insulted him, swords were drawn, and the young Scotsman killed the Sicilian on the spot, and, to escape the consequences, fled to the favourite wife of the viceroy, Mehemet Ali, and procured her protection. She gave him a purse of money, and sent him disguised to her second son, Tusoun Pasha, born at Kavala, in Macedonia (where Mehemet's father had been head of the police), and he took Keith into his service, pleased to find that he was a skilful armourer and master of the Arabic language.

Though little else than a boy, Tusoun (we are told by the author of *Egypt and Mohammed Ali*) had a fiendish temper, and on Keith incurring his sharp displeasure by some omission of duty, he ordered the latter to be assassinated in bed, and beset the house with armed slaves, whose instructions were to mutilate him and bring away his head. But Keith was prepared for them!

Ere they could enter his room he was out of the doorway, which he had barricaded, and which he defended for half-an-hour with his sword and pistols, till a pile of dead lay before him; then seizing a lucky moment, when they shrank from that ghastly barrier, he leaped into the street, and brandishing his bloody sabre, once more sought the protection of Tusoun's mother.

She effected a reconciliation between them, and the savage young prince, in admiration of his courage, appointed him *Aga* of his body of Mamelukes, a post of importance, in which he displayed many brilliant qualities. "In the bearded *Aga* of the Mamelukes, who shaved his head in conformity to the rules of the Prophet, it might have been difficult to recognise the kilted Ross-shire Buff of a year or so before; but now his former military experience made him of vast service in infusing a species of discipline among the Mamelukes and other wild and barbarous horsemen in the *pasha's* army, while his knowledge of all kinds of weapons, his bodily strength, bravery, and hardihood, made him almost their idol. Thus he stood high among the *Agas* of the *pasha* of Egypt."

Freed from the British, the latter now began to adopt warlike measures against the Wahabees, who had plundered many caravans, and forbidden people to pray in their mosques for his master the *sultan*—being in the East not unlike the Puritans under Cromwell.

It was on the 1st March, 1811, just before Tusoun was to begin his march against these people in Arabia, that the dreadful massacre of the Mameluke Beys and their soldiers took place at Cairo. Keith escaped that event, warned, it is supposed, by Tusoun to absent himself, as he was to command the latter's cavalry; but, if in the capital, he must have been cognisant of that awful scene in the citadel, when (as Ebers relates) from every window and loophole musketry and cannon volleyed on these gorgeously-accoutred horsemen, till hundreds with their horses lay in the narrow way wallowing in blood, though some snatched sword and pistol but in vain, and in unutterable confusion men and chargers, living, dying, and dead, rolled in one mighty mass—at first shouting and screaming, then silently convulsive, and more silent and still, and 480 lives were quenched, one alone escaping by leaping his horse over the terrific rampart—Ameer Bey.

Leading Tusoun's cavalry, as Ibrahim Aga, Thomas Keith, then only in his eighteenth year, had under him 800 sabres, chiefly Bedouins, while the infantry, 2,000 Arnaouts in the kilt, were led by Saleh Bey. In October they attacked Yembo, on the Red Sea, and Keith's Bedouins pillaged the town. In January, 1812, Tasoun and Keith set out to attack the city of Medina, and on their march by the sandy caravan route, after capturing Bedr-Honein and Safra, in a narrow defile between two rugged mountains, they were attacked by more than 20,000 fanatical Wahabees.

The infantry took to flight, the Bedouins followed fast, all abandoning the prince save Keith and one other horseman. The three broke, sword in hand, through the enemy, reached the camp in the rear at Bedr-Honein, and escaped to the Red Sea, the whole shore of which was now swept by the victorious Wahabees; but Keith for his fidelity in the Pass of Jedeida was appointed treasurer to Mehemet Ali, by orders from whom he lavished gold to detach the Bedouins from the Wahabees, against whom Tusoun marched again in 1812, accompanied by Keith.

They stormed Medina, the latter leading the Arnaouts, sword in hand, in his twentieth year. "At Medina," says the *History of Arabia*, "he fought with courage, being the first man who mounted the breach, and after distinguishing himself on many other occasions he was made governor of the city in 1815." But nowhere did he do so much than in the repulse of the Turks before Taraba, when 14,000 of them were killed or wounded. Keith captured a cannon in a charge, and served it with his own hands. In 1816 he was in command at Mecca, near where, on one occasion, 5,000 human heads were piled before the tent of the victorious Mehemet. In the cavalry fight at El Bass, Keith, while succouring Tusoun, slew four with his sabre in quick succession, but was unhorsed, cut to pieces, and beheaded on the spot.

His comrade, "Osman" the drummer, long survived these events, and the strongest feature of his character, says one who met him, was his intense nationality. "In vain men called him *Effendi*; in vain he swept along in Eastern robes, and rival beauties adorned his *harem*. The joy of his heart lay in this:—that he had three shelves of books, and that *these books were thorough-bred Scotch*; and, above all, I recollect that he prided himself upon the 'Edinburgh Cabinet Library.'" (*Traces of Travel.*)

So lately as 1854, Colonel Cannon, son of the Rev. Dr. Cannon, minister of Maine and Strathmartin, and Colonel Ogilvy of Tanuadyce, entered the Turkish service. The former, known as Behram Pasha, commanded the Turkish Light Division at Silistria while Naysmith was there, and also at the Battle of Giurgevo.

Later still, in 1868, Mr. H. B. Frost, a native of Aberdeen, held a high office in the gun-factories at Constantinople under Sir John Anderson, and for his great services and improvements in gunnery was made brigadier-general, with the rank of *pasha*; "and, commenting on a *sabre d'honneur* to Abdul Kerim Pasha, the *Invalide Russe* declares that the real conqueror of Servia was not Abdul, but Arthur Campbell Pasha, a military agent, who, with six British officers, was the real leader of the Turkish troops." (*The World*, 1877.)

In 1886 Borthwick Pasha was appointed a member of the *Gendarmerie* Commission; and in the *Scotsman* for August, 1876, we read that Blacque Bey, a Catholic, then director of the Press at Constantinople, and formerly the Turkish Minister at Washington, is of Scottish descent from a Mr. Black who followed King James VII to France. European discipline was first introduced into the Persian army by two Scottish officers during the early part of the present century. The first Persian artillery corps was organised by Lieutenant Lindsay of the Madras army, who had every difficulty thrown in his way by the prejudices of the Mahomedans. But the then *Shah* gave him unlimited powers. The *serbaz*, or infantry, were organised by Major Christie of the Bombay army, an officer of the greatest merit, who inspired them with an *esprit de corps* never before known in Persia.

The surgeon-general of the army of the Prince Abbas Mirza, when encamped on the frontiers of Yam, in Azerbijan, in 1810 and 1816, was Dr. Campbell, a Scotsman, as Morier states in his *Travels*; and it was from these officers that the Persian buglers and trumpeters acquired the British "calls" in the field, the use of which by them perplexed our troops—particularly the Ross-shire Buffs—at the Battle of Khooshab, when Sir James Outram so thoroughly routed the Persians under Shooja-ool-Moolk. In 1831 Dr. Littlejohn, another Scot, on leaving India, entered the service of Daood Pasha at Bagdad, and, accompanying the army of Abbas Mirza in the Kermon campaign, commanded the garrison of Azerbijan, but was compelled to surrender to the Firman Firma, after which he remained to the day of his death at Shiraz.

In 1840 Sir Henry Lindsay-Bethune, Bart., of Kilconquhar, was a general officer in the Persian service, and a major-general in Asia, In 1821 the governor of Tripolizza, which under the Turks had been the capital of the Mores, was Sir Thomas Gordon Knight, previously an officer of the Scots Greys. The town had been sacked by the Greeks in the same year. On the breaking out of the war between France and Russia he had served as a volunteer in the army of the latter, and was an A.D.C. on the retreat from Moscow. He afterwards returned to Scotland, and then taking £20,000 with him, went to the Morea to fight for Greece, and is "now at the head of Yps Tlonti's staff and commandant of Tripolizza, (as at time of first publication)." (Ed. *Weekly Journal*, No. 1253.)

CHAPTER 13

The Scots in Denmark

In the times of which we chiefly write, when our countrymen rose to rank and power in nearly every European court and army, the favourite creed and toast of these wanderers were, "Peace at home and plenty wars abroad," while the old Highland version was, we are told, "O Lord, turn the world upside down, that honest fellows may make bread out of it."

In northern Europe, Denmark was a favourite field for some of these military spirits.

In 1379, Haco, King of Denmark, created Sir Henry Sinclair of Roslin, Earl of Orkney, a title confirmed by Robert II, while these isles were still a portion of Scandinavia. Sir Henry was the only son of that Sir William Sinclair who perished in battle against the Moors at Teba in 1331. According to Sir Robert Douglas, he married Florentina, daughter of the King of Denmark; and Nisbet in his *Heraldry* adds that he was made by Christian I, Lord of Shetland, Duke of Oldenburgh (in Holstein), a statement doubted; and that he was Knight of the Thistle, the Cockle, and the Golden Fleece—the gift of the different sovereigns of these orders. The old tradition, that before one of this family died the beautiful chapel of Roslin appeared to be full of light, is supposed to be of Norse origin, imported by them from Scandinavia, as the tomb-fires of the North are mentioned in many of the Sagas.

In 1469 James III married Margaret, daughter of the King of Denmark, Sweden, and Norway, whose dowry was Orkney and Shetland.

In 1606, when Sir David Sinclair directed his body to be buried in the cathedral of St. Magnus, at Kirkwall, his golden chain of office as a chief captain of the palace of Bergen, which post he held with that of "Governor of Hetland," under the Scottish crown, was bequeathed to the altar of St. George, in the Domskerke of Roes Kilde, the ancient capital of Denmark.

In 1506 we find James IV interfering in behalf of his ally, John, King of Denmark, Norway, and Sweden, against whom the latter country had revolted, and despatching conciliatory letters to the Archbishop of Upsala and the citizens of Lubeck, who were about to assist the Swedes—letters which were models of elegance and vigour (Pinkerton)—and by his influence the insurrection was suppressed; but when war with England came, in 1613-15, inspired only by ingratitude, neither Denmark nor France responded to the Scottish government. Yet, in 1618, Christian II applied to it for assistance in suppressing an insurrection which had broken out among his Swedish subjects, and asked for 1,000 Highlanders. This request was declined, on the plea that the disposition of the English court was uncertain. In this matter Christian sent as his ambassador Alexander Kinghorn, a Scottish physician, established in Denmark.

In 1519, however, a body of Scottish troops, with plenty of ammunition, was sent to Copenhagen under James Stewart of Ardgowan to fight in that war which saw the massacre of Stockholm, the adventures of Gustavus Vasa, and the termination of the Union of Calmar. In the dead winter of 1520 the army under Otto Krumpe, composed of Germans, Scots, and French, passed the Sound; and fought the peasantry under Sture, who was slain by a cannon-ball. The Swedes were cut to pieces, and all who fell were refused the rites of Christian burial, and Christian was crowned King at Stockholm, where he placed the Scottish and German troops in garrison; but the tyrannical conduct of Christiern (or Christian), which ultimately led to his deposition, and the piratical seizure by Danish privateers of a rich merchant-ship belonging to Leith, completely alienated his Scottish allies, who returned with the Laird of Ardgowan (*Epist. Reg. Scot, et.*), whose representative is now Sir Michael S. Stewart, Bart., of Ardgowan and Blackball.

With the army of which they formed a part, Paraselsus was the principal physician. The capital of Denmark (says Schiern) "had, as we learn from 'a grace for the Scottish nation,' issued in 1539 by Christian III, an entire guild of Scotsmen, which, among other institutions, formed an hospital in Copenhagen for 'their sick countrymen,' and during the first half of the century many of these were professors of the university there, to wit—Peter David and Johannis Maccabeus (John MacAlpin) for theology; Alexander Kinghorn, medicine; Thomas Alame, philosophy; while many Danish students were attending the University of Aberdeen."Thus the fugitive Bothwell had doubtless a warm welcome in Denmark in 1560.

Before this crisis in his misfortunes, Bothwell had been in Denmark, and there had met the Lady Anne, whoso father, Christopher Throndson (of the Rustung family), was admiral of Christian III, and whose mother, Karine, was daughter of the deacon of Trondheim.

In Resen's *Annals of Frederick' II*, under date June, 1560, information is given that the Lord James, Earl of Bothwell, High Admiral of Scotland, came to Denmark, and was well received by the king, by whom and the Duke of Holstein he was conducted through Jutland, as he wished to travel in Germany. In the same year he was in Prance.

Anne complained that Bothwell "had taken her from her fatherland and home into a foreign country, away from her parents, and would not hold her as his lawful wife, which with hand, mouth, and letters he had promised to do," at the time when it was rumoured at home he was making a rich match in Denmark. (F. Shiern, *Life of Bothwell*.)

Though the Earl of Bothwell, who was latterly the evil star of Mary's life, was not a soldier of fortune, his connection with Norway and Denmark is so little—if at all—known in Scotland, that we may be pardoned for inserting it here.

In Suhm's *Samlinges*, or *Collections for the History of Denmark*, we find it stated that the famous—or infamous—"earl was married early in life to a Norwegian lady, Anne, daughter of Christopher Throndson, prior to his marriage with Lady Jean Gordon, of the house of Huntly, and that his possessing, through the former, certain estates in Orkney was reason for his being made duke of these Isles in 1567.

After his flight from Orkney, and his defeat at sea by the gallant Kirkcaldy of Grange, Bothwell sailed into Karmesund, a harbour, when he was found by Captain Christian Alborg, commander of a Danish warship named the *Biornen*, or Great Bear, who demanded his licences for sailing an armed ship in Danish waters, and, as he failed to produce them, compelled the earl to accompany him up the Jelta Fiord to Bergen. Captain Alborg in his declaration records that "among the Scottish crew there was one disguised in old and patched boatswain's clothes, who stated himself to be the chief ruler of all Scotland."

This was the earl, with whom he reached the castle of Bergen, or Bergenhaas, on a tongue of land in the Byefiorden. The governor of the fortress, a wealthy Danish lord named Erick Rosenkrantz, appointed a committee of twenty-four gentlemen to interrogate the prisoner. These met on the 23rd September, 1567. Among them were the bishop and four councillors of Bergen, from whom Bothwell obtained permission to reside in the city.

Magister Absalom Beyer, the pastor of Bergen, who left behind him a diary entitled *The Chapter Book,* running from 1533 to 1570, recorded therein the following, which is inserted by Suhm in his *Samlinges:—*

1567, *September 2.*—Came in (to Bergen) *Royal David,* of which Christian Alborg is captain. He had captured a Scottish noble, James Hepburn, Earl of Bothwell, Duke of Orkney and Shetland, who had been wedded to the Queen of Scotland. He was suspected to have been in the plot against the king's life. The council of the kingdom having revolted against the queen, this earl escaped, and has come hither to Norway.

1567, *September 17.*—I upbraided the Lady Anne, daughter of Christopher Throndson, that this Earl of Bothwell had taken her from her native country, and yet would not keep her as his lawful wife, which he had promised to do, with hand, mouth, and letters, *which letters* she caused to be read before him; and whereas he has *three wives living*—first, herself; secondly, another in Scotland, from whom he has bought (divorced?) himself; and thirdly, Queen Mary. The Lady Anne opined 'that he was good for nothing.' Then he promised her an annual rent from Scotland, and a ship with all her anchors and cordage complete.

September 26.—The earl went to the castle, when Erick Rosenkrantz did him great honour.

September 30.—The earl departed on board the *David* and was carried captive to Denmark, where he yet remains in the castle of Malmo, at this time, 1568.

October 10, 1567.—Part of the earl's men were returned to Scotland on board a small pink which Erick Rosenkrantz had lent them, and it is said they were all put to death on their landing.

The only discrepancy here is in one statement of the pastor and the committee: the former calls the Danish ship the *David,* and the latter the *Biornen;* but perhaps Captain Alborg commanded *two* so-named.

Other passages in the *Chapter Book* record that in 1563 the Lady Anne moved in the best circle in the province, which she could not have done as Bothwell's mistress; and that she was known as the *Skot-tifruen*, or Scottish lady. Her second sister, Dorothy, was married to John Stewart, a gentleman of Shetland; and her third, Elsie, was thrice married—the last time to Axel Mouatt, a Scottish gentleman settled in Norway.

The royal order issued by King Frederick for imprisoning Bothwell in Malmo was issued from Fredericksborg, 28th December, 1567. (*Les Affairs du Comte de Bodeul.*)

He lived two years after his well-known confession, and died in the fortress of Dragsholm, on the northern coast of Zealand, between Halbek and Kallondsborg, in April, 1578, and was interred in the church of Faareville.

According to the *Privy Seal Register*, Axel Wiffirt, a servant of the King of Denmark, Frederick II, was licensed to levy 2,000 soldiers in Scotland, and to convey them away armed as *coulvreniers* on foot "as they best can provide them," to serve the Danish monarch in his war against the Swedes. The accoutrements of these troops were a habergeon with sleeves, a matchlock, salade, sword, and dagger. This was in July, 1568.

In 1571, Crawford states in his *Memoirs* that Captain Michael Wemyss, an experienced soldier, was coming from Denmark with his company, consisting of a hundred men, to serve under the Earl of Morton against the adherents of Queen Mary: probably the former were some of Axel Wiffirt's levy.

During Bothwell's captivity in Denmark a Scottish officer named Captain John Clark made a great figure there. He had commanded a body of soldiers in the insurrection which ended at Carberry Hill; and in the subsequent autumn passed, with 80 Scots, into the service of Frederick II, who on the 15th June, 1564, gave him a commission, dated at Bordesholm, over 206 Scottish cavalry. He is described by Resen as a brave and well-trained captain, who, with his lieutenant, David Stuart, after a bloody encounter, stormed the castle of Halmstad, which commanded the Kattegat, from the Swedes. In a letter dated Roskilde, Oct., 1568, he styles himself—

I, John Clark, commander of the Scottish military detachments (Schiern), when engaging to produce the murderers of Darnley to the Scottish government.

In 1569, he with his Scottish troops was quartered at Londskrona, on the coast. His lieutenant then was Andrew Armstrong. They quarrelled with Frederick II about commissariat matters, Clark demanding 17,000 dollars on his discharge; and for this and other matters he was summoned to appear for examination at Copenhagen, before a court of which Alexander Durham, Richard Scougal, and Cagnioli, a kinsman of Riccio, were members, while his "Scottish Riflemen," to the number of 300 or more, were nearly perishing of hanger in Jutland—the reward of their service during Frederick's Seven Years' War.

Clark died in 1575, a prisoner of state, in the castle of Dragsholm, in Denmark; the king of which had come, says Schiern, "to regard the Scottish soldiers with a strange dislike."

In 1605 the King of Denmark sent three ships, of which John Cunningham, a Scotsman, was admiral, to Greenland. They went a great way up Davis' Straits. In a place called Cunningham's Ford they found stones, out of a hundredweight of which they extracted 26 ounces of fine silver. They brought with them three of the natives of Greenland to Denmark. (*Atlas Geographicus*, vol. i)

During the reigns of seven kings, traces of the former had been lost, having become inaccessible by floating ice. The fiord and a cape still bear the name of Cunningham, (as at time of first publication).

Many Scots now went to Denmark. A Highland regiment, raised among the Mackays, embarked for service there in March, 1625, for the service of King Christian. In June, Sir James Leslie levied another of 1,000 men, and Captain Alexander Seaton raised 500 more. The forces of Leslie and Mackay soon mustered in all 4,400 men; and a letter of Philip Burlamachi, a London merchant, shows that he paid, by the king's order, £3,000 for their transport from Scotland to Hamburg.

In 1626 the king paid £8,000 to the Earl of Nithsdale, the Lord Spynie, and Sir James Sinclair of Murkle for levying three regiments of 3,000 men each "for his unkell the King of Denmark's service," making 13,400 soldiers sent by Scotland to that country in two years. In three years Mackay's regiment had 1,000 men and 30 officers killed or wounded.

Colonels Sir Donald Mackay, Seaton, and Forbes, wounded at Oldenburg; Captains Boswal and Learmouth of Balcomie, killed at Boitzenburg; Sir Patrick M'Ghie, Forbes of Tulloch and Munro, wounded at Oldenburg; Forbes and Carmichael killed at Bredenburg; Mackenzie of Kildare and Kerr, wounded at Eckernfiord; Lieutenant

Martin, killed at Boitzenburg, and six others at Stralsund and else-where; seven ensigns were wounded at Oldenburg and one at Stral-sund, where the quartermaster, chaplain, and 600 Highlanders fell. (*Munro's Expedition with Mackay's Regiment*, fol., 1637)

"The regiment received colours whereon his Majesty (Christian IV) would have the officers to carry the Danish cross, which the of-ficers refusing, they were summoned to compeare before his Majestie at Raynesburg to know the reason of their refusal." Captain Robert Ennis was sent home to learn the wish of James VI, "whether or no they might carrie, without reproach, the Danish Crosse on Scottish Colours, Answer was returned that they should obey the orders of him they served." (*Ibid.*)

The escort of the Duke of Holstein's ambassadors to Muscovy and Persia in 1637 would seem to have been mostly Scottish soldiers, and one of them, a sergeant named Murray, distinguished himself amid a brawl that ensued in the Persian capital, when, among several others, a Danish gunner was killed as he was in the act of levelling a cannon against the enemy.

Sergeant Murray, "being eager to avenge his death, charged the natives so furiously that he slew five or six of them, till, an arrow tak-ing him directly in the breast, he plucked it out, and, having killed another with his firelock, fell dead upon the spot." (*Voyaye du Chev, Chardin, etc.*)

Sir Thomas Gray, one of the many Scots who in several capaci-ties served Christian IV, was military governor of the castle of Ber-gen, where, in 1647, he hospitably entertained the fugitive Marquis of Montrose, who went from there across the Norwegian Alps to obtain an interview with Christian IV,

At the close of the century the chief huntsman of Frederick II was a Scotsman named Graham, when the latter sumptuously entertained Queen Elizabeth's envoy, Mr. Vernon, at Yagersburg, a few miles from Copenhagen, as we are told in *Travels through Denmark in 1702*.

Under Christian VII the governor and commandant of Rends-borg, a strong border fortress between Holstein and Schleswig, was Sir Robert Keith, Bart., of Ludquhairn, a major-general in the Danish army, and there he died on the 14th January, 1771. He was a gallant veteran, and had been A.D.C. to his kinsman. Marshal Keith, for many years.

The killing of the Danish Count Rantzau Aschberg by a Scottish officer made some noise in Europe in November, 1773. The count was concerned in some way with the administration of Struenzee, who so soon became hateful to the nobility and cabinet, and whom a plot to overthrow had been formed, under the queen-mother, by which he was ultimately disgraced and brought to the scaffold, with his friend Count Brand.

The cause of Rantzau's death was involved in some mystery.

Before leaving his seat of Aschberg he received a letter without any signature, informing him not to set out on a journey he intended, as a certain person would follow, and certainly slay him on the road. Disdaining this anonymous hint, the count departed for Switzerland, whence he was travelling to Spain by way of France. When on the frontier of the former country he was suddenly confronted by a Scots-man, Lieutenant Osborne, of the Danish service, who stopped his carriage on the highway and offered him a brace of pistols, desiring him to choose one and fight a fair duel, "as he owed him satisfaction."

The count, having no second with him, refused to fight, on which Osborne shot him through the head and rode away. Says a print of the time:

> As the count was brought up at the court of Denmark, and consequently knew the secret history of the Danish cabinet; his journey, in the present critical period, to France and Spain, after his falling into disgrace; his being killed thus by a zealous Scotsman, and the notice taken of the matter by the courts of France, cause his death, attended with all these circumstances, to make a great deal of noise.

We have not traced Osborne's career further in this matter; but, as in Sweden, many Scottish names are still to be found in Denmark; thus, in March, 1886, we find the Danish frigate *Eyen* is commanded by Captain D. MacDougall, who exchanged salutes with our batteries on the 3rd of that month at Portsmouth, when sailing from Naples to Copenhagen.

CHAPTER 14

The Scots in Spain and Portugal

When the illustrious Robert Bruce lay dying at Cardross, by his desire, after his demise, his heart was taken out, as all know, embalmed, and given to his firm friend and brother patriot, the noble Sir James Douglas, for conveyance to the Holy Land, whither the long war with England had prevented the king going in person. Douglas had that true heart, which had so often beat high in battle for Scotland, enclosed in a silver casket, which he constantly wore suspended from his neck by a chain of the same metal; and having made his will, and settled all his affairs, he set sail from Scotland, attended by a splendid and gallant retinue of knights, among whom were Sir William Sinclair of Roslin, Lockhart of Lee, and others famed in Scottish war. This was in 1329.

Anchoring off Sluys, the great emporium of Flanders, expecting to find companions bound on the same pilgrimage, he kept open table on board his ship, with royal munificence, for twelve days. Froissart says he had with him eight Scottish knights, one of whom bore his banner; twenty-six esquires, "all comely young men of good family; and he kept court in a royal manner, with the sound of trumpets and cymbals. All the vessels for his table were of gold and silver."

At Sluys he heard that Alphonso, the King of Leon and Castile, was at war with Osmyn, the Moorish King of Granada, and as this was reckoned a holy strife, he resolved to take Spain on his way to Jerusalem; thus, after landing at Seville, he marched with the Spanish army to the frontiers of Andalusia, and in the great battle fought at Teba the vanguard was. assigned to him—the Scottish hero and veteran of Bannockburn.

Teba lies about forty miles north-west of Malaga, in the midst of the rocky Sierra Camorra, and has still its Moorish castle which was made defensible by the French in 1810.

The Moorish cavalry were routed and took to flight, and Douglas with his comrades, pursuing them too eagerly, were separated from the Spanish army. The Moors, perceiving the small number that followed, rallied and surrounded the Scots. Douglas, with only ten survivors, cut his way through, and would have made good his retreat had he not turned to assist Sir William Sinclair, whom he saw surrounded and in dire peril. In attempting to save his friend, he was cut off and overwhelmed. On finding himself inextricably involved, he took from his neck the casket containing the heart of his king, and threw it before him with the memorable words, "Now, pass onward as thou wert wont, and Douglas will follow thee or die!"

He rushed to where it lay, and was there slain, with the Laird of Roslin, Sir Robert and Sir Walter Logan, two brothers. Next day the body of the hero of *seventy* battles—Fordoun says he was thirteen times defeated by, and fifty-seven times victorious over, the English (Book xiii)—was found with the casket and brought home by his few surviving friends. He was laid among his forefathers in Douglas Kirk, and the heart of Bruce in Melrose Abbey.

At the court of Alphonso there was a knight of high renown whose face was seamed with scars, and who expressed surprise that a soldier of such renown as Douglas had none to show. "I thank God," said the latter, "that I always had hands to protect my face." (*Barbour.*) His sword is still preserved, and is referred to by Scott in the notes to *Marmion*. On the blade is the date 1329—the year of Teba.

When Seville was captured from the Moors by the Spaniards in 1247, after one of the most obstinate sieges mentioned in Spanish history, in which the wooden bridge of the Guadalquiver perished, one of the bravest knights in the army of the King of Castile was a Scottish wanderer named Sir Lawrence Poorè (Powrie?), called in the Spanish annals Lorenzo Poro, who, after the storming of the city, was the first man to ascend La Giralda, a tower still 250 feet in height. His descendant, the Marquis de la Motilla, still owns his ancestral mansion in the Calle de la Cuna at Seville, says Forde in his work on Spain, and adds that "a Scottish herald will do well to look at the coats of arms in the Patio."

In 1495-6 ambassadors were sent from James IV to Spain. In the High Treasurer's accounts for that year there is an entry to "George Murehead—4 ells of Rissili's brown, for a gowne to him, when he went to Spain with the Secretary."

Sir John Seton of Barnes, Knight of St. Jago, the direct descendant of George IV. Lord Seaton was Master of the Household to Philip II, 1556-98; but was home in Scotland in 1609. (*House of Seaton, etc,*)

In 1618, Archibald, Earl of Argyll, who commanded the royal forces at Glenlivat in 1594, "not being able to give satisfaction to his creditors," according to Scotstarvit, entered the service of Spain, had a command in West Flanders, and distinguished himself at the capture of several strong places from the States of Holland, but changed his religion. Thus Craig, a forgotten poet, wrote of him:—

Now Earl of Guile and Lord Forlorn thou goes,
Quitting thy prince to serve his foreign foes;
No faith in plaids, no trust in Highland trews,
Camelion-like, they change so many hues.

About two years after this, one of the Semples, of whom little more than the name is known, founded the Scottish College of Valladolid, the revenue of which is now about £1,000 *per annum*, and the lands of which are to be held off the Spanish Crown while vines shall continue to grow upon them, Six miles from the city is the country villa (of the college) which Wellington occupied for a night on the retreat from Burgos.

Ludovick, "the Loyal Earl of Crawford," after the king's fortunes had reached the lowest ebb in 1646, finding himself penniless and destitute, returned to Spain, the theatre of his early fame, "to crave," says Guthry, "arrears due to him" by Philip IV, who gave him command of an Irish regiment, in which a Don Diego Leslie had a company—a follower of his own.

He was at Badajoz in 1649. Two years after he was in Paris fighting valiantly in the wars of the Fronde, and guarding the Cardinal de Betz in Notre Dame, with fifty other Scottish officers *qui avoient été des troupes de Montrose*, and in these wars he is supposed to have perished. (*Memoirs of Montrose*, 1858.)

In 1706 a Scotch officer rendered such valuable services in succouring the city of Denia, in Valencia—a place of difficult access, and strongly defended by walls and a double port—that he won the gratitude of Charles III. This was Commodore James Moodie, of Melsetter, who ran from school in his boyhood, and entered on board a man-of-war. How well his services were appreciated by the Spanish king may appear from the following letter which the latter addressed to Queen Anne on the subject in French:—

Madame, my sister,

Captain James Moodie, who commands the vessel *Lancaster*, has rendered me services so important that I owe almost entirely to his zeal the preservation of my city of Denia, which, being destitute of all kinds of provision, would not have held out against a siege of five weeks, unless the said captain had furnished a supply at the request of those who commanded on my part. I doubt not but your Majesty will make him a handsome and generous return, both on account of the said services and of this my pressing intercession; to which I shall only add the assurance of that respect and sincere attachment with which I am, *madame*, my sister, your affectionate brother,

Charles.

How the commodore was rewarded we know not; but from the old *Statistical Account* we learn that when close on his eightieth year he was murdered in the streets of Kirkwall at the instigation of the Jacobite, Sir James Stewart.

During the war in Catalonia, John Wauchope of Niddrie-Marischal, a general of Spanish infantry, was slain in 1718. His brother, in the same service, has already been referred to as the governor of Cagliari, in Sicily. The *earl-marischal* at this time, and till 1788, and several other Scottish officers, his companions in loyalty and misfortune, were serving in the Spanish army. Among them was Sir John Macdonald, who afterwards landed in Moidart with Prince Charles.

The earl was offered the rank of lieutenant-general, but declined it, until his services should prove his capacity and merit—an instance of modesty and disinterestedness that filled with astonishment the ambitious Alberoni. The earl then proceeded to Rome, where he received the Order of the Charter from King James; and in 1733 he was again in the army of Spain when war broke out between that country and the emperor. Some years after he seems to have quitted the Spanish service again and lived for a time in obscurity, though in 1750 he was sent by Charles III of Spain to negotiate for the peace of Europe, but failed in the attempt. As stated elsewhere, he was governor of Neufchatel.

He was the last *earl-marischal*, and with him ended a family the most ancient in Europe, after serving Scotland in a distinguished capacity for above *seven hundred years*. Then the old prediction attributed to Thomas the Rhymer was said to be fulfilled:—

Inverugie by the sea,
Lordless shall thy lands be!

The prints of 1759 record that Don Pedro Stuart, lieutenant-general of the naval forces of Spain, left Madrid in November for Carthagena, whence he sailed with sixteen ships of the line to convey home his Sicilian Majesty. (*Caledon Mercury.*)

It was no doubt a son of this officer that we find so prominently referred to by Schomberg and Brenton in their naval histories.

On the night of the 19th December, 1796, Nelson, then a commodore, having been despatched by Sir John Jervis in *Le Minerve*, 38-gun frigate, accompanied by the *Blanche*, 32 guns, to Porto Ferrajo, fell in with two Spanish frigates, and directed Captain Cockburn to attack the one that carried a large poop light. This was off Carthagena. The *Blanche* kept up a running fight with one of the frigates; but the *Minerve*, says Sir Jahlel Brenton, "proved more fortunate, and subdued her antagonist, which on being boarded proved to be the *Santa Sabina*, an 18-pound frigate of 40 guns, commanded by Don Jacobo Stuart. During the action the contending and chasing ships had run close into Carthagena, with the wind dead upon the land. The Spanish captain was therefore no sooner on board the *Minerve* than the *Sabina* was taken in tow. This was scarcely accomplished when the *Minerve* was brought to action by another Spanish frigate."

The hard and gallant fighting that followed—fighting for which Nelson presented a beautiful gold-hilted sword to Captain Cockburn—lies apart from the story of Don Jacobo Stuart, who, before he struck his colours, had lost his mizzen-mast, and had 164 killed and wounded out of a crew of 286—by his valour exciting the admiration of Nelson. Schomberg gives the date of this frigate-battle the 19th December, 1796; Brenton, the 1st of June in the same year.

In the early part of the present century, Sir John Downie, a Scotsman in the Spanish army, took a prominent part in several political events. He went to Spain in the first instance with Sir John Moore, and with the survivors of that officer's ill-fated expedition returned with Sir Arthur Wellesley. Having entered the Spanish service, he won such reputation in Estramadura that a legion of 7,000 men, collected by his influence alone, served under him with great success during the rest of the Peninsular war. This force was named the Estremena Legion, on the formation of which he expended 200,000 dollars. (*London Courier,*)

In the attack on Seville, in 1812, he led the advanced column, which his legion formed, and for this King Ferdinand VII promoted him to the rank of field-marshal, loaded him with honours, and made him knight of St. Ferdinand, Carlos III, with seven crosses, for distinguished actions in the field. He was made governor of the palace of Seville and captain-general of Andalusia. On visiting London the Prince Regent (afterwards George IV) knighted him for his Spanish services; but his decided preference for Spain gave offence in some quarters, though he had many attached friends in the British army, among them notably the gallant Sir Thomas Picton, who fell at Waterloo.

When the troubles of Ferdinand began, Sir John Downie and his nephew were arrested at Seville in 1823, on suspicion of being engaged in a plot to rescue the king and royal family, about the time that a French army crossed the Bidassoa and occupied Madrid, while the king and Cortes retired to Seville, and thence to Madrid.

He was subjected to many grievous indignities, and imprisoned for a time in the Four Towers, at the arsenal of Curacca, on an island near Cadiz, with a sentinel placed over him. But these sufferings were temporary, and his honours were restored to him.

Sir George Napier, in his *History of the Peninsular War*, gave great offence to the relatives of Sir John Downie by terming him "an adventurer," and drew forth a retort from one, who asserted that he "was lineally descended from Sir Duncan Forrester of Arngibbon, in Perthshire, an extensive landed proprietor, who in the year 1492 was Comptroller of the Household to King James IV," and that he was also descended from the Maxwells of Brediland, in Renfrewshire.

He was born on his father's property of Blairgorts, near Kippen, in Stirlingshire, and was a man of very commanding presence.

He died in Spain in 1826, and was interred with every honour that the King of Spain could bestow.

In 1879 there died at Madrid Donna Maria Manula Kirkpatrick of Closeburn, the mother of the Empress Eugenie, and daughter of a Mr. Kirkpatrick, who was British consul at Malaga during her marriage with the Condé de Montijo, an officer of the Spanish army, connected with the Duke de Frias, representative of the ancient Admirals of Castile, of the Duke of Fyars, and others of the highest rank, including the descendants of the kings of Arragon.

Her great-grandfather (according to the *Times*) died on the scaffold in 1746, in consequence of having joined the loyal Highlanders under Prince Charles Edward. His son emigrated and settled at Ostend, whence his family passed into Spain and settled in the south. The Countess-Dowager, who died in her 86th year at the Alba Palace, was married to a brother of the Count of Montijo and Teba (the same Teba where "the good Sir James Douglas" fell), and on the death of the latter without issue her husband succeeded to the title. The law of Spain makes it necessary to inquire into the descent of any lady before she can be espoused by a noble, thus certificates were obtained from Scotland proving that the countess was a Kirkpatrick of Closeburn, and her ancestor had been created a baron by Alexander II.

From these parents the Empress Eugenie inherited the title of Teba. The Counts of Montijo and Teba were of the same origin as the Dukes of Medina-Sidonia, the family name of both being Guzman. ... The counts appear among the most illustrious warriors of Spain in past generations, back as far as 1492, and during the wars of the first French Empire the owners of the title fought under the standard of Napoleon.

The first Scotsman we can trace in the Portuguese service is Captain Forbes of Skellater, in Strathdon, who served at the siege of Maestricht, and in the Seven Years' War with the Prussian army, after which he entered that of Portugal, where he was the chief means of introducing the principles of that discipline which he had learned under Frederick the Great and Marshal Keith.

He enjoyed the confidence of four successive sovereigns of Portugal, who nobly rewarded his integrity and virtue. He rose to the rank of general, and commanded the army at Roussillon, at the commencement of the Revolutionary war. He attained the highest rank and honours the King of Portugal could award him; and when the royal family retired to Brazil he accompanied them, and died there, on the 8th of January, 1808, in his 67th year.

The influence of Forbes in the Portuguese army drew other Scotsmen to its ranks. Among these were William Sharpe, a native of St. Andrew's, who in 1764 was made brigadier-general and governor of Olivenza, and died in London a baronet; in 1780 governor of the province of Minho, and colonel of the Monça regiment of infantry; Colonel James Anderson, who in 1763 commanded the battalion of Lagos, and died at Viona in 1771; Major Bethune Lindsay, who died at Falmouth in February, 1776; and Colonel John McDonell, commander of the regiment of Peniche in 1765—a corps for steadiness surpassing even those of Prussia. Says a writer in the *Edinburgh Advertiser*, vol. iii:

> I am told that Colonel McDonell has been indefatigable, and that, with the assistance of three or four of his own relations who have seen service, he has in a few months brought that regiment to its present perfection, from being one of the worst in Portugal. The king publicly expressed his satisfaction, and thanked the colonel at the head of his regiment.

There was also Lieutenant-General MacLean, who was appointed governor of Lisbon in 1763, and ten years after succeeded Don José Francis Lobo, Count of Oriolo, as governor of Estramadura, the first military honour in Portugal, and never before given to any but a noble of the highest rank.

In 1764, Captain Forbes, the antagonist of the notorious John Wilkes, entered the Portuguese service, after having been in the French; and there was also the gallant Brigadier John Hamilton, who was drowned in 1767, when returning home in the *Betsy*, of Leith, which foundered off the coast of Lincolnshire.

CHAPTER 15

The Scots in Holland and Flanders

Like France and Sweden, Holland and the Low Countries were a spacious area for the development of Scottish valour and military enterprise, for thither in thousands flocked those whose swords peace with England left idle at home. As one song has it:—

Oh, woe unto those cruel wars
That ever they began,
For they have swept my native shore
Of many a pretty man:
For first they took my brethren twain.
Then wiled my love frae me.
Oh, woe unto those cruel wars
In Low Germanie!

Another girl sings thus of her love:—

Repent it will I never
Until the day I dee.
Though the Lowlands o' Holland
Hae twined my love and me.

Between Scotland and the Low Countries intercourse took place at a very early period.

James Bennett, Bishop of St. Andrew's, when a fugitive from the party of the usurper Baliol, took shelter there, and dying in 1332, was buried in the Abbey of St. Eckchot at Bruges.

The market of trade for Scotland in the Low Countries was changed several times. It had been originally fixed at Campvere, in Zealand (on the north coast of Walcheren), the count of which had married a daughter of James I. "The Scots are allowed the use of the old parish church here," says a work of 1711; "it has frequently been in danger by the sea, which overturned a tower on the side of the harbour in 1650." From thence the staple was taken to Bruges, which in the 15th century was the centre of all European trade, and became eventually the seat of the Conservator of Scottish Privileges in Flanders.

The *Ledger of John Hallyburton*, who held this office, and which runs from 1492 to 1503, is perhaps one of the most interesting commercial relics in Europe. John Home, the author of *Douglas*, was, we believe, the last who held this office. He died in 1808.

When passing along the Quai Espanol at Bruges, in September, 1873 (to quote a previous work of our own), we met a vast crowd defiling across the old bridge that leads thereto from the Rue des Augustines, preceded by women strewing the way with flowers, for it was St. Giles' Day—the 1st of the month—the patron of the parish wherein lies the Scottish quarter of the old city. Preceded by the *curé* with censers and acolytes, and escorted by the 2nd Belgian Infantry with fixed bayonets, and preceded by all the drummers of the Civic Guard, came the curious relic of the saint on a pedestal borne by four men—the left hand and arm of St. Giles cased in silver, and fixed upright from the shoulder.

The *right arm*, we need scarcely inform Scottish readers of Knox's *History*, was the chief relic of the sister church in Edinburgh, where, till the Reformation, it was enshrined in silver, weighing over five pounds, and the right of bearing which, on the Saint's day, was hereditary in the family of Preston of Gourton. In the Bruges procession there is borne St. Giles in effigy, accompanied by his fawn, a supporter of the Edinburgh arms; and, saluted by all guards and wayfarers, the procession parades the city till evening, when it returns to the old church of St. Giles (near the great canal), before the altar of which lies William de Camera, sub-prior of St. Andrew's, in Fifeshire, who died at Bruges in 1417.

There the Scottish factory was established in 1386, according to the old folio *Chronyke Van Vlanderen*. It has long since been demolished, but near its site, in the *Histoire de Bruges,* 1854, we find still extant the Schotte Poorte, Schottinen Straet, Schotte Bolle Straet, Schottile Straet, Zottine Straet, *de l'Eglise St Gilles*, all of which were the abode or resort of Scottish traders and seamen in the middle ages.

In 1408, Alexander, styling himself the Earl of Mar, though he had no right to that title save a charter from Isabel, his first wife, raised "a large company of gentlemen," says Douglas, and carrying them into

Flanders, under John, Duke of Burgundy, performed great feats of chivalry at the siege of Liége, in that contest in which 36,000 Liégeois are said to have been slain. He married Jane, Duchess of Brabant, whose subjects refused to submit to him as a foreigner, especially as she died within a year or so of this marriage. Enraged by this, he fitted out a fleet, swept that of the Brabanters from the sea, and steering elsewhere, according to Drummond, pillaged and destroyed Dantzig, after which he returned with a vast booty to Scotland.

Among those who accompanied him was Sir William Hay of Nachton. (*Notes to Border Minstrelsy.*)

From Rymer's *Fœdera* we learn that William, Lord Graham (ancestor of the Duke of Montrose), was at Bruges in December, 1466. While there he borrowed £80 Scots from Sir Alexander Napier of that ilk, who was then selecting a suit of fine armour for James II, and was present at the nuptials of Charles the Bold in 1468, when the brilliant tournament of the Golden Fleece was held. (*Merchiston Papers.*)

We have now come to the year 1570—the epoch when the old Scots brigade of gallant and immortal memory, a corps that existed for 258 years until 1818, and took its rise at a time when the power of Maurice, Prince of Nassau, drew to his standard the best and bravest of those Scottish spirits whose swords failed to feed them at home—a time when the Spanish armies with which they warred were the finest troops in the world, but when the musketeers, pikemen, and *cuirassiers* of the Marquis de Spinola, of Alexander, Prince of Parma and Placentia, Cordova, Mansfeldt, and John of Austria were all men of the highest soldierly qualities, with a love of military glory; but, unhappily, added to these a bigotry in religion, a ferocity and cruelty previously almost unknown in war.

It was chiefly by the aid of the Scottish troops that Maurice of Nassau was able to meet the tide of Spanish invasion. Among those who led these Scots in 1670 were Sir Walter Scott of Buccleugh, one of the bravest of Border chiefs, who had exasperated Queen Elizabeth by storming the castle of Carlisle to release Armstrong of Kinninmont, and his son Walter, afterwards created by James VI Earl of Buccleugh; Sir Henry Balfour of Burleigh, whose brother David, a captain in his regiment, perished at sea *en route* to Holland; John Halkett of Pitfirran, knighted by James VI, and progenitor of all the Halketts in that country; and Colonels Stewart, Hay, Douglas, Grahame, and Hamilton, whose names are given by Grose in his *Military Antiquities,* The first year of their service was distinguished by a brawl concerning their countryman, George, sixth Lord Seaton, who was accused of tempting them to revolt and join the Spaniards in the cause of his mistress, Mary Queen of Scots.

The Dutch authorities threatened to put him to the rack; he was brought before it, when the Scottish officers, with their men, surrounded the house, and threatened, if he was not set at liberty, "to go off in a body to the Spanish general." (Crawford's *Memoirs,*) He was thereupon released, and the matter ended.

The war in which these troops came to bear a part was caused by Philip II, the successor of Charles V, a bigoted Catholic, appointing his sister, the Duchess of Parma, Regent of the Netherlands, on which the discontent of the people reached an alarming height. The Prince of Orange, with Counts Egmont and Home, remonstrated against the establishment of the Inquisition and the new bishops, and insisted upon the states-general being assembled to consider the complaints of the people; but ere long it was evident that the courts of Spain and France had no other object in view than the destruction of Protestantism.

A general combination was now formed for the removal of grievances, and the sword was once more drawn on the great battlefield of Europe, "the Lowlands of Holland," and "no mean part of the merit of overthrowing the Spanish power in the Netherlands is justly attributable to the Scots brigade," many of whom had served in those civil wars at home which ended in the fall of the castle of Edinburgh after the siege in 1573.

In the Church of St. Walburga at Bruges there was shown till 1780 the tomb of a Scottish warrior of those days. Beneath no less than sixteen shields, each of which was surmounted by a coronet, was carved the epitaph of "William Foret, a native of Scotland, Chevalier of the Order of St. Andrew in that kingdom, during his life captain of 150 lances in the service of their Highnesses, the States of Flanders in the quarter of Bruges, *'lequel il passa le 6 Juillet, 1600; et Dame Marguerite Despars, fille de noble homme Louis Despars,'* his wife, who died 20th December, 1597." (*Sepulchral Memorials.*)

This name is little known in Scotland, but seems to have belonged to Fifeshire.

In the first five years of the 17th century four recruits, who made some figure in Scottish history, joined the brigade. These were William Dalrymple, a poor student, the hero of Scott's Ayrshire Tragedy y in 1602; and in 1605, Angus Macdonald of Isla, Maclean of Duart, and

Tormod Macleod of Lewis, who had undergone a tedious captivity in Edinburgh Castle since 1589 to keep the Isles quiet.

Dalrymple having had the misfortune to be unwittingly the bearer of that message by which the Laird of Auchindrane lured to his doom Sir Thomas Kennedy of Culzean, near Maybole, was, by means of the former, enlisted in the regiment of Buccleugh, with which he served some years as a soldier; but on returning home he became a source of dread to the savage baron, who had him murdered and buried in the sand near Chapel-Donan. The corpse, speedily unearthed by the tide, was carried out to sea by the waves, which afterwards cast it on the shore near the scene of the murder, which soon came to light, and the guilty were brought to an ignominious death. (Pitcairn's *Trials*.)

In the April of 1607 there is recorded the arrest of a ship conveying to Flanders several fresh companies for Buccleugh's regiment. It is mentioned in a letter among the Denmylne MSS. in the Advocate's Library, which records that the states of Flanders owed several great sums to "*umquhile Capitayne Achisoun*" for his service in their wars, and that his heirs had arrested this ship in the harbour of Leith; and the king was requested to use his influence that the arrestment should be "*lousit*," which no doubt was the case.

In 1609 a twelve years' truce was concluded between the states-general and the King of Spain, and the first article of the document bore that his Catholic Majesty treated with the lords states-general of the United Provinces "in quality of, and as holding them to be, free countries, provinces, and states, over which he pretended nothing."

In 1621 the war was renewed by the Spanish army, under the Marquis of Spinola, who won in several encounters, but was sharply repulsed by the brigade under Colonel Henderson when besieging Bergen-op-Zoom in 1622. He attacked that great fortress, the barrier between Holland and Zealand, with fury and confidence, pouring about 200,000 shot into it; but was compelled to raise the blockade after three months, with the loss of 12,000 men, on the approval of Prince Maurice of Nassau. In the course of this siege Colonel Henderson was killed; and it is probably a son of his, James Henderson, of whom we read as proceeding, with the rank of admiral, with the Dutch expedition to take Angola from the Portuguese in 1641, at the head of twenty ships, having on board 3,100 soldiers and seamen—an object in which he succeeded, capturing the place, and finding therein a vast amount of booty. (Ogilby's *Africa*, fol., 1670.)

During the progress of the new war, in 1624, old Sir Andrew Gray, whom we left in London soliciting military employment, after the struggle in Bohemia arrived from Dover at the head of 11,000 English auxiliaries in Holland, where, according to Balfour's *Annals*, "the most part of them died miserably with cold and hunger." The scarcity of food brought on a pestilence, and in their small transports the soldiers were literally "heaped one upon another." They perished in thousands, and their bodies lay unburied in piles upon the sandy shores of Zealand, where their limbs and bowels were torn and devoured "by dogs and swine, to the horror of beholders." (*Acta Regia.*)

After this we hear no more of old Sir Andrew Gray, unless he is the same who is mentioned by Sir Thomas Urquhart of Cromarty in his list of Scottish colonels serving Louis XIII of France. (Hepburn's *Memoirs.*)

In 1629 the three battalions of the brigade, commanded respectively by Colonels Sir Henry Balfour, Bruce, and the chieftain of Buccleugh, accompanied the Prince of Orange in his successful attempt to reduce Hertogenbush (otherwise Bois-le-Duc), where the Spaniards had concentrated all their munitions of war; and thus by one stroke gave a mortal blow to the Spanish power in the Low Countries. On this occasion so greatly did the Scots cover themselves with glory that the Prince of Orange styled them "The Bulwark of the Republic." (*Grose,*)

Walter, first Earl of Buccleugh, who had so long commanded the first regiment of the brigade, died on the 11th June, 1634, and his body was landed at Leith for conveyance to his own house of Branxholm, whence the funeral set out for Hawick. "A striking sight it must have been that long heraldic procession which went before the body of the deceased noble, along the banks of the Teviot on that bright June day. First went forty-six *saulies* in black gowns and hoods, with black staves in their hands, a trumpeter in the Buccleugh livery following and sounding his trumpet. Then came Robert Scott of Howshaw, fully armed, riding on a fair horse, and carrying on the point of a lance a banner of the defunct's colours, *azure* and *or*.

"Then a horse in black, led by a lackey in mourning, a horse with a crimson foot-mantle, and the trumpets in mourning sounding sadly." Then came the gun pheon, lances, spurs, and gauntlets, the great pencil standard and coronet, all borne by gentlemen of the Clan Scott. "Last came the corpse, carried under a fair pall of black velvet, decked with arms, tears, cypress of satin, and on the coffin the defunct's helmet, with a coronet overlaid with cypress to show that he had been a soldier. And so he was laid among his ancestors in Hawick Kirk." (*Dom. Ann, Scot.*)

Colonel Sir William Brog was a man of some distinction among the Scottish troops in Holland. A rare print of him by Queboren was engraved in 1635. He died in the Low Country wars, and a dispute among his heirs was before the Lords of Session in 1639—according to *Durie's Decisions*, 1690.

During the German campaign which succeeded, the vexed question of precedence between the Scottish and English auxiliaries of Holland, with priority of rank, appears to have been discussed for the first time, and it was decided that the order and ranking should be according to the antiquity of the respective regiments; but this right was never contested in the matter of the Scots brigade until the year 1783.

Under Cardinal Richelieu, France in 1635 joined the Protestant League; but the outrageous cruelties of the French troops, particularly at the siege and sack of Tirlemont, in Brabant, so exasperated the Netherlanders that they flew to arms on every hand, and compelled the invaders to retreat.

George Douglas (a son of the Earl of Morton), who had borne the Royal standard under Montrose at Alford, in 1645, joined the brigade soon after, and died in high military rank (baronage); and the great marquis's friend and chaplain, afterwards Bishop of Edinburgh, was chaplain to one of the battalions in 1648.

After the peace of Westphalia, which was signed at Munster in that year, the Thirty Years' War ended, and Holland was declared to be "a free state, independent alike of Spain and the Empire."

The Dutch disbanded their forces, but "the Bulwark of the Republic," their Scottish troops, remained intact, and the civil wars at home sent so many trained recruits to their ranks that the brigade was eventually increased to six battalions.

CHAPTER 16

The Scots in Holland and Flanders (Continued)

Their first encounter with the enemy was at Gembloux, in the province of Namur, where, on the 20th of January, 1578, the Spanish troops obtained a complete victory over them and the Belgic insurgents—a defeat avenged on the 1st of August in the same year at the great Battle of Mechlin, when, as Famiana Strado tells us in his Belgic Wars, the Scots threw off their half-armour, let slip their belted plaids, and fought naked—"*nudi pugnant Scotarum multi*," his words are. This was probably owing to the heat of the weather; but, according to the Dutch historians, the hardest work and heaviest loss fell upon the Scots, ere the brigades of Don John of Austria were put to the route and driven across the Dyle.

In the great church of the city there was then to be seen a monument with the date obliterated, and an inscription stating that there lay "Margaret, daughter of Henry Stuart, by H.R.H. the Duchess of Orleans, daughter to George Stuart, of the illustrious house of Stuart and Lennox in Scotland, by Dame Mary de Baqueville of Normandy." (*Atlas Geo.*, 1711.)

From the Privy Council Register we learn that in 1678 Captain John Strachan was empowered to levy 200 additional men for the service of the Low Countries, "friendis and confederatis of this Realme"; that "loose women" were not to be transported there, and that the "great reputation" won by Scotsmen there was duly recorded in 1581; that a dispute among the officers was remitted to themselves; and another, in which Colonel Balfour was concerned, was remitted to the judges in Flanders.

In the same year, William I, Prince of Orange, sent an ambassador to Scotland to compliment James VI upon the valour of the brigade, which now marched to assist in the ineffectual attempt to raise the siege of Antwerp, which had then been invested for more than a year by the Prince of Parma, while the Dutch merchants of Amsterdam basely used secret means to prevent assistance being given to their rival brethren.

Here fire-ships were used, and a prodigious mine exploded, according to Strada and others, "the shook of which was so dreadful that it made the earth tremble for several miles, and threw the water of the river a great way beyond its banks." In the explosion 500 men perished, and the city surrendered in the following year; but the brigade was more successful in the case of Bergen-op-Zoom, from which the Prince of Parma was compelled to beat a retreat.

Meanwhile a body of Scots, under Colonel Seaton, and of English, under Colonel Norris, were disposed about Ghent, according to Cardinal Bentivoglio, who tells us that at the siege of Tournay, "some days after the assault Colonel Preston, a Scotsman, forcing his way through the German companies of the king's camp, got some horse into the city," and thus gave heart to the besieged, though he informed them that there was no hope of succour from France. (*History of the Wars in Flanders*, fol.)

In the commission granted in 1684 to Captain William Stewart (afterwards Lord Pittenweem) as colonel of the Guards to James VI it is stated that the officers and soldiers of that corps had previously served in the Netherlands, where they had been "permitted and licensiatt to assist the Prince of Orange and the States in their wieris" for twelve years; but, in default of wages, had endured poverty and hunger, whereby many perished, leaving widows and orphans—which affords a glimpse that the brigade had found but indifferent paymasters in the states-general of Holland at that crisis. (*Acts Parl.*, Jac. YI, fol.)

At Gertruydenberg, on the Maes, after the storm and capture of the strongly fortified town, the brigade suffered so heavily in three months that it was ordered to remain in garrison till recruited from Scotland; and on the return therefrom of the States ambassadors, who had gone to congratulate James VI on the birth of his son in 1594, they took back with them 1,500 recruits to bring up its strength. (Grose's *Antiquities*,) And five years after saw the brigade cover itself with glory at the siege of Bommel, a strongly walled town, which was twice attacked by the Imperialists in 1589 and 1599, but on both occasions they were repulsed with heavy losses.

By the year 1600 the Low Countries were cleared of the invaders, and the operations of the war were almost confined to Flanders; but in these brief accounts the names or numbers of the slain are not fully recorded.

In that year, at the Downs of Nieuport, eight miles from Ostende, the brigade served at the attack of the town under Maurice, Prince of Nassau, when the Archduke Albert of Austria, who advanced to relieve it, was defeated with the loss of 7,000 slain.

On this occasion the Scots brigade lost heavily. It formed part of a column detached to hold some bridges over which the enemy had to pass to reach the scene of operations, and the sluices by which the country could be laid under water; but its numbers proved too weak for the duty assigned them, and they were forced to retire, "the whole loss having fallen on the Scots, as well as on their chiefs and captains, as on the private soldiers, insomuch that 800 remained (dead) on the field, amongst whom were eleven captains, many lieutenants, and other officers."

In the *History of the Republick*, 1705, it is stated that at the siege of Nieuport many discontents concerning the division of booty and prisoners took place among the Protestant troops, and that many of the captured "were barbarously killed in cold blood by the Scots."

In 1601 the brigade served at the famous siege of Ostende—a task which lasted three years, and in which more than 100,000 men are said to have perished on both sides.

So slightly was it fortified at first, that the Princess Isabella averred she would not change her dress till the Dutch and their Scottish allies surrendered, and when it fell "it was reduced to a heap of rubbish. The Spaniards shot so many ballets against the sandhill bulwark that it became as a wall of iron, and dashed all the fresh ballets to pieces when they hit it."

The governor was changed every six months. The assaults and cannonading daily were frightful; the forts called the Hedgehog and Gullet of Hell were carried by storm by the Spaniards and Italians; the Germans carried the Sandhill, though they saw the first stormers blown by scores into the air amid the smoke of the conflict that mingled with the fog from the canals. Ultimately the place surrendered on honourable terms, and 3,000 Dutch and Scots and a few English capable of bearing arms marched out, with four field-pieces in front, and took their way to Sluys, upon the Maes.

One account gives the roll of slain on this occasion at 76,961 of the assailants, and 50,000 of the besieged; and by Prince Maurice of Nassau the gallant survivors of the latter were welcomed as conquerors, and every officer and man was rewarded.

The first governor of Surinam, when the Dutch got possession of it in 1667, was an officer of the Scotch brigade, Robert Baird, of the Sauchtonhall family, whose brother Andrew, also in the Dutch service, fell in the East Indies. (*The Surname of Baird.*)

In 1672, when Louis XIV poured his troops under Luxembourg, Condé, and Turenne into the Low Countries, the brigade consisted as yet of three regiments, commanded by the father of the first Lord Portmore (who had relinquished the name of Robertson for that of Collier), Colonel Graham, and Colonel Hugh Mackay of Scoury, a member of the Reay family, and formerly an ensign in the 1st Royal Scots. In 1673 he married Clara, the daughter of the Chevalier Arnold de Bie, in whose house he had been billeted.

Subsequently he was present at the Battle of Seneff, when, in August, 1674, the army of the Prince of Orange was defeated by that of the Prince of Condé. In his battalion, Graham of Claverhouse (the future Viscount Dundee) received a captaincy for saving the life of the Prince of Orange, in whose Guards he was then a cornet. A vacancy taking place soon after in the command of a Scottish regiment, Claverhouse applied for it. His request was refused, whereupon he quitted the Dutch service, saying, "The soldier who has not gratitude cannot be brave," and, returning to Scotland, he raised a regiment of horse to serve against the persecuted Covenanters.

The ill-judged appointment of some Dutchmen to commissions in the brigade caused much discontent therein against the Prince of Orange, the future William III, from whom the force was demanded by James VII, when the time of the Revolution of 1688 drew nigh. (*Grose.*)

In February, 1688, the Scottish Privy Council, by request of James VII, forbade the officers of the brigade, "under the highest pains, to beat up for recruits." "This," says Lord Fountainhall, "was looked upon as the forerunner of a war; but the pretence was that our king intended (to have) levies of his own."

In the April following, 10,000 stand of arms, "with ammunition conform," were ordered from Holland by the three Estates, then levying men against King James. (*Eglinton Memorials*, vol. ii.)

It had now been raised to six battalions, and when the luckless king appealed to their loyalty only 60 officers out of 290 responded, while "the rank and file, being chiefly recruited from those whom the disturbed condition of the country had driven from Scotland, remained with the Prince of Orange, and formed one of the most valuable portions of the force with which he invaded Britain."

Three battalions came over with him under General Hugh Mackay, but the operations in which they were engaged, at the siege of Edinburgh Castle, at Killiecrankie, and Aughrim (in Ireland), lie apart from our narrative. The death of the *last* survivor of that force. Colonel William Maxwell of Cardoness, "who came over with our glorious deliverer. King William," is recorded in the Edinburgh Chronicle for 1759, as having occurred in 1752, in his 95th year.

In 1692 the three regiments of the brigade rejoined the others in Flanders, where the contest between Louis XIV and William of Orange was about to be renewed in the spring, when the former suddenly appeared before Namur with 46,000 men, while Marshal Luxembourg with another army covered the siege of that important place, which holds the confluence of the Sambre and the Maes. William was unable to prevent its fall, and then came the Battle of Steinkirk, in which the brigade was severely engaged.

It was now ordered that the grenadiers of each regiment should alone wear caps; that there were to be fourteen pikes in each company of sixty men; that each captain was to carry a pike, each lieutenant a partisan, and each ensign a half-pike.

At Steinkirk there were ten Scottish regiments in the field, led by Lieutenant- General Mackay, and fifteen English. Among the former was the brigade; Mackay led the way, and his Scots were all victorious. They first encountered the Swiss infantry, and a deadly struggle ensued, for "in the hedge-fighting," says D'Auvergne in his *Campaigns*, 1692, "their fire was generally muzzle to muzzle, the hedges generally only separating the combatants."

In this battle, which, through William's bad leading, was a series of blunders, there fell 5,000 of the allies, and of these 3,000 were Scots and English. Bishop Burnet relates that General Mackay, being ordered to take ground which he deemed untenable, remonstrated, but the orders were enforced. "God's will be done!" exclaimed the veteran, and a minute after he fell from his horse dead.

In 1854 there died at his *château* of Ophemert in Guelderland, Berthold, Baron Mackay, at the age of 81 years, of whom we have the following notice:—

"A MINUTE AFTER HE FELL FROM HIS HORSE."

The baron was the descendant of General Hugh Mackay of Scoury, who commanded the Williamites at Killiecrankie, and fell at the Battle of Steinkirk. Lord Reay's second son, the Hon. Æneas Mackay, was colonel of the Mackay (Scots) Dutch regiment, and his family have since resided at The Hague, where they had obtained considerable possessions and formed alliance with several noble families. Their representative, Baron Mackay, the subject of this notice, married the Baroness Van Renesse Van Wilp, and died at a patriarchal age, after a life of great piety and usefulness. By his death the Baron Æneas Mackay, late chamberlain to the King of Holland, become next heir to the ancient Scottish peerage of Reay after the Hon. Eric Mackay, now master of Reay, who succeeded his brother Eric, late Lord Reay, who died unmarried at Goldings, in Hertfordshire, in July, 1847.

At Neerwinden, in 1693, the brigade again suffered heavy loss, and William was compelled again to give way before the white-coated infantry of France with the loss of 10,000 men. "During many months after," wrote the Earl of Perth to his sister (as quoted by Macaulay), "the ground was strewn with skulls and bones of horses and men, and with fragments of hats, shoes, saddles, and holsters. The next summer the soil, fertilised by 20,000 corpses, broke forth into millions of scarlet poppies."

The treaty of Ryswick, concluded in 1697, was followed by five years of peace.

The brigade shared in all the perils and honours of the subsequent war of the Spanish succession, under the command of John, Duke of Argyle. At Ramilies, in 1706, says the *Atlas Geographicus*, "the Dutch troops, but more particularly the Scots in their service, distinguished themselves by their extraordinary gallantry." Among the few prisoners taken by the enemy was Ensign Gardiner, of one of the Scottish regiments, who afterwards fell a colonel at the Battle of Prestonpans.

At Oudenarde, in 1708, where the French were defeated by Marlborough, and where "charge succeeded charge," states the record of the Scots Royals, "until the shades of evening gathered over the conflict, and the combatants could only be discerned by the red flashes of musketry that blazed over the fields and marshy ground," the Scots brigade was among the steadiest troops in the field; and at Malplacquet, in the same year, when Villars was totally defeated, and where the hapless descendant of James III and VIII was serving as a simple volunteer, yet charged twelve times, says Smollett, at the head of the household troops, the brigade fought well and loyally.

John, Marquis of Tullibardine, eldest son of the Duke of Athole, fell at the head of one of its regiments , and among others there also fell two sons of Alexander Swinton, Lord Mersington; Charles, colonel of a battalion; and James, one of his captains, who had married a lady in Holland. Both brothers died within the French lines or trenches. (*Douglas Baronage.*)

In the arts of peace the Scots were not unknown in Holland. Among the many filling chairs in the continental universities in the 17th century, now utterly unknown at home, few stood higher than David Stewart, professor of philosophy at Leyden, who is mentioned with honour in *Soberiana* (Paris, 1732), a work in which M. Sorbier records many of the pleasant Sunday evening *conversazioni*, wherein Stewart figured, at the house of M. and Madame Saumoise.

CHAPTER 17

The Scots in Holland and Flanders (Continued)

The peace of Utrecht, which was concluded in 1713, continued until 1744, when the British ministry again plunged into a continental war, for which they were severely reprobated, and in the following year, by order of the states-general, eight new companies were added to each regiment of the brigade, and recruited for in Scotland. Their first service was at the siege of Tournay, then deemed one of the strongest and finest citadels in Europe. The allied army, consisting of 126,000 men, took the field; but Sluys and Hulst fell, and the Dutch, terrified by the progress of the French, clamoured against their rulers, and compelled them to declare the Prince of Orange *Statholder*.

The brigade fought at Roucaux, at Val, and Laffelot. At the latter, an account of the battle printed at Liége states "that the French king's brigade carried the village of Lauberg, after a repulse of 40 battalions successively." A letter from an officer states:

> . . . . that this brigade consisted of Scots and Irish, who fought like devils; that they neither took nor gave quarter; that observing the Duke of Cumberland to be extremely active in the defence of that post, they were employed in the attack at their own request; that they in a manner cut down all before them, with a full resolution to reach his Highness, which they certainly would have done had not Sir John Ligonier come up with a party of horse and saved the duke at the loss of his own liberty. (*Scots Mag.*, 1747.)

The "hero" of Culloden was routed, with the loss of many colours and sixteen guns.

In July, 1747, Count Lowendahl commenced the siege of Bergen-op-Zoom, which cost him 20,000 of the finest French troops. On the 14th his batteries opened against the place, the garrison of which consisted of six battalions, including two of the Scots brigade, with whom Colonel Lord John Murray, Captain Fraser of Colduthil, Campbell of Craignish, and several other officers of the 42nd obtained permission to serve, as their regiment was then in South Beveland. (*Records of the Black Watch.*)

In the lines were 18 more battalions, with 250 pieces of cannon, and the assailants mustered 86,000 men, thereby exciting such terror that the governor and the whole of the troops, except the two Scots and one Dutch battalion, abandoned the town, to which, by oversight or treachery, Lowendahl gained access, after a two months' investment.

The three regiments maintained a desperate contest with the enemy, single-handed, as it were, for several hours at this eventful crisis. From the 15th July till the 17th September the siege had been pushed without intermission, and the French losses were dreadful. During all that time 74 great guns and mortars had hurled their iron showers upon the works, in many instances red-hot, to fire the streets and churches; but, on the 25th July, London's Highlanders, who were posted at Fort Rours, covering the lines, made a sally, claymore in hand (says the *Hague Gazette*), destroyed the enemy's grand battery, and slew so many that Count Lowendahl beat a parley for the burial of the dead. This was refused, so the latter had to lie where they fell. The town was now in ashes, the trenches full of carnage and pools of blood, and hour by hour the roar of cannon and the red explosion of bombs went on.

The stand made by the two battalions of the Scots brigade enabled the governor and a few of the garrison to recover themselves after the surprise of the town, says General Stewart, otherwise the whole would have been killed or taken. "The Scots," according to the *Hague Gazette*, " assembled in the market-place, and attacked the French with such vigour that they drove them from street to street, till fresh reinforcements pouring in compelled them to retreat in turn, disputing every inch as they retired, and fighting till two-thirds of their number fell upon the spot, killed or severely wounded, when the remainder brought off the old governor and joined the troops in the lines."

This was through the Steenberg gate, and they marched with colours flying and drums beating. Of Colliers' battalion, originally 660 strong, only 156 men remained alive; and of General Marjoribanks' battalion, originally 850, only 220 survived the slaughter.

The *Hague Gazette* says that:

> The two battalions of the Scots brigade have, as usual, done honour to their country, which is all we have to comfort us for the loss of such brave men, who from 1,450 are now reduced to 330, and those have valiantly brought their colours with them, which their grenadiers recovered twice, from the midst of the French, at the point of the bayonet. The Swiss have also suffered, while many others took *a more speedy way to escape danger*.

The brigade had 37 officers killed and wounded. Coxe's *History of the House of Austria* has it that 330 Scots fought their way out. Two lieutenants, Francis and Allan Maclean, sons of the Laird of Torloisk, were taken prisoners, and brought before Count Lowendahl, said he:

> Gentlemen consider yourselves upon parole. If all had conducted themselves as you and your brave corps have done, I should not now have been master of Bergen-op-Zoom.

Allan Maclean afterwards left the brigade, and raised the 114th Highlanders for the British service in 1750, and the 84th Highlanders subsequently. At the head of the latter he served under Wolfe, and was the chief cause of our victory at Quebec.

In Amsterdam there was collected £17,000 in one day for distribution among the survivors of the two battalions, and as during the siege every soldier who carried off a gabion from the enemy's works was paid a crown, some of the Scots gained ten per day in that desperate work, while those who drew the fuses from burning bombs received twelve *ducats* for each fuse.

The *Edinburgh Herald* for 1800 records the death of John Nesbitt, at Oldhamstocks, in his 107th year, an old brigademan who had been wounded by a bayonet at the famous siege of Bergen-op-Zoom.

So many captains and lieutenants had fallen there, that ensigns received companies; but purchase was unknown in the Scots brigade, which, after the peace of 1748, remained, as usual, on duty in the Dutch garrisons; bat changes took place.

Thus, when in 1752 the states-general agreed to reduce their forces of the Scots brigade, four of the junior companies of each battalion were reduced, and incorporated with the old ones to form Drumlanrig's regiment, the second battalion of which had been already reduced in 1749. By the new regulations "there are reduced of the Scots 28 captains, 56 second lieutenants, and 70 ensigns; the captains pensioned at 900 *guilders* a year, and obliged to serve; the subalterns at 300, with leave to go where they will. But the gentlemen who have companies now are between 40 and 50 pounds sterling a year better than formerly." (*Scots Mag.*)

The list of the principal field-officers of the six battalions is given thus, March 25, 1752:—

1st Battalion—colonel, Lieutenant-General Halkett; 2nd colonel, John Houston, died at Edinburgh, in 1788, as lieutenant-general.

2nd Battalion—colonel, John Gordon; 2nd colonel. Earl of Drumlanrig, who shot himself in 1754.

3rd Battalion—colonel, Major-General Strewart; 2nd, Colonel Graham.

4th Battalion—Colonel Mackay; Lieut.-Colonel Forbes.

5th Battalion—colonel, Major-General A. Marjoribanks, died at The Hague in 1774; 2nd colonel, Lieutenant-Colonel Cunningham.

6th Battalion—Colonel Mackay; Lieutenant-Colonel Maclean, died at the Brill in 1752.

Between the middle and end of the last century there died the following Scotsmen of rank in the service of the states-general, each and all after a long career of military experience:—

In 1758—Lieutenant-General Halkett, at The Hague.

In 1767—Major Farquhar of Dalwhinnie, in his 87th year.

In 1768—at Venloo, Lieutenant-General Sir George Colquhoun of Tillychewan; at Montpellier, Colonel Fergus Hamilton; at Castleton, in Skye, Colonel Donald Macdonald, in his 75th year; at Standhill, Colonel Robert Turnbull of Standhill.

In 1784—Colonel C. Craigie Halkett, Lieutenant-Governor of Namur.

In 1786—at Zutphen, in Gueldreland, Colonel Sir James Gordon of Embo, Bart.

In 1789—Major-General Ralf Dundas, lately commanding Gordon's regiment; Major-General W. J. H. Hamilton of Silvertonhill, at Gorcum-on-the-Maes.

In 1798—at Talisker, aged 80, Lieutenant-General John Macleod.

In 1804—Lieutenant-Colonel Sutherland, of the Hon. John Stuart's regiment.

In 1755 the brigade was somewhat disappointed at not being recalled in a body to Britain; but it had now been so long in the Dutch service that it had become a matter of dispute whether there existed a right to recall it.

In 1768, the field-officers of the brigade addressed a strong remonstrance to the British Secretary for War, expressing a desire for removal from Holland "on account of indifferent usage," but their request was not successful; and four years before this time we find that their officers, when beating up for recruits in Scotland, were obstructed by the Convention of Royal Burghs and the magistrates of Edinburgh, on the plea that men were required for labour at home. (*Edinburgh Advertiser*, No. 32.)

In 1797 there died in his 62nd year a distinguished officer of the brigade. Captain J. G, Stedman, who commenced his career in the British navy, but joined a regiment of the former as lieutenant, when he served with the force sent to suppress the insurgent negroes in Surinam. Inspired by a desire for exploring a part of the world then little known, and in the hope of preferment by the states-general, he volunteered for service with a regiment of seven companies formed as marines, and was appointed captain therein by the Prince of Orange under Colonel Tourgeoud, a Swiss.

He landed at Surinam in 1773, and there formed an attachment to a handsome *mulatto* girl in her 16th year (daughter of a Dutch planter), "whose goodness of heart and faithful attachment to him were more endearing than all her personal attractions; but by the laws of the settlement she could not be redeemed from slavery or brought home to Europe, but died of poison, a victim to jealousy, before the captain left her," (*Ann, Reg.,* 1797.)

After undergoing incredible toils, witnessing horrible cruelties, and having many strange adventures, he returned to Scotland, and, shortly before his death, published a narrative of the five years' expedition against the revolted negroes of Surinam, 1772-1777, in two volumes *quarto*, with eighty drawings by himself, published at London in 1796. He left a widow and five children, some of whose descendants are now in Scotland.

The king in 1776 requested the states to give him their six Scottish battalions for service against his rebels in America; but the Dutch objected, on the plea that they would have to raise six others in their place; and a confused series of negotiations went on till 1782, without avail. In 1776 the Society of Amsterdam for the Recovery of the Drowned bestowed their gold medal upon Dr. John Stoner, of the Hon. General Stewart's regiment, for the recovery of one who was to all appearance dead. (*Edin. Weekly Mag.*)

In 1779 the brigade again offered its services to the British government, being unwilling to linger in garrison towns when Britain's foes were in the field; but the states-general were resolved that on and after the let of January, 1783, it should be incorporated with the Dutch army. By that time the brigade had been 213 years in this service, and in all the battles and sieges in which its soldiers fought had never lost a colour.

On the 8th December, 1782, the Prince of Orange issued an order to the colonels of the brigade, directing them to assume blue uniform instead of the scarlet they had hitherto worn, to provide themselves with orange sashes, new *gorgets* and *espontoons*, and their sergeants with new halberts, with the British arms engraved thereon; and lastly—a most vexed point—*new colours*, "painted with the arms of the generality, or of the province upon the establishment of which the battalion is paid; as on the 1st January next the said regiment must begin to be commanded in Dutch, from which day, likewise, the said regiment is to beat the Dutch and *not* the Scottish march."

The indignation of the brigade at these changes soon took a practical turn. On General Welderen assembling the officers of Houston's and Stuart's battalions at The Hague, and delivering to them these orders, they declared themselves to be British subjects, and refused to obey them. So time was given for deliberation, and by a letter from Lord Grantham, addressed to Colonel Ferrier, it was stated that those who chose to return to Britain would be welcomed by the king, while those who chose to stay in Holland would not forfeit his regard. On this 60 officers returned from the Dutch service, and came to London in search of military service, and were presented to the king; while it was arranged that the colonels commandant of the three regiments of two battalions each. Generals Houston, Stewart, and Dundas, should receive pay for life, without subscribing the Dutch oath of allegiance. (*Edinburgh Advert.*, vol. xxxi.)

The next demand of the regiment was the restitution of their Scottish colours and to have them sent to the king; and Lieutenant-

Colonel Cunningham was at The Hague in April, 1783, to receive them for that purpose. A long and somewhat angry correspondence ensued, and in 1784 the states ordered the said colours to be deposited in the arsenal at The Hague, adding that if the colours were transmitted to Britain they declined to employ Lieutenant-Colonel Cunningham. (*Pol. Mag.*, vol. vi.)

In 1793 the brigade came back to Britain in a body and was placed on the British establishment, and from that year till 1809 wore the kilt. On the 9th October, 1794, they were numbered as "the 94th regiment, or Scots Brigade," under General Francis Dundas, and in the following June a new set of British colours was presented to the corps in George Square, Edinburgh, by Lord Adam Gordon, commanding the forces in Scotland. By this time several Dutchmen were in the ranks; in one company alone there were 23 rank and file, all foreign. The three colonels commanding were Francis Dundas, Frederick Halkett, and Islay Ferrier.

As the 94th they maintained their ancient reputation at the Cape, in India, and the Peninsula, but were unfortunately disbanded in 1818. Reimbodied at Glasgow in 1823, on which occasion their old colours were unfurled and borne by one of the Black Watch, a vain attempt was made to identify the new corps with the old; but even the new one has passed away; as, under the recent and helplessly defective scheme of army reorganisation, it is "muddled" up, under a new name, with the old 88th or Connaught Rangers!

Through the kindly influence of Lord Reay, a stand of colours belong to the old brigade (not taken in 1782) was lately given to the magistrates of Edinburgh for preservation in the parish church of St. Giles. But such is the story of that splendid old corps, which existed for 248 years—"The Bulwark of the Republic."

CHAPTER 18

The Scots in Sweden

At the funeral of Carl Gustaf the Scoto-Swedish nobles appeared in strength. Baron Forbess led the Princess Euphrosyne, and in the procession were Colonel Leighton, John Clerk, Jacob Spens, Adolf Stewart, who bore the banner of Ravenstein, Forbess that of Holland, Douall that of Gothland; and forty Swedish cavaliers of the second class were there, among whom were the names of Barclay, Klerk, Spens, Hamilton, etc. The families of thirteen Scottish nobles, some of whose titles yet exist, are given at length by Marryat.

Among the untitled Scottish noblemen was Thomas Gladstone of Dumfries, colonel in Sweden in 1647; and all are frequently styled mysteriously of *Tatilk*—i.e., "of that ilk."

The first of the Swedish Spens family was James, who raised in 1611 a Scottish regiment for service in Sweden, to the indignation of the Danes, who sent 200 horse to slay him and his attendants in Zealand.

At Skug Kloster, the *château* of General Wrangel, and now the residence of Count Brahe, the lineal descendant of the great astronomer, there are preserved portraits of many of Wrangel's comrades in the Thirty Years' War, inscribed with their names. Among these are Captain Kammel (Campbell), David Drummond, King (Lord Eythen), Patrick, Earl of Forth, Major Sinclair, who died serving Charles XII. "The best families in the kingdom are of Scottish descent," says Bremner (*Denmark and Sweden 1840*); "Leslies, Montgomeries, Gordons, Duffs, Hamiltons, Douglases (lately extinct), Murrays—in short, all the best names of Scotland are to be found in Sweden, having been introduced by the cadets of our noble families who served under Gustavus Adolphus in the Thirty Years' War."

In 1850 there were Count Hamilton of Christianstadt and Baron

Hamilton of Boo; and John Hugh, Baron Hamilton, was Adjutant-General of Sweden in 1803, and *premier écuyer* to the Duchess of Sudermaine.

The most famous cannon-founder in Sweden was Sir Alexander Hamilton of the Redhouse, in Haddingtonshire. In the time of Gustavus his gun-forges were at Orebro. His invention, the *canon à la Suédois*, was used in the French army till 1780. He became famous in the wars of the Covenant, and in his old age perished when the castle of Dunglass was blown up by the treachery of an Englishman.

According to Sir Thomas Urquhart, there was in the time of Gustavus upwards of sixty Scottish governors of castles and towns in the conquered provinces of Germany; and he had at one time no less than four field-marshals, four generals, three brigadiers, 27 colonels, 51 lieutenant-colonels, 14 majors, and an unsown number of captains and subalterns, all Scotsmen, "besides seven regiments of Scots that lay in Sweden and Livonia, and six elsewhere. The Dutch in Gustavus's service were many times glad to beat the old Scotch march when they designed to frighten or alarm the Dutch; and it is observed that Sir John Hamilton abandoned the army though earnestly pressed by Gustavus to stay, only because the Swedes and Dutch were ordered to storm the enemy's works before him at Wurtsburg, after he and his men had boldly hewn out a way for them." (*At, Geo.*, 1711.)

Robert Munro of Foulis commanded two regiments, one of horse, the other of foot; and of his surname there were three generals, 24 field officers, 11 captains, and many subalterns in Sweden. (*Old Stat Acct.*)

It has been written that "the reproach of a mere mercenary spirit would be unjust to the memory of these brave men, whom a peace with England compelled to draw their swords in other lands; and it must be remembered that military service, no matter under whom or where, was a necessary part of a Scottish gentleman's education. The recruiting in all parts of Scotland continued during most of the Thirty Years' War with the greatest spirit, for the love of military enterprise and hatred of the Imperial cause were strong in the hearts of the nation; and thus, until the era of the Covenant, the drams of the Scoto-Swedes rang in every glen from Caithness to the Cheviots."

We have now to describe one of the greatest calamities of the time—the massacre *to a man* of an entire Scottish regiment among the Norwegian Alps.

In the year 1612 Gustavus Adolphus procured several companies of

COLONEL GEORGE SINCLAIR'S FORCES LAND IN NORWAY

infantry from Scotland, and formed them into two regiments. According to Puffendorf, he had also sixteen Scottish ships of war, by which he captured the town of Drontheim (or Trondeim), in Norway, and cleared the southern shores of Sweden. His Scottish troops served him faithfully in his Russian war, particularly at the storming of Pleskov and Kexholm, at the mouth of Lake Ladoga; and in 1620 he had still a stronger body of these auxiliaries, led by Colonel Seaton and Sir Patrick Ruthven, afterwards field-marshal and Earl of Forth, who won high honours at the capture of the Livonian capital and the storming of Dunamond and Mitau, in Courland.

In the March of 1612, by permission of James VI, Colonel George Sinclair raised in his native county a body of 900 men for the Swedish service. A soldier of fortune, he had been early in the army of "The Bulwark of the North," and was a natural son of David Sinclair of Stirkoke, and nephew of the Earl of Caithness.

The antecedents of the colonel were somewhat remarkable. According to Calder's *History of Caithness*, before embarking for Norway he was engaged in a somewhat desperate affair, the circumstances of which are briefly these:—John, eighth Lord Maxwell of Nithsdale, having, it is said, treacherously slain Sir James Johnston of that ilk, fled to France and then to Caithness, where he lurked for some time; but a price being set upon his head, he attempted flight again, but was captured near the southern boundaries of the county by Colonel Sinclair, and sent to Edinburgh, where he was beheaded at the Market Cross on the 21st of May, 1613. His *Good Night*, a pathetic ballad in which he takes leave of his lady, Margaret Hamilton, and his friends, is printed in the *Border Minstrelsy*; and when the hand of fate overtook Sinclair, it was deemed but a just retribution by the whole Johnston clan.

He embarked with his regiment to join Gustavus by the way of Norway, and after a four days' voyage landed on the coast near Romsdal. The object of the expedition was to assist Gustavus in the conquest of Norway, and for this purpose Colonel Monkhoven, with another body of 2,300 Scots, had not long before landed at Drontheim, and cut a passage into Sweden. (Geyers' *Histoire de Suède*.)

Sinclair's second in command was Alexander Ramsay, who had under him two other officers—Jacob Mannerspange and Henrick Brussey, supposed to mean Henry Bruce, according to the Norwegian accounts—and he was accompanied by *Fru* (or Lady Sinclair); and they note an insolent speech alleged to have been made by Sinclair on his landing—"I will recast the old Norway lion, and turn him into a mole that dare not venture out of his burrow!"

He pursued his march along the valley of Lessoo, under the shadow of the tremendous Dovrefelt, 8,000 feet high, and is said to have given the country to fire and sword, thereby infuriating the Norse, who sent abroad the *Budstick* (or message-rod)—a signal like the Scottish fiery cross—summoning all to arms; and a great body of boors, armed with matchlocks and axes, under Burdon Segelstadt of Ringebo, near Elstad, took possession of the narrow mountain gorge through which the Scots had to pass at Kringellen. The road was only a mere footpath, exceedingly narrow, and overhanging a deep and rapid stream that flowed beneath. According to Norwegian tradition, a mermaid appeared to Colonel Sinclair by night and warned him of death if he advanced; but he replied that "when he returned in triumph from the conquest of the kingdom, he would punish her as she deserved." According to Calder's *History*, the mermaid is supposed to have been the *Fru* herself in disguise.

Be that as it may, the Sinclairs marched on, and the air which their pipes played is still remembered in Norway (*Calder*), and it was certainly their own dead march. Night was closing, and the deep Norwegian fiords and the pine forests that overhung them were growing dark, when the regiment entered on the narrow path described. The stillness and loneliness, together with the difficult nature of the place, caused the Sinclairs to straggle in their march, and they had just attained the middle of the black defile when the roar of more than a thousand long matchlocks reverberated among the impending cliffs, filling all the chasm with fire and smoke.

Then came the crash of half-hewn trees and loosened masses of rock, urged over by levers, that swept away whole sections and hurled them into the mountain torrent that foamed below. Among the first who fell was Colonel Sinclair, when gallantly essaying to storm the rocks, claymore in hand. Among those hurled into the stream, say the Norwegians, was the *Fru*, "but, being supported by her ample robes, she was able to carry her infant son safe across in her arms,"

In the pass all perished save sixty and the adjutant. These were at first distributed among the inhabitants, but the latter grew tired of supporting them, and, marching them into a meadow, murdered them in cold blood, all save two, who escaped and got home to Caithness. Accounts differ, and Laing in his *Norway* is at variance with the native narrative in some points. Colonel Sinclair was buried in the church of Quam, near the valley of Vüg, but his regiment all lie in a remote

Sinclair's men would have looked similar to these Scottish soldiers in the service of Gustavus Adolphus

solitude near the fatal pass. Above the remains is a cross with a tablet inscribed thus:—

> Here lies Colonel Jorgen Zinclair, 900 Scots dashed to pieces like earthen pots by the boors of Lessoo, Vauge, and Foroen, under Berdon Segelstadt of Kingebo. (*Von Buch.*)

Here we are strongly tempted to give Ooclenschalager's ballad, which is not much known in this country:—

Child Sinclair sailed from Scottish land
Far Noroway to brave;
But he sleeps in Gulbrand's rocky strand.
Low in a bloody grave.
Child Sinclair sailed the stormy sea,
To fight for Swedish gold;
'God speed thy warrior hearts and thee,
And quell the Norseman bold!'
He sailed a day, and two, and three,
He and his gallant band;
The fourth sun saw him quit the sea
And touch Old Norway's strand.
On Romsdal's shore his soul was fain
To triumph or to fall;
He and his twice seven hundred men,
The gallant and the tall,

O stern and haughty was their wrath,
And cruel with sword and spear;
Nor hoary age could check their wrath,
Nor widowed mother's tear.
With bitter death, young babes they slew,
Though to the breast they clung;
And woeful tidings, sad, but true,
Echoed from every tongue.

On hill and rock the beacons glared.
To tell of danger nigh;
The Norseman's sword was boldly bared—
The Scots must yield or die!
The warriors of the land are far,
They and their kingly lord;
Yet shame on him who shuns the war,

133

Or fears the foreign horde!
They march—they meet—the Norwayan host.
Have hearts both stern and free;
They gather on Bredalbigh's coast—
The Scots must yield or flee.
The Langé flows in Leydéland,
Where Kringen's shadows fall;
Thither they march, that fated band,
A tomb to find for all.

In the onslaught first, Child Sinclair died,
And ceased his haughty breath,
Stern sport for Scottish hearts to bide,
God shield them from the death!
Come forth, come forth, ye Norsemen true,
Light be your hearts today!
Fain would the Scots the ocean blue
Between the slaughter lay!

Their ranks yield to the leaden storm,
On high the ravens sail—
Ah me! for every mangled form
A Scottish maid shall wail!
They come a host with life and breath,
But none returned to say,
How fares the invader in the strife
He wars with Old Norway?

There is a mound by Langé's tide,
The Norseman lingers near,
His eye is bright—but not with pride—
It glistens with a tear!

Robert Chambers, who in his tour through Norway visited the scene of this slaughter, says:

> In a peasant's house here were shown to me, in 1849, a few relics of the poor Caithness men—a matchlock or two, a broadsword, a couple of powder-flasks, and the wooden part of a drum.

In 1869, I was shown, by an officer of the Norwegian artillery, several others m the arsenal at Aggerhous; but the long matchlocks had been refitted with locks for the flint.

Among others who now joined the army of Gustavus Adolphus

was Captain Sir James Hepburn of Athelsteinford, who brought with him the survivors of old Sir Andrew Gray's Scottish band that went to Bohemia in 1620; and he was accompanied by his cousin, James Hepburn of Waughton, who soon attained the rank of lieutenant-colonel. The Swedish artillery at this time consisted of 4, 6, and 12 pounders. The musketeers wore morions, gorgets, buff coats, and breastplates, swords and daggers; the pikemen were similarly armed and accoutred. Ammunition was for the first time made up into cartridges, regiments were formed into right and left wings, with pikes in the centre to guard the colours. Gustavus formed his ranks six deep, Wallenstein thirty. Each battalion had four surgeons and two chaplains. For a time the private chaplain of Gustavus was the then well-known Bishop Murdock Mackenzie. The hair was shorn short, but *mustachios*, like swords and spurs, were of great length. All officers of rank wore a gold chain, and rich armour from Parma and Milan was quite the rage. A day's march was eighteen miles. Says Harte:

> In a journal of each day's marching which a Scottish regiment made for six years successively, I find that quantity to establish the medium. (*Life of Gustavus.*)

Each Swedish and Scottish regiment consisted at this time of eight companies; in each company were 72 musketeers and 54 pikemen.

In 1625 Gustavus appointed Sir James Hepburn colonel of his old Bohemian comrades, now represented by the 1st Scots Royals, of which his name as 1st colonel, under date in France, 1633, can yet be seen in any Annual Army List. Says Defoe:

> He was a complete soldier indeed, and was so well-beloved by the gallant king that he hardly knew how to go about any great action without him.

When Gustavus renewed hostilities with Sigismund of Poland, in 1625, Hepburn's Scottish regiment formed part of the allied force which invaded Polish Prussia, captured many strong places, and ended by the total rout of the Poles on the plains of Semigallia in Courland.

Gustavus, resolving to effect the relief of Memel, in Prussia, when his garrison was closely blockaded by 30,000 Poles, entrusted the duty to Hepburn and Count Thurm. The former had only three Scottish regiments of infantry, and the latter but 500 horse for this desperate task, which; after a long march, they began in the night, "at push of pike." A terrible discharge of bullets, arrows, and stones was opened

GUSTAVUS ADOLPHUS

on the Scots by dense hordes of Cossacks and Heyducks, clad in mail shirts, and Hepburn was compelled to take post on a rock, around which the wild horsemen surged and shouted, "The Scottish curs cannot abide the bite of the Polish wolves!"

On that rock Hepburn defended himself for two entire days against the whole Polish army led by Prince Udislaus, till Gustavus in person achieved the relief of the town, on which the Poles gave way unpursued. It was computed that each of Hepburn's Scots killed a man, yet lost only a seventh of their own number.

In the following year the Scots fought gallantly at Dantzig under General Sir Alexander Leslie of Balgonie (the future Earl of Leven), a veteran of the Dutch and Bohemian wars. His pikemen broke through the dense masses of Sigismund's cavalry twice, cut to pieces 400, capturing four troop standards, and retired with little loss; but this movement brought on a battle which ended in the total rout of the Polish army, with the loss of 3,000 men. (Puffindorf's *Sweden,*)

In 1627 Hepburn's Scots accompanied Gustavus again into Prussia, and were at the storming of Kesmark on the Vistula and the defeat of the Poles at Dirschau. In the following year Sweden obtained fresh levies from Scotland. Among these was a strong regiment led by Alexander Lord Spynie. These, with a few English, made 9,000 men. Spynie's regiment was added to the garrison of Stralsund, then blockaded by the Imperialists, who aimed at nothing but the total subversion of German liberty and extirpation of the Lutheran heresy by fire and sword—a scheme including the conquest of all Scandinavia, which attracted the attention of all Europe.

Thus Stralsund, which had taken no part in the war, was exposed to a vigorous siege, and the two Northern kings resolved to forget their jealousies and relieve it. Led by the Laird of Balgonie, 5,000 Scots and Swedes cut a passage into the town and supplied the starving people with food. A gallant defence now began, though Wallenstein vowed he would possess Stralsund "even if God slung it in chains between heaven and earth!"

Nowhere did the Scots do their duty more nobly than there, and medals were struck in their honour, while Hepburn was knighted. Says Munro:

Here, was killed the valorous Captain Macdonald, who with his own hands killed with his sword five of his enemies before he was killed himself. Divers also were hurt, as was Captain

137

Lindesay of Bainshaw, who received three dangerous wounds; Lieutenant Pringle and divers more, their powder being spent; to make good their retreat falls up Captain Mackenzie with the old Scottish blades of our regiment, keeping their faces to the enemy while their comrades were retiring; the service went on afresh, when Lieutenant Seaton and his company alone, led by Lieutenant Lumsden, lost about 30 valorous soldiers, and the lieutenant, seeing Colonel Holke retiring, desired him to stay a little and see if the Scots could stand and fight or not. The colonel, perceiving him to jeer, shook his head and went away. In the end Captain Mackenzie retired slowly with his company till he was safe within the walls; and then he made ready for his march towards Wolgast, to find his Majestic of Denmark. (Munro's *Expedition*, 1637.)

In the end Wallenstein was forced to raise the siege and begin a shameful retreat.

CHAPTER 19

The Scots in Sweden—(Continued)

At this date (1630) Gustavus had now in his army more than 1,000 officers and 12,000 men, all Scots. "Amongst these forces," says Richard Cannon—and many of them, under Leslie, were sent to drive the Imperialists out of the Isle of Rugen—

> Colonel Hepburn's Scots regiment appears to have held a distinguished character for gallantry on all occasions: and no troops appear to have been found better for this important enterprise than the Scots, who proved brave, hardy, patient of fatigue and privation, frugal, obedient, and sober soldiers. (1st Royals—War Off. Records.)

Rugen was captured at a stroke, after which the regiment was quartered "in Spruce."

Sir Donald Mackay, of Strathnaver's regiment, 1,500 strong, raised for the Danish army in the country of Lord Reay in 1626, now volunteered for service in Sweden, and was ordered by Oxenstiern to embark at Pillau, under Lieutenant-Colonel Monro, and proceed towards Wolgast, in Pomerania.

Monro (a cousin of Foulis) embarked his men on board of two Swedish vessels—the *Lilynichol* and *Hound*. On the former were the companies of Robert and Hector Monro and Bullion; on board the latter, those of Major Sennot, Captains Learmonth and John Monro; while their luggage, horses, and drums were on board a third and smaller craft. When night came on there blew a tempest, and the expedition found itself among shoal water, with the rocks and reefs of Pomerania to leeward; and Monro's ship was all but water-logged, though relays of 48 Highlanders were constantly at the pumps. This was on the 19th of August.

A little before midnight the *Lilynichol* foundered on the Isle of Rugen, parting in two; but after incredible exertions the soldiers got ashore, the colonel being the last to abandon the wreck, from which he brought off all the arms and armour. He found himself on the picturesque Isle of Rugen—the last stronghold of paganism in the North, and where to this day may be seen the sacred wood and lake mentioned by Tacitus in his treatise on Germany, and where human sacrifices were offered up to a gigantic monster-god named Swantovit. He was 80 miles from the Swedish outposts. All the forts were again in the possession of the Imperialists; he was without ammunition, and, as he tells us, "had nothing to defend us but swords, pikes, and wet muskets." In addition to this his soldiers were soaked, exhausted, and starving.

On his application, the *seneschal* of Rugenvalde, a castle belonging to the Duke of Pomerania, sent him fifty dry matchlocks and ammunition. With men armed with these, and his pikemen, Monro fell briskly upon a night picket of Imperial horse, all of which he slew or captured, thus rewinning the isle for Duke Bogislaus IV. He blew up the bridge, strengthened the castle of Rugenvalde by turf batteries, and then defended himself for nine weeks, till Hepburn's "Invincible Regiment" advanced to his relief from Polish Prussia by order of the chancellor Oxenstiern.

On the 6th November 500 of Monro's Highlanders were ordered to defend to the last Colberg, a half-ruined castle and town on the coast of Pomerania. He threw up redoubts, barricaded the approaches, and ere long the place was assailed by 8,000 Imperialists led by the famous Count de Monteculculi, under whom were the splendidly accoutred regiments of Goetz and Sparre, Charles, Wallenstein, Isolani, and Coloredo. Three troops of *cuirassiers* in white armour led the van, with three of Croats and 1,000 *arquebussiers*, all of whom were hurled back in confusion by the steady Highland fire. On being summoned to treat for the surrender of the post, Monro replied:

> The word *treaty* has been omitted in my instructions; thus I have only powder and ball at the service of the Count de Monteculculi.

A dreadful strife ensued. The whole town was laid in ashes. The Reay regiment retired into the castle, and, despairing of success, the count drew off in the night, under cover of a mist, thus admitting that 500 Highlanders could repel *sixteen* times their number of Germans.

On the 18th November another deadly struggle took place, amid mist and darkness, between the Imperialists—7,000 strong—and the Swedish infantry, under the young Graf of Thurn. They fled almost without firing a shot, but the Scottish muleteers of Lord Reay and Hepburn held their ground, and poured in their volleys steadily till the unaccountable flight of the Swedish cavalry left their flanks uncovered, and they too fell back, with the loss of 500 men, many shooting their comrades in the confusion, says Harte.

In 1631, Gustavus, on representing his desire to free Germany from the oppression of the Emperor Ferdinand, received from England and other countries £108,000, with a promise of 6,000 infantry, raised by the Marquis of Hamilton, who, previous to his departure, received the Order of the Garter from Charles I.

Colonel John Monro of Obsdale now offered another regiment of Highlanders for the Swedish service, and Colonel Sir James Lumsden (brother of Invergellie) brought over a battalion of Lowland infantry. His eldest brother, the laird, was senior captain of a company, in which the ensign was the famous Sir James Turner, the cavalier memorialist. Robert Lumsden was murdered in cold blood by the English at the sack of Dundee twenty years after, but Monro of Obsdale was slain in battle at Wettereau, on the banks of the Rhine. (*Scots Nation Vindicated,* 1714.)

Robert Scott was quartermaster-general of the Swedish army, and afterwards general in Denmark. His bust in Lambeth Church has been engraved. David Barclay of Mathers and Anthony Haig of Beimerside, the latter with 50 horse, with three sons of Boswell of Auchinleck, John and Robert Durham of Pitkerow, and Francis and Alexander Leslie of Wardis, all joined the Swedish army at this time. "Mackay, our countryman, is in great honour," wrote James Baird, the commissary, to his brother Auchmedden, in 1631, "and is general over three regiments, and captain of the King of Sweden's Guards, quhilk consist of 100 horse and 100 foot, *and sall be all Scotsmen*" (*Surname of Baird.*) There, too, came George Buchanan of Auchmar, a captain. He vanquished an Italian swordsman in single combat, for which he was made major, but was killed in action soon after. (*History of the Buchanans.*) Thus in the second campaign against the empire the Swedish army, according to Burnett, was almost entirely led by Scottish officers.

The love and spirit of adventure must have been keen in those days which lured so many brave Scots abroad at a time when locomotion was tedious and difficult, and even all ideas of locality beyond their native hills and glens were vague and dim indeed.

SIR JAMES TURNER,

In the March of 1631 Sir James Hepburn, in his 30th year, was at the head of the Green brigade, as it was named, comprising the four finest battalions of the army, *viz.*, his own old regiment, the Reay Highlanders, Lumsden's musketeers, and Stargate's corps. The brigade was so termed from the colour of its scarfs and plumes, as the other brigades were—white, blue, and yellow. With the green, Hepburn led the van of the Swedish army, which, with armour burnished, colours flying, and matches lit, began its march for Frankfort-on-the-Oder, as Monro says (in the words of Dalgetty), under "the Lyon of the North, the invincible King of Sweden of never-dying memory." (*Exped.*)

After distinguishing themselves at the capture of the castle of Trepto, where Major Sinclair was left with two companies, the Scots captured Dameine, and then followed their defence of New Brandenburg, when 600 of Lord Reay's men were placed in garrison under his lieutenant-colonel, Lindsay, who had been thrice dangerously wounded at the defence of Stralsund.

After nine days' resistance against the most overwhelming odds, all mercy and quarter being refused them, the entire wing of the Reay Highlanders was savagely cut to pieces—a circumstance that inspired all the Scots in the army with fury against the Imperialists and their ruthless leader, Count Tilly.

Colonel Lindsay fell pike in hand in the breach, and there every officer and man perished by his side, save two—Captain Innes and Lieutenant Lumsden—who swam the wet ditch in their tartans and armour, and reached Hepburn's brigade, then pushing on to Frankfort, where Count Schomberg barred the way with 10,000 veterans. As the Highland marching song has it—

In the ranks of great Gustavus,
With the bravest they were reckoned,
    Agus O, Mhorag!
Ho-ro! march together!
    Agus O, Mhorag!

Longing for vengeance, Hepburn's brigade was, as stated, in the van of a column consisting of 18,000 men, which, with 200 guns and a pontoon bridge, followed the course of the Oder to Frankfort, where Count Schomberg, who had laid waste all the adjacent district, commanded, while Marshal Horne held the Pass of Schwedt to prevent Tilly from harassing the Swedish rear. Directed by the advice of Hepburn (according to Monro), Gustavus made his dispositions for the investment, and every column marched to its place—the horse with trumpets sounding, the foot with drums beating, matches lit, and pikes advanced.

All the artillery and stores not required were in rear of Hepburn's brigade. In Frankfort, we have stated, were 10,000 men under Schomberg, Monteculculi, and others, while the weakest point was assigned to a regiment of Irish musketeers, led by that Walter Butler to whom we have referred in Austria. When reconnoitring with Hepburn, the king narrowly escaped capture by a party which made a dash at him, but was repulsed by Hepburn's musketeers, led by Major John Sinclair, who drove in the Imperialists under cover of their batteries and made some prisoners. After the Guchen Gate had been reconnoitred by twelve Scottish soldiers, and the batteries on every side, on the 3rd of April the king ordered a general assault under cover of the smoke.

"Now my brave Scots," cried he, as he called to Hepburn and Sir James Lumsden by name, "remember your countrymen who were slain at New Brandenburg!" (*Swedish Intelligencer*, 1632.) On swept the stormers under a storm of lead, iron, and brass bullets, led by Hepburn and Lumsden, having each a petard holding 20 pounds of powder. These blew the gate to fragments, and in that quarter the Scots fought their way in.

Elsewhere Monro's Highlanders crossed the wet ditch, where the water rose to their necks, planted their ladders against the scarp, and stormed the palisades with pike and sword; while the Blue and Yellow brigades, all led by Scotsmen, swept away Butler's Irish and all who opposed them.

Hepburn was wounded, says Monro, "above the knee that he was lame of *before*."

"Bully Monro," cried he, "I am shot!"

A major took his place, but was shot dead. Then Lumsden and Monro, having joined, pushed on, turned their own cannon on the Austrians, and blew their heads and limbs into the air. To their cries of "quarter" on every hand the grim response was—

"New Brandenburg! Remember New Brandenburg!"

One Scottish pikeman (says the Swedish Intelligencer) slew eighteen Austrians with his own hand, and Lumsden's regiment captured *nine* pairs of colours. Fifty of Hepburn's men were charged by a regiment of *cuirassiers* in a burying-ground; but Major Sinclair formed them back to back, and repulsed the assailants. Twice the Imperialists beat a parley, but it was unheeded. "Still the combat continued, the carnage went on, and still the Scots brigade advanced in close columns of regiments, shoulder to shoulder, like moving castles, their long pikes levelled in front, while the rear ranks of musketeers volleyed in security from behind."

Schomberg and Monteculculi, escorted by a few *cuirassiers*, fled by a bridge towards Glogau, leaving 40 officers and 3,000 men dead behind them, while hundreds threw themselves into the Oder and were drowned. But Gustavus lost only 300 men, and had only two officers of wounded—Sir John Hepburn and Baron Teuffel. The former took possession of the ramparts and posted guards round the city, of which Major-General Leslie was made governor, and his first task was to bury the dead—100 in every grave.

The capture of Landsberg, on the Warta, was the next task—the key of Silesia. Hepburn invested it on one side. Marshal Home on the other, while Monro ran the parallels, and got his men entrenched, with the loss of six only, before dawn on the 5th, their long lines of matches shining like glow-worms in the dusk. The town was attacked in the dark, and the Austrians under old Count Gratz were hemmed in on every side, as Hepburn stormed the chief redoubt in three minutes, and Monro cut off a sortie with the loss of only 30 Highlanders. Gratz marched out next morning with the honours of war, accompanied by no less than 2,000 female camp followers.

Hepburn's brigade was next at the investment of Berlin, and was afterwards encamped among the swamps of Old Brandenburg, 34 miles from the capital. There, amid the miasma of the Havel, 34 of Monro's men died in one week—among them Robert Monro, a quartermaster-sergeant, and Sergeant Robert Munro, son of Culcraig. But July saw the brigade leave that district of frowsy fogs, where only sour black beer could be had, to cross the Elbe, beyond which the Swedish cavalry captured Wolmerstadt; while the Laird of Foulis stormed the castle of Blae at the head of his Highlanders, and Banier took Havelberg from the garrison of Pappenheim, on whose person there were said to be the marks of a hundred wounds. (*Scots Mag.*, 1804.)

CHAPTER 20

The Scots in Sweden—(Continued)

In these warrs, if a fort be to be stormed, or any desperate piece of service to be set upon, the Scottish have always had the honour and the danger to be the first men that are put upon such a business. (*Swedish Intelligencer*, part ii.)

Colonel Robert Monro of Foulis, to whom we refer so often, was a well-trained soldier, and began his career as a private gentleman in the French Guards, and he tells us:—

I was once made to stand, in my younger years, at the Louvre Gate in Paris, for sleeping in the morning when I ought to have been at my exercise, from eleven before noon to eight of the clock at night, sentry, armed with corslet, headpiece, bracelets, being iron to the teeth, in a hot summer day, till I was weary of my life, which always made me more strict in punishing those under my command.

The coming contingent of 6,200 men under the Marquis of Hamilton, then a very young man, was delayed in its departure by an accusation of treason brought from Holland against Hamilton by Lord Ochiltree, son of the notorious Captain Stuart, who, during the minority of James VI, had usurped the estates of the Hamilton family. The malicious fabrication averred that Colonel Ramsay, the agent of Gustavus, had told Lord Reay that the troops, instead of being destined for Germany, were to be employed in raising Hamilton to the throne of Scotland. A challenge was the result; but the duel—a public one— was forbidden. The expedition sailed on the 4th August, after the Scots from Leith had joined the English in Yarmouth Beads, and safely reached the banks of the Oder. The rumour that it consisted of

20,000 men had a material effect on the campaign. Soon there were none but Scots left of the contingent, as the English all perished, says Harte, on the march between Wolgast and Werben, by overeating themselves with "German bread, which is heavier, darker, and sourer than their own; they suffered too by an inordinate fondness for new honey; nor did the German beer agree with their constitutions." There were now four regiments, consisting each of ten companies, in each of which were 150 pikes and muskets. They had several pieces of cannon, including some of Sir Alexander Hamilton's, known by the Scots as "Sandy's Stoups." (*Memoirs of the House of Hamilton, etc.*)

The marquis was hard-visaged, wore his hair cut short, and adopted often a *calotte* cap; was sombre in expression, and fond of quoting Gustavus. (Warwick's *Memoirs*,)

After a conference with the latter, the young marquis marched his contingent towards Silesia, and after storming the frontier town of Guben, in Brandenburg, he advanced to Glogau, a strongly fortified city (60 miles from Breslau), which his Scots would have taken easily, as it was insufficiently garrisoned; but he was recalled by Gustavus to Custrin, and despatched to assist in the reduction of Magdeburg. His force, reduced now by causalities to 3,500 men, took possession of the town, which the aged Pappenheim abandoned; but Hamilton's force continued to dwindle, till, by pestilence, privation, and the sword, there remained of it only two battalions commanded by Colonel Sir Alexander Hamilton and Sir William Bellenden of Auchnoule (afterwards Lord Bellenden of Broughton, near Edinburgh). These were incorporated with the column of the Duke of Saxe-Weimar, while the marquis rode as a mere volunteer on the staff of the Swedish king. (*Harte, Burnett*, etc.)

The latter was now marching toward the Pass of Wittenberg, *en route* recalling from Havelburg the regiment of the Laird of Foulis, who had been joined by a fresh body of Scottish recruits, chiefly under Robert Munro of Kilternie, who died at the former place of marsh fever, and was buried by his clansmen with military honours.

On the plains of Leipzig—*God's Acre*—the same ground on which Charles V overthrew the Emperor of Saxony on the memorable 7th of September, 1681, the army of Gustavus, 30,000 strong, encountered that of Count Tilly, numbering 44,000. On that eventful day the Scottish brigades covered the advance and rear of the attacking force.

In the van were the Scottish regiments of Sir James Ramsay the

Black, the Laird of Foulis, and Sir John Hamilton, which on crossing the Loben found themselves face to face with the splendid Imperialists—chiefly *cuirassiers*, whom Ramsay at once engaged.

Hepburn commanded the reserve, which included his own brigade, which marched with colours flying the Green brigade displaying four. "*God Mitus!*" was the war-cry of the Swedes; "*Sancta Maria!*" that of the Imperialists, before whom rose a flight of birds, taken as an omen of victory.

The Saxons, who formed the Swedish left, gave way, on which Tilly prepared to charge the Swedes and Livonians at the head of his main body; "but now Gustavus selected 2,000 musketeers of the brave Scottish nation," says the old Leipzig account, and covered each flank with 1,000 horse, while the Scottish officers formed their men into columns of about 600 each—three front ranks kneeling, three standing erect, and all pouring in their fire together—a platoon method adopted for the first time, which struck terror, amazement, and destruction in the Austrian ranks. (Harte's *Gustavus*.)

Thus they closed up, till Hepburn gave the order "Forward, pikemen!" Then muskets were clubbed, pikes levelled, and the regiments of Hepburn, Lumsden, Ramsay, and Monro, each led by its colonel, burst like a whirlwind through the Austrian ranks, when all order became lost and their retreat began amid disorder, dust, and smoke. Wrote Monro:

We were as in a dark cloud, whereupon, having a drummer by me, I caused him beat *the Scots' March* till it cleared up, which recollected our friends to us.

This old national cadence on the drum was the terror of the Spaniards in Flanders, so much so, that it was often beaten "by the lubberly Dutches," we are told, "when they wished their quarters to be unmolested in the night."

All Tilly's baggage, cannon, and standards were taken, and 7,000 at least of his men were slain.

The Scots made great bonfires of the broken waggons and tumbrils, the shattered stockades and pikes that strewed the field; and the red glow of these as they blazed on the plains of Leipzig, glaring on the glistening mail and upturned faces of the dead, was visible to the Imperialists as they retreated towards the Weser.

By this decisive victory the whole German Empire was laid open to the invaders, from the Baltic to the Rhine, and from the mouth of the Oder to the sources of the Danube, and terror was struck to the heart of the Catholic league; 100 captured standards were hung in. the Ridderholm Kirche at Stockholm; and Colonels Lumsden and Monro, Majors Monipenny and Sinclair, and others, were rewarded for their merit in that day's victory, which Gustavus won, says old Monro, enthusiastically, "with the help of a nation *that never was conquered by a forraine enemy*—the invincible Scots!"

Three days after, at the capture of Mersberg, when 1,500 were killed or taken, Colonel Hay's regiment stormed the outworks; but Major-General Thomas Kerr was slain, and Captain Mackenzie of Suddie wounded through his helmet, after which he killed his assailant by a pike-thrust. On the 11th September, at the capture of Moritzberg, Captain William Stuart, of Monro's regiment, led the musketeers and prayers were offered up in the cathedral church of St Ulric; while at an entertainment that followed, Gustavus presented his Scottish officers to the Elector of Saxony and other Protestant princes. Taking the Laird of Foulis by the hand, said he:

Monro, I wish you to be master of the bottles and glasses tonight, and bear as much wine as old Major-General Sir Patrick Ruthven, that you may assist me to make my guests merry. (Naylor's *Mil, Hist of Germany, Harte*, etc.)

As the war went on, when Hepburn's brigade approached the capital of Franconia, he marched in peacefully, according to terms he had granted to Father Ogilvie, a venerable priest of the Scottish cloister, who had visited him on behalf of the bishop and citizens.

At Marienburg on the Maine the passage of Gustavus was disputed by the castellan, Captain Keller, "a brave, good fellow, who hated all Protestants, and believed that none could reach him unless they had wings as well as weapons"; but Sir James Ramsay had orders to capture the place at all hazards. He sent Lieutenant Robert Ramsay, who spoke German well, to procure some boats; but his rich costume exciting suspicion, the latter was made prisoner.

The guns of Marienburg enfiladed the bridge of the Maine, the broken central arch of which was crossed by a plank admitting but one man at a time, where sixty might have marched abreast before, and fifty feet below rolled the dark river. On the 6th October, Ramsay's undaunted soldiers advanced to the assault, led by Major Bothwell, of the family of Holyrood House, who with his brother was shot dead at the gorge of the *tête-du-pont*, where most of their soldiers perished with them; but Hamilton and Ramsay, with the main body of the regiment, passed the stream in boats under a cannonade, and bivouacked in their armour on the bank under the fortress, which they escaladed at daybreak. The stormers were chiefly officers, armed with a partisan and a brace of pistols in their sword-belts. Ramsey had an arm broken, but Hamilton led them on, and, after a two hours' conflict, the half-moon battery was won, when it was heaped with corpses and slippery with blood and brains.

"Give them Magdeburg quarter!" was the cry of the Swedish supports as they came up; and then Gustavus ordered the Scots to retire and the Blue brigade to advance. Perhaps he thought they had done enough; but this was an affront which the Scottish troops never forgave, for Sir John Hamilton resigned his commission on the spot. Sir James Ramsay received a large grant of land in the Duchy of Mecklenburg, with the government of Hainan (Lord Hailes, from *Locen. Hist.*); and the two Both wells were interred with all honours, side by side, in the church of St. Kilian the Scot) in the city; and so ended the storming of Marienburg.

The next service of the Scots was the defence of Oxenford on the Maine, to prevent the vast force of the Imperialists, said to be 50,000 strong, from crossing the river. Hepburn, who commanded, undermined the bridge, threw up works, out down trees that might impede his fire, and made every preparation for a vigorous defence in the early days of a stormy October, till the enemy came on, with their shouts, drums, and trumpets—"making such a noise as though heaven and earth were coming together," says Monro.

Thirty-six Scots musketeers of Lumsden's corps, who had been advanced with *videttes* under Sergeant-Major Monipenny, were driven in, and the armour of the latter was sorely battered by pistol-balls; and when day broke, Hepburn discovered that the whole Imperial army had taken the route for Nuremberg by the way of Weinsheim.

The king now reinforced him with 500 men, and sent orders to abandon the town in the dark, pass the Imperialists, and occupy the place they were approaching—to wit, Weinsheim: orders which were obeyed with alacrity. Hepburn blew up the bridge, and with pikes and muskets at the trail retreated at the double just as day dawned on the mountains of Bavaria.

His Scots formed the van of the army, which, after a five days' march through a fertile country, reached in the middle of November Aschaffenberg, a stately city of the Bishop of Mentz, on which 300 of Ramsay's regiment, led by Major Hanna (of the family of Sorbie, we believe), had already hoisted the three crowns of Sweden; while 200 Scots of Sir Ludovick Leslie's regiment took possession of Russelsheim on the Maine, and held it under Captain Macdougal.

Two more Scottish regiments, under Sir Frederick Hamilton and Alexander, Master of Forbess, had now joined Gustavus, who had thus thirteen entire Scottish battalions of infantry.

He had five others, composed of English and Irishmen, officered chiefly by Scotsmen; and he resolved now to turn his arms against the Palatinate, then held by a body of Spanish troops under Don Philippo de Sylvia. He entered the Bergstrasse and reached the Rhine, when Count Brahe, with 300 Swedes and 300 Scots of the regiments of Reay, Ramsay, and the Laird of Wormiston, crossed the stream and entrenched themselves, after repulsing no less than fourteen squadrons of Imperial *cuirassiers*, who fled to Oppenheim. Seventy years afterwards, a marble lion was erected on a column 60 feet in height, to mark the spot where Gustavus, with his Swedes and Scots, passed the great river of Germany. (*Schiller, Harte,* etc., etc.)

On the Imperial side of the Rhine rose the town and castle of Oppenheim. On the other was a strong redoubt girt by double ditches full of muddy water; these were crossed by a narrow bridge. A thousand resolute Italian and Burgundian veterans held it, and Hepburn's brigade was ordered to capture the place, thus to facilitate the passage of the army.

On Sunday, the 4th December, 1631, he broke ground before it, and, just as the king was about to order an assault, the promise of some boats led to a countermand. The White brigade crossed thus in the night, and, with drums beating, marched towards Oppenheim as day broke. Meanwhile, the Scots near the redoubt had lit fires behind their earthworks, when Hepburn and Monro supped together, enjoying, we are told, "a jar of Low Country wine," when the light shining on their armour attracted the Imperials, who fired in their direction a 32-pound shot? which knocked to pieces Colonel Hepburn's coach, while a second killed a sergeant of Monro's, "by the fire drinking a pipe of tobacco," as the colonel curiously phrases it; and now many men of the brigade were cut in two or torn to pieces by roundshot, which dyed with blood all the snow through which the parallels were cut. At midnight 200 Burgundians made a desperate sally, but the Scots were on the alert, and, after some gallant fighting, sharply repulsed them.

On seeing the White brigade approaching Oppenheim, the cavalier who commanded in the redoubt, fearing that his retreat would be cut off, sent a little Italian drummer with articles of capitulation to Sir John Hepburn, who permitted him to march out by the way of Bingen, but to leave all cannon behind him. The redoubt was now occupied by 200 of Lumsden's musketeers and 100 of Reay's, while 200 of Ramsay's captured the gates of Oppenheim just as Gustavus assailed the castle. Ramsay's wound caused his absence, but his regiment was led by Lieutenant-Colonel Douglas; and so sharp was the service it saw, that, though originally 2,000 strong, only 200 survived at the close of the war, and of these few ever saw Scotland again. (Fowler's *Southland*, 1656.)

Hepburn, having procured 107 boats, brought over his own brigade and the Blue, and as these approached the castle they were surprised to hear discharges of musketry *within* it, and to see the garrison leaping over the outworks and seeking to escape in every direction.

It would seem that the two hundred Scots who had captured the gates of Oppenheim had discovered a secret passage to the castle. Led by Lieutenant-Colonel Douglas, they drove in the station guards, and, reaching the heart of the place, engaged in a desperate hand-to-hand conflict with the garrison. Nine companies of Italians, each 100 strong, were taken prisoners in the redoubt, and "the king," says Harte, "made a present of them to Hepburn (whose kindness and humanity were equal to his bravery) to refit his broken brigade." But they all deserted *en masse* from Beyerland a few months subsequently. Gustavus, on entering the castle, which had been taken ere he could reach it, was received with a salute by Ramsay's musketeers.

"My brave Scots!" he exclaimed, "why were you too quick for me?"

A "Handbook" of 1843 states that a ruined chapel within the churchyard of Oppenheim is half-filled with the skulls and bones of those who fell on this occasion; and it was to Scottish valour that Gustavus owed nine pair of colours, the first he had ever taken from the Spaniards. *The Swedish Intelligencer* exultingly records how they fell on here, with "such tempest and resolution."

The following Sunday saw Hepburn's Scots before the walls of Mentz, deemed then by the Germans their best bulwark against France, and held by 2,000 chosen Castillian troops under Don Philippe de

Sylvia. "Colonel Hepburn's brigade (according to use) was directed to the most dangerous posts next the enemy," whose fire from the citadel slew many of his men ere they got under cover of their parallels. Then Colonel Axel Lily, a Swedish officer, came next night to visit Hepburn and Monro, and being invited to sup with them, "in a place from which the snow had been cleared away, the three cavaliers sat down by a large fire that the soldiers had lighted, and regaled themselves on such viands as the foragers had procured, spitted upon old ramrods or sword-blades. Every moment the flashes broke brightly from the citadel, and the cannon-shot boomed away over their heads into the obscurity of the night, or plashed into the deep waters of the Rhine behind them. They were all discoursing merrily, when Axel Lily said to Hepburn, laughing as he listened to the Spanish cannon, and ducking his head as a ball passed, "If any misfortune should happen to me now, what would be thought of it? I have no business here, exposed to the enemy's shot."

Soon after a ball earned off one of his legs; but the king heaped so many sinecures upon him that his Scottish comrades could not help envying him, though he had ever after to march "with a tree or wooden legge." (Monro's *Expedition, etc,*)

Mentz surrendered; the bells of the glorious cathedral saluted Gustavus, and Hepburn's brigade exchanged the snowy trenches for quarters in the city, where they spent the Christmas; and the king's court was attended by twelve ambassadors and the flower of the German nobles.

In Mentz the Green brigade remained till the 5th March, 1632, getting more recruits from Scotland, and the regiment, vacant by the resignation of Sir John Hamilton, was now commanded by old Sir Lodovick Leslie.

Previously (in February) Gustavus had marched against Creutzenach, on the Nahe, a well-built town, defended by a castle; and on this expedition he took with him 300 of Ramsay's musketeers, under Lieutenant-Colonel Robert Douglas, of whom his secretary. Fowler, has left us an ample account in his folio work, dated 1656, in his "*Life of Sir George Douglas, Knight, lord ambassador extraordinary for the peace between Sutherland and Poland.*"

This officer was the son of Sir George Douglas of Mordington (a cadet of the house of Torthorwald) and Margaret Dundas of Fingask. Passing a party of English volunteers under Lord Craven, who held the trenches, where they certainly suffered severely, he stormed the

"Devil's Works," as they were named, at Creutzenach, of which he was made governor till the recovery of Ramsay from his wound. Douglas incurred the displeasure of Gustavus before the Battle of Lutzen, and, after being the ambassador of Charles I, died in 1635. At the capture of Creutzenach 47 of Ramsay's men were killed, including Captain Douglas, shot through the heart.

CHAPTER 21

The Scots in Sweden—(Continued)

Sir Patrick Ruthven having been made governor of Ulm, Monro with some of his regiment was dispatched to Bingen on the Rhine, which, with the "Massive Tower" (of Bishop Hatto's old legend), was then held by a wing of Ramsay's regiment. Drawing off a captain with 100 Scots, he marched to the succour of the Rhingrow at Coblentz, where with twenty troops of horse he was about to be attacked by 10,000 Spaniards from Spain. Four of their regiments of horse fell suddenly on his cantonments, which were in several open villages, but these were so resolutely charged by only *four troops* of Swedes, led by Rittmaster Hume of Carrelside, that 300 of them were slain, and the Count of Napau was taken prisoner. (*Intelligencer,*)

Soon after this, two small towns on the Rhine, named Bacharach, which was encircled by antique walls, with twelve towers, and Stahleck, the ancient seat of the Electors Palatine, were stormed by Ramsay's musketeers, led by Major Hanna, who, in consequence of the resistance be met, put all within them to the sword, the officers excepted. According to Hope, the beautiful church of St. Werner at Stahleck, was demolished on this occasion, but the pointed windows still show the most delicate tracery.

In the Swedish force of 14,000 horse and foot, now elsewhere moving up the Elbe, were five battalions of Scots, *viz.*, one of Lumsden's, under Lieutenant-Colonel Robert Stuart; the Master of Forbess's regiment, under Lieutenant-Colonel Sir Arthur Forbess; Sir Frederick Hamilton's regiment; Colonel Monro of Obisdale's regiment; and Colonel Robert Leslie's Old Scots regiment, with one of Englishmen, led by Colonel Vavasour. This force cleared the whole Duchy of Mecklenburg, storming castles and capturing towns; and so great was the terror now generally excited by their achievements, that, on the advance of Gustavus towards the Moselle, the presence of so many Presbyterian soldiers alarmed Cardinal Richelieu, and furnished him with a powerful argument for seeking to turn Louis XIII from the Swedish alliance. The spring of the year saw old Sir Alexander Leslie of Balgonie—the future champion of the Covenant—with his Dutch and Swedish veterans hovering like a crowd over the fertile plains of Lower Saxony. He was then field-marshal, and governor of all the cities on the Baltic coast.

Major-General Sir David Drummond was then governor of Stettin. The Earl of Crawford, Colonels Baily, King, Douglas, Hume, Gunn, and Hugh Hamilton, had all Dutch regiments; also two Colonels Forbess, John and Alexander, called the Baldy with many more too numerous to mention.

The early days of March saw Hepburn's brigade and the other Scots with Gustavus on the march to Bavaria, while the chancellor, Oxtenstiern, who had remained with a strong force to guard the conquests on the Rhine, repelled the enemy near Frankenthal, in which affair the Dutch, who formed the first column, when they saw the Spaniards, resorted to their old ruse of beating the *Scots' March* to intimidate the enemy, and yet basely fell back! But immediately upon this the Scottish regiment of Sir Lodovick Leslie and the battalion of Sir John Buthven, "whose officers were all valiant Scots, Lieutenant-Colonel John Lesly, Major Lyell, Captain David King, and divers other resolute cavaliers," fell on with sword and pike, driving back the Spaniards in confusion. So furious was their charge and so complete their victory that the chancellor of Sweden in front of the whole line "did sweare that had it not beene for the valour of thet Scots Briggad they had all beene lost and defeated by the Spaniard." (*Monro*, part ii.)

The 26th of March saw Gustavus before Donauwörth, the key of Swabia, where he was joined by the Laird of Foulis with his two regiments. The place guarded a fortified mountain, and was rendered strong by its embattled walls and deep ditches, commanding the bridge across the Danube.

The Duke of Saxe-Lauenberg occupied the city with 2,500 men. A toll was levied then, and he vowed the toll paid by Gustavus in passing the river would be the lives of his bravest soldiers—though the works were without cannon. A handsome street led to the town-gate, and in the former Gustavus placed 500 musketeers to prevent a sortie, and completed a twenty-gun battery, guarded by a body of infantry under the Scottish Captain Semple. In the gloom of a dark night, a troop of Cronenberg's Reiters issued from the town-gate, hewed a passage through the musketeers, and fell upon Semple's artillery guard, cutting it to pieces. Semple was put under arrest, but pardoned on the intercession of other Scottish officers.

Hepburn now urged a flank movement, and, drawing off his own brigade with its field-pieces in silence, took up such an excellent position on the Swabian side that the captain of the place became assured. While his guns opened on the town, Gustavus assailed the *Lederthor*, and the former, leading his brigade across the corpse-strewn bridge— ably seconded by Major Sidsorf, of Ramsay's regiment—cut a passage in about daybreak; thus the Scots won the key of Swabia, while the Swedes were still fighting in the Leothergate. Says the *Intelligencer:*

> Sir John Hepburn being thus gotten in, and having first cut to pieces all resistance, his souldiers fall immediately to plundering, when many a gold chain, with much other plate and treasure, were made prize of.

By sunrise the carnage and uproar were over, and the king sent for the leader of the Scots.

Through streets encumbered by rifled waggons, dismounted cannon, broken drums and arms, and terrified citizens wandering wildly among dead and dying soldiers, he made his way to a handsome house which had escaped the cannon-shot, and where he found Gustavus with Frederick of Bohemia, the long-bearded Augustus of Psalzbach, and other men of rank, resting after the fatigue of the past night, with armour unbuckled and flagons of Rhenish before them.

In their presence he thanked Hepburn for taking the town in flank with his Scots by the Hasfort bridge, after which the brigadier recrossed the Danube to throw up a battery at a point that was deemed of the first importance.

After resting four days at Donauwörth Gustavus advanced at the head of 32,000 horse and foot to complete the passage of the Lech.

In these Swedish wars were no less than 155 generals and field-officers, all Scotsmen, whose names are given at length in the *Memoirs of Sir John Hepburn*; while the number of Scottish captains and subalterns will never be known.

Among some of the most notable of the former were Generals Sir Andrew Rutherford, afterwards killed at Tangiers when Earl of Teviot;

Sir James Spence of Wormiston, afterwards Count of Orcholm, Lord of Moreholm, and chancellor of Sweden; George, Earl of Crawford-Lindsay, who was slain by a lieutenant of his regiment whom he had struck with a *bâton*; yet "General Lesly, being then governor of Stettin, when the earl was buried, caused him (the lieutenant) to be shot at a post." (*Scots Nation Vindicated.*) Another general was Sir James King of Barrocht, in Aberdeenshire, governor of Vlotho, on the Weser, who had to leave Scotland in 1619 for slaying Seaton of Meldrum, with whom his family was at feud. He was created Lord Eythen in 1642, but died childless and in obscurity. His title is extinct.

Prior to the passage of the Lech, Hepburn's Scots, penetrating into a rocky gorge three miles from Donauwörth, captured the castle of Oberndorff—a grim edifice of the middle ages, situated amidst the gloomiest scenery—killing or capturing 400 men; but the count, "a mailed Hercules," hewed his way out and escaped. Hepburn then rejoined to assist in the passage of the Lech, which formed the last barrier of falling Bavaria—a swift mountain torrent that rises in the Tyrol, and is in full flood, sweeping down rocks and timber, in May.

On the 5th of April the two armies came in sight of each other, and the eyes of all Europe might be said to be fixed upon their movements. On the Imperial side 70 pieces of cannon protected the passage of that terrible stream, and thick, like fields of corn, the dense battalions of Tilly and the Elector—pikes and musketeers—held the point upon which Gustavus was marching, and the guns opened upon him.

With 72 he replied, and for six-and-thirty hours the crossfire was maintained, till rocks and trees were dashed to pieces. The Bavarians were thrown into disorder, 1,000 of them were killed, with Count Merodi, and a bullet carried away a leg of old Count Tilly; and then, amid the smoke of the batteries and that created by heaps of damp wood and ignited straw, Gustavus ordered his infantry to pass the stream, Hepburn and his Scots—as usual on every piece of desperate work—forming the van. Captain Forbes with thirty musketeers led the immediate way, and found the enemy had retired beyond gunshot, the Bavarian Elector retreating towards Ingolstadt, where the veteran Tilly expired, after resigning his *bâton* to Wallenstein, the great Duke of Friedland.

The invasion of Bavaria struck the Catholics of Europe with alarm; but in its progress, says Monro, old Sir Patrick Ruthven, "with the young cavaliers of the Scots nation that followed him, such as Colonel Hugh Hamilton, Colonel John Fortune, Lieutenant-Colonel Gunne,

Lieutenant-Colonel Montgomerie, Majors Ruthven, Bruntisfield, and divers other Scots captains, such as Dumbarve, who was killed by the boores," overran all Swabia, and laid every town under contribution from Ulm on the Danube to Lindon on the Lake of Constance.

The Green brigade—in these details we adhere chiefly to the Scots—occupied eight days in besieging Ingolstadt, beyond which lay the Elector of Bavaria. On the 19th April a sally was expected, and all night the brigade lay under arms, from sunset till sunrise—a night the longest in the year, it seemed, says Monro, "for by one shot I lost twelve men of my own companie, not knowing what became of them. He who was not that night afraid of cannon-shot might next day without harm have been brayed into gunpowder!"

Gustavus had his horse shot under him, 300 men were killed, yet the Scots never flinched; a work defended by 1,500 Bavarian arque-buses was stormed; but the Margrave of Baden-Dourloch lost his head by a cannon-ball, and was buried beside Captain Ramsey of the Green brigade, who died of fever on the advance to Gesegnfeld.

Hepburn and Count Home, with 8,000 troops, now invested Landshut, a fine city in Lower Bavaria, and on the march there the Scots suffered from the fanaticism and ferocity of the Bavarian boores, who murdered about fifty soldiers on the way by Augsburg, tearing out their eyes, cutting off their noses and hands, in revenge for which the Swedes and Scots shot all who fell into their hands. Hepburn was made governor of Landshut, honour being all he won; but Home lev-ied 20,000 dollars on his own account from the citizens.

On the 7th May, 1632, the army of Gustavus entered Munich. Hepburn's brigade were the first troops in, and he was made governor of that beautiful capital, which no troops were allowed to occupy but his own brigade, and the Lord Spynie's Scots regiment, which entered with the king. To prevent plundering, five shillings per day was given to every man above his usual pay.

Leaving Hepburn with his Scots to hold the Bavarian capital, Gus-tavus advanced to Augsburg to give battle to the Imperialists; but they fell back towards the Lake of Constance, followed by the troops of Sir Patrick Ruthven.

Colonels Forbes and Hamilton now raised two Swiss regiments; but the latter were routed and scattered, and the two former were made prisoners.

On the 4th June Hepburn's Scots relieved Weissenburg, a place of great importance; after which he encamped at Furth, and was engaged in many defensive operations. Gustavus, having to confront an army of 60,000 men with only 20,000, formed an entrenched camp round Nuremberg, which had then six gates and walls armed with 300 pieces of cannon. Under Wallenstein the Imperialists endeavoured to cut off the supplies till the 21st August, when Gustavus attacked the heights of Altenberg, and the Scots were severely engaged in their attempt to storm the castle—an affair in which 1,000 Scots and Irish musketeers, who served the Emperor under Gordon and Major Leslie, proved their most active antagonists.

Monro was wounded; Captain Patrick Innes was shot through the helmet and brow; Colonel Mackean was killed; Captain Trail, of Spynie's regiment, shot through the throat; Hector Monro of Cadboll through the head; and Captain Vaus, of Foulis' regiment, in the shoulder. Both Gordon and Leslie were taken and brought into the Swedish camp, where they were hospitably entertained by Hepburn, Munro, and other countrymen for five weeks, after which they were released. We have already referred to these officers in detailing the murder of Wallenstein, in the now ruined castle of Egar, in Bohemia.

The two armies confronted each other till the 8th of September, when Gustavus retired, and 600 of Hepburn's Scots, commanded by Lieutenant-Colonel Sinclair, covered the retreat at Neustadt.

A few days afterwards the Marquis of Hamilton, being about to return to London, Sir John obtained leave to accompany him, having had a quarrel with the King of Sweden, of the real details of which no exact account has been preserved. In a fit of anger Gustavus is said to have upbraided Hepburn with his religion and the richness of his arms and apparel (Anderson's *France*, vol. v). Schiller adds that the brigadier was offended with Gustavus for having not long before preferred (to Sir John Hamilton?) a younger officer to some post of danger, and rashly vowed never again to draw his sword in the Swedish quarrel.

But Hepburn would seem not to have been the only Scottish officer with whom the great Gustavus seriously quarrelled. One day he so far forgot himself as to give a blow to Colonel Seaton, of the Green brigade, who, quitting his service, at once set out for the frontiers of Denmark. Says Lord de Ros, condensing this anecdote:

> The king, ashamed of the insults he had put upon a brave and excellent officer, soon followed on a swift horse and overtook him. 'Seaton,' said he, 'I see you are justly offended; I am sorry

for it, as I have a great regard for you. I have followed to give you satisfaction. I am now, as you know, out of my own kingdom— we are equals; here are pistols and swords; avenge yourself if you choose.' But Seaton declared he had already received ample satisfaction; nor had the king ever a more devoted servant, or one more ready to lay down his life for this prince who had so generously redeemed his hasty and inconsiderate passion.

On the bank of the Bavarian Rednitz Gustavus erected three powerful batteries on the 22nd of August, and for the whole of that day cannonaded the Austrians under Wallenstein, who remained motionless, hoping, by famine, to conquer him; but, after a time, Gustavus crossed the river with his whole force in order of battle, and took up a new position near Furth, a small open town in Middle Franconia, which enabled him to menace the left flank of the Imperialists.

Hepburn had resigned, but when a battle was imminent he could not, with honour, remain idle in the rear, but, arming himself completely "in his magnificent inlaid armour, with *casque*, gorget, breast and back pieces, pouldrons, vambraces, and gauntlets, as if going on service," he mounted, and rode near the king, but by the side of Major-General Rusteine, who was shot dead when the advance began.

On the rooky summits of the Alta Feste, at the base of which flowed the Rednitz and the Biber, the Imperialists were entrenched behind breastworks and palisades, over which their long lines of polished *morions*, tall pikes, and arquebuses glittered in the sunshine, while 80 brass cannon peeped grimly forth from every bnsh and tree, over which circles of ravens were wheeling, marking where already a dead soldier or a charger lay. When the Swedes advanced in dense battalions, and the deadly strife began, shrouding the heights and the dominating ruins on the Altenberg in fire and smoke, Hepburn, serving as a simple volunteer, faced it all, while his old brigade advanced as stormers.

"I will not believe there is a God in heaven if they take that castle from me!" exclaimed the impious Wallenstein, while, shading his eyes with a gauntleted hand, he watched the approach of four columns, each 500 strong, to assail the ancient fortress, which was the key of his position.

"Selecting 2,000 chosen musketeers, chiefly Scotsmen," says Colonel Mitchell in his life of Wallenstein, these stormers, leaving their colours at the foot of the mountains, and supported by a column of pikes, advanced under a fire of 80 guns, that crashed through them,

"'SEATON,' SAID HE, 'I SEE YOU ARE JUSTLY OFFENDED.'"

often sweeping entire sections away, for "the Scots knew well that if *they* failed no other troops would attempt it."

"Exposed to the whole enemy's fire, and infuriated by the prospect of immediate death," says Schiller in his *Thirty Years' War*, "those intrepid warriors rushed forward to storm the heights, which were in an instant converted into a flaming volcano."

They were compelled to waver, even to retire down the steep precipices, where their killed and wounded were falling and rolling in scores; but five other Scoto-Swedish columns came upward in fierce and furious succession; and here Gustavus had a jack-boot torn off by a cannon-ball.

Sheathed in light armour, Wallenstein's *cuirassiers* came filing forth under cover of the smoke, took the assailants in flank, captured General Tortensohn, and rode fairly through the Swedish infantry, through Cronenberg's "Invincibles," 1,500 heavily-mailed horse, and were routed by only 200 Finland troops, who drove them under the guns of the Altenberg, on which those of Gustavus are said to have fired 200,000 rounds that day.

The most practicable assault was one suggested by Duke Bernard of Saxe-Weimar; but an officer was required to reconnoitre the ground, and for this duty Sir John Hepburn offered himself. (*Harte*,)

"Go, Colonel Hepburn; I am grateful to you," said Gustavus.

"Sir, it is practicable," reported Hepburn after he had ridden over the ground, exposed to the fire of the enemy, by which a faithful old sergeant was slain by his side.

On this the Scottish regiments of Hamilton and Bellenden carried the heights by storm, driving in the Austrians with terrible loss; and 500 musketeers of the old Scots brigade, under Monro, kept the position till 500 more of their comrades, under Colonel John Sinclair, came up to reinforce them, "and these 1,000 Scots maintained their dangerous post all night."

"Our brigades of foot had seven bodies of pikemen left to guard their colours," says Monro. The mutual losses were about 5,000 on both sides; "neare sixe thousand," according to Sir James Turner's military memoirs.

Night fell, and the Swedish troops at the base of the hills were in peril of being cut off; on this Gustavus asked Hepburn to carry orders to them to withdraw.

"Sir, I cannot decline this duty, *as it is a hazardous one*," he replied, and rode forward (*Schiller*), But for Hepburn's skill or decision these troops would have been utterly cut off; but he marched them to the king's post in the dark, and then, sheathing his sword, said, according to *Modern Hist.*, vol. iii, "And now, sire, never more shall this sword be drawn for you; this is the last time I will ever serve so ungrateful a prince."

Yet, when day drew near, and it was reported that the Scottish musketeers of Sinclair and Monro lay too far in advance among the ruins of the Altenberg, he went by the king's request to see after them.

"Sir," he reported, "I found the Scottish musketeers almost buried among mud and water; but have discovered ground from whence four pieces of cannon might be brought to bear against the Altenberg at 40 paces' distance."

But, after taking council, Gustavus ordered a general retreat; he went in person to draw off the advanced Scots, and carried the half-pike of Colonel Monro, who was so severely wounded as to be scarcely able to walk.

CHAPTER 22

The Scots in Sweden—(Continued)

On the 14th September, after his troops had suffered terribly from scarcity of food, Gustavus, leaving 500 men (including the Laird of Foulis' regiment) in Nuremberg, began his retrograde movement, with drums beating and colours flying, towards Neustadt, leaving no less than 10,000 citizens and 20,000 soldiers dead behind him in and around the great Bavarian city—the casualties of war. "Dead bodies," we are told, "infected the air; and bad food, the exhalations from a population so dense, and from so many putrefying carcases (when summer came), together with the heat of the dog-days, produced a desolating pestilence, which raged among men and beasts, and, long after the retreat of both armies, continued to load the country with misery and distress."

"We have thus shown how the valiant Sir John Hepburn left the Swedish army.

But there would seem to have been at this time some discontent among the Scottish officers concerning the Marquis of Hamilton, who, they deemed, had been treated ungenerously; but still more concerning Colonel Douglas of Modrington (the hero of Creutzenach), whom Gustavus had sent to a common prison for presenting himself unceremoniously in a tennis-court when he and the Elector of Bavaria were at play—a punishment which the British ambassador, Sir Henry Vane, and all the Scots, resented as an insult. (Fowler's *Southland*,)

When the gallant Hepburn and several other Scottish officers, including colonels Sir James Hamilton of Priestfield, now Edinburgh; Sir James Ramsay, called "The Fair," took leave of their comrades, Monro informs us that the separation was like that "which death makes betwixt friends and the soul of man, being sorry that those who had lived so long together in amity and friendship, also in mutual

165

dangers, in weal and in woe; the splendour of our former mirth was overwhelmed with a cloud of grief and sorrow, which dissolved in mutual tears."

The command of the brigade now devolved, on the death, at Ulm, of Colonel Monro of Foulis, on Robert Monro (brother of Obisdale), whose regiment was now so weak as to consist of seven companies instead of twelve as originally. Major John Sinclair, afterwards killed at Neumosk, was made lieutenant-colonel, and Captain William Stewart, major. This was "in Schwabland," on the 18th August, 1632, and at the end of September the Green brigade marched to the relief of Rayn, on the Acha, then besieged by the enemy, who abandoned it at the approach of Gustavus. The fact of there being in the army of the latter 27 field-officers and 11 captains of the clan of Monro causes some confusion with their names.

The Scots brigade was now so much exhausted and thinned in numbers by hard service that he left it in quarters of refreshment in Bavaria, while he marched into Saxony. Before his departure he expressed "his approbation of the conduct of these valiant Scots or Moccosions, and exhorted the commanding officers to use every possible expedition in replacing the casualties in their respective regiments; but this proved the final separation between the great Gustavus and these distinguished Scots regiments. His majesty marched to Saxony and was killed at the Battle of Lutzen, when the chief Scots in the field were only Sir John Henderson, in the reserve, with the Palatian cavalry, on the 6th November, 1632.

The king fell with eight wounds, one in the head, after having three horses shot under him, and being several times in the power of the enemy, but was always rescued by his own men. "Long have I sought thee," cried an Imperial cavalier, as he put a final shot through the body of the dying hero, and was shot down in turn by the Smoland cavalry. The last words of Gustavus were, "My God! My God!" One of those mysterious boulders which have been transported from the mountains of Scandinavia, sheltered by a few poplars, and still called the *Schnadenstein*, or Stone of Sweden, marks the site of this catastrophe. With him died the hopes of the Elector Frederick.

One of his swords is shown at Dresden, a second at Vienna, and a third was long in use by St. Machar's Masonic Lodge at Aberdeen. (*Edinburgh Advertiser*, 1768.) It was probably brought home by his *aide-de-camp*, Colonel Hugh Somerville, with his large rowelled spurs, taken off him on the field, and now preserved in the Museum of Scottish

Antiquities at Edinburgh, to which they were presented by Sir George Colquhoun, Bart., in 1768. Monro's work contains fully four folio pages of lamentation on his death.

After that event this Green or old Scots brigade served for a short time under the weak Elector Palatine, and distinguished itself at the siege and capture of Londsberg on the Lech, in Upper Bavaria, before which a foolish dispute about precedence arose between it and another, the brigade of Sir Patrick Ruthven. "But," says Monro, "those of Ruthven's brigade were forced, notwithstanding their diligence, to yield the precedence unto us, being older blades than themselves, for in effect we were their schoolmasters in discipline, as they could not but acknowledge."

Colonel Sinclair, of Monro's, commanded the breaching battery at Londsberg, when two gaps were effected. The town was abandoned and entered by Major-General Ruthven. The sufferings of the troops were great about this time. After taking Londsberg they bivouacked for two months in the open fields, without tents or cover, in the extremity of cold and rough weather.

In February, 1633, the brigade crossed the Danube at Memmengen, and was quartered on the estates of Sir Patrick Ruthven. But their houses took fire in the night; they saved their cannon and ammunition, but lost their baggage; and then drove back the enemy, in sight of the snow-covered Alps. At the capture of a castle near Raufbeuren Captain Bruntisfield and Quartermaster Sandilands were taken prisoners and sent to London. Then the brigade formed part of the army which, under Marshal Home and the Duke of Saxe-Weimar, marched to the relief of Nordlingen, where the fortitude of the Swedes remained unconquered on the 26th August, 1634, but "where they suffered so severely that, among others, Monro's once glorious regiment of Mackay, Lord Reay, was literally cut to pieces, *one* company alone surviving.

After the battle this handful of men retired to Worms, on the left bank of the Rhine, and, Marshal Home having been taken prisoner, the remnants of the veteran Scots remained under the orders of Bernard, Duke of Saxe-Weimar.

The event of the Battle of Nordlingen almost ruined the Protestant interests in Germany, and all the fighting of Gustavus and his veterans seemed to have been in vain.

Monro, a lieutenant-general in after years, was concerned in Glencairn's expedition to the Highlands against the Cromwellian troops in 1653-4, and fought & reckless duel with the earl. From Balcairn's *Memoirs, touching the Revolution of Scotland*, he would appear to have been alive in 1688, as he was then at the head of the militia, "but knew little more of the trade than these newly raised men, having lost by age, and being long out of service, anything he had learned in Gustavus's days, except the rudeness and austerity of that service." (*Memoirs*, edited by Lord Lindsay, 1841.) Several of his political and military pamphlets are preserved in the British Museum.

Sir Alexander Leslie of Balgonie, as field-marshal, Sir Patrick Ruthven of Bondean, Sir Robert Douglas, and others still wielded their high rank in the Swedish army under Queen Christina, the young daughter of the great Gustavus, but their names only occur incidentally.

Thus, when the talented Chancellor Oxenstiern held the reins of government during her minority, and was animated by an eager desire to obtain for Sweden possession of Pomerania and the bishopric of Bremen, in the war which was waged the Saxons marched to the Elbe to give the Swedes battle, but Banier defeated them, and Sir Patrick Ruthven was detached with nearly all the Swedish horse and 1,000 musketeers to secure Domitz, a town at the influx of the Elde with the Elbe, and having ditches by which the adjacent country can be laid under water.

Ruthven fell with his horse upon the Saxons, cut them off, captured 2,500, and forced them to serve in the Swedish army. It was now resolved that Wrangel should command a column on the Oder, Field-Marshal Sir Alexander Leslie another in Westphalia, and Banier on the Elbe, where he routed twelve Saxon battalions. Baron Kniphauser lost his life and a battle elsewhere; but Leslie mustered his defeated regiments, and with these and his own made himself master of Minden. He then formed a junction with other Swedish troops who had been in the service of the Duke of Lunenberg, cleared Westphalia, relieved Hanau, and marched towards the Weser.

He then joined Wrangel and Banier, attacked the Saxons in their fortified camp at Perleberg, and slew 5,000 in defeating them. He routed also eight Saxon regiments near Edenburg, and out off 2,000 men at Pegau; but his services on the Continent were drawing to a close.

The unwarrantable interference of Charles I and the English with the religion of the Scots had now brought about the army of the Covenant, and Marshal Leslie, with hundreds of other trained officers who had been serving on the Elbe, the Oder, the Weser, and the Rhine, came flocking home to offer their swords and experience for the defence of Scotland. Noble indeed was the patriotism of those Scottish officers who came home to lead the armies of the Covenant. Says Gordon of Ruthven:

> In the armies of Gustavus there were found more commanders of Scots gentlemen than all other nations besides. This did well appear in the beginning of the Covenant, when there came home so many commanders, all gentlemen, out of foreign countrayes as would have seemed to command one armie of *fyftie thousand* and furnish them with all sorts of officers, from a generall doune to a sergeant or corporall. (*Britones Distemper*, 1639-1649.)

Sir John Seaton of Gargunnock, colonel of Scots in Sweden, on being invited by Charles to join his army made that noble reply, which ought to have stung the king to the soul:

"No, sire— not against the country that gave me birth!" (*Newes from England*, 1638.)

The Swedish war still raged, and in 1644 Torstenson had secret orders to march into Holstein, whence the Danes had wrought the Swedes much mischief. He afterwards made a truce with the Elector of Saxony, and, marching into Bohemia, engaged the Imperialists at Jonkowitz on the 24th February, 1645, and defeated them with the loss of 8,000 men. Then his cavalry were led by Sir Robert Douglas (of the Whittingham family), who commanded the left wing, and his cavalry charge is celebrated in military history "as being the first charge *en muraille* (that is, firm, steady as a wall) ever executed against a formed body of infantry, and on this occasion it decided the fate of the day." (*Life of Wallenstein*)

Ferdinand, says Schiller, depended upon his cavalry, which outnumbered that of Douglas by 3,000 men, "and upon the promise of the Virgin Mary, who had appeared to him in a dream, and given him, he asserted, the strongest assurances of complete victory." (*Thirty Years' War*,) In 1648 came the Peace of Munster, when such was the state of Sweden that she could maintain 100 garrisons in Germany, ruling it from the Baltic to the Lake of Constance, besides supporting a veteran army of 70,000. How much Scottish valour contributed to this end these pages, perhaps, may show.

Lord Reay died about 1660, governor of Bergen; but his body was brought home and interred among his kindred in Strathnaver.

When Charles X, in 1655, entered upon a war with John Casimir, King of Poland, he forced the latter to retire into Silesia and abdicate the Polish crown. In this war he gave orders to Sir Robert Douglas to make himself master of Mitau, an ancient fortified town in Courland, and to secure the person of the duke so named, as he had broken the neutrality. Douglas obeyed his orders with brilliant success, and brought the duke prisoner to Riga, from whence he was sent to Ivangorod, where he continued till the end of the war.

Sir Robert Douglas was the son of Patrick Douglas of Standing-Staines, in East Lothian, and nephew of the Baron of Whittingham, a lord of session, whose representative in the male line he became. His brothers, William, Archibald, and Richard, all died in the service of Sweden. Sir Robert was governor of East Gothland, and married a daughter of Count Steinbeck, according to Wood. He died a field-marshal in June, 1662, and his funeral was celebrated at Stockholm with great solemnity. It was attended by four squadrons of horse in armour, five companies of infantry, "their muskets under their left arms and trailing their pikes"; hundreds of officials in mourning cloaks; his arms and armour borne on cushions; a marshal went before the hearse, which was borne by 24 colonels and followed by the queen-consort and all the court.

A herald proclaimed his titles, as privy-councillor of Sweden, field-marshal, counsellor to the College of War, Lord of Thalby, Hochstaten, Sangarden, and Earl of Shonegem; and at the lowering of the coffin 120 pieces of cannon were fired, and all the horse and foot "gave two pales of shot." (*Spottiswoode Miscell.*) His eldest son, Count William, succeeded him in all his titles, and was A.D.C. to Charles XII, with whom he was taken prisoner at the Battle of Pultowa in 1709. He had two other sons, one of whom became a general in the Russian service, and the other a captain in the Royal Swedish Guards.

In that war, when Charles XII, at the age of sixteen, left Stockholm with only 8,000 Swedes to defeat eventually 100,000 Muscovites, he was first under fire at Copenhagen at the head of his guards, and his closest attendant was Major Stuart.

The young king, who had never before heard the discharge of loaded musketry, asked that officer "what that whistling noise meant?"

"It is musket-balls," replied the latter.

"That is right!" said Charles; "henceforward it shall be my music."

At that moment Major Stuart received a ball in the shoulder, and a lieutenant who stood on the other side was shot dead. (*Life of Charles XII*, 1733.)

Subsequently, at the passage of the Duna and defeat of the Saxons, there was, says Voltaire, a young Scottish volunteer who was master of German, and offered himself as a means to discover the intentions of the Emperor of Russia and the King of Poland. "He applied to the colonel of the regiment of Saxon horse, which served as guards to the *Czar* during their interview, and passed for a cavalier of Brandenburg, his address and well-placed sums having easily procured him a lieutenancy in the regiment. When he came to Birsen (*sic*) he artfully insinuated himself into the friendship of the secretaries of the ministers, and was made a party in all their amusements; and whether it was that he took advantage of their indiscretion over a bottle, or that he gained them by presents, he secretly drew from them all the secrets of their masters, and he hastened to give an account of them to Charles XII."

His information eventually led to the successful passage of the river by the latter, and the subsequent conquest of Courland and Lithuania.

At Pultowa, in 1709, among the prisoners taken by the Muscovites were several Scottish officers; among them the unfortunate Major Malcolm Sinclair, whom they basely sent to Siberia for thirteen years, and General Count Hamilton, who had commanded a column at the Battle of Narva in 1700.

In 1723, Salmon, in his *Chronology*, notes the death at Stockholm of "Hugo Hamilton Esq., of Scotland, general of artillery to the King of Sweden." He was in his 70th year, and had entered the service as a lieutenant.

Few events created a greater sensation in Sweden than the tragic fate of Major Malcolm Sinclair in 1739. One of the most favourite officers of King Frederick, he was basely assassinated by Russia on his way to Constantinople with important despatches with reference to a treaty between Sweden and the Porte. In his memoirs Baron Manstein relates the matter thus:—

Bestucheff, who resided at Stockholm in quality of the minister of Russia, gave advice to his court that Major Sinclair had been sent to Constantinople, whence he was to bring back the ratification of this treaty. Upon this news Count Munich, by order of the cabinet, sent certain officers, accompanied by some subalterns, into Poland with orders to disperse themselves in different places and try to carry off Sinclair, take away all his letters and despatches, and kill him in case of resistance. These officers, as they could not be everywhere, employed some Jews and some of the poor Polish gentlemen to get information of the arrival of Sinclair; thus he had warning from the governor of Chockzine (in Bessarabia) to take care of himself, as there were lying in wait for him several Russian officers, particularly at Lemberg, by way of which he proposed to pass.

Upon this Sinclair changed his route, and the *Bashaw* of Chockzine gave him an escort to Broda, where the crown-general of Poland gave him another, with which he entered Silesia. There he thought himself safe, but, being obliged to stop a few days at Breslau, the Russian officers, who learned by spies the road he had taken, pursued and overtook him within a mile of Neustadt. There they stopped and disarmed him, and, having carried him some miles further, assassinated him in a wood. After this ignoble stroke they took away his clothes and papers, in which, however, nothing of consequence was found.'

The infamous Russian court, having examined the despatches, coolly sent them, *via* Hamburg, to that of Sweden. Then the excitement became great. At Stockholm the population rose and wrecked the houses of Catherine's ambassador, crying out "that they were inspired by the soul of Sinclair." The remains of the latter were placed in a magnificent tomb, inscribed thus, by order of King Frederick:—

"Here lies Major Malcolm Sinclair, a good and faithful subject of the kingdom of Sweden, born in 1691, son of the worthy Major-General Sinclair and Madame Hamilton. Prisoner of war in Siberia from 1709 to 1722. Charged with affairs of State, he was assassinated at Naumberg, in Silesia, 17th June, 1789.

Reader! drop some tears upon this tomb, and consider with thyself how incomprehensible are the destinies of poor mortals. (*Scots Mag.*, 1740.)

In 1759 Colonel Ramsay commanded the Swedish garrison of Abo.

In the Seven Years' War great progress was made in 1768 by the Swedish army in Pomerania, under the command of Count Hamilton, who recovered, by force of arms, all Swedish Pomerania, and even made hot incursions into the Prussian territories; thus Frederick the Great advanced against him in person at the head of 10,000 men from

Berlin, while the Prince of Bevern menaced him with 5,000 men from another quarter.

In a conflict at Forhellia the Swedes were compelled to retreat and quit Prussian ground. Retiring by the way of Stralsund, Count Hamilton, "either disgusted by the restrictions he had been laid under," says Smollett, "or finding himself unable to act in such a manner as might redound to the advantage of his reputation, threw up his command, retired from the army, and resigned all his other employments." (*Hist. of England*, vol. vi.) General Lantinghausen succeeded him.

We presume this is the same officer. Count Gustavus David Hamilton, field-marshal of Sweden, who died in his 90th year at Stockholm, in 1789, and who is recorded in the *Edinburgh Advertiser* for that year as having entered the Swedish army in 1716, and having fought in several battles under different powers.

In 1776 General Ramsay (the same officer who commanded at Abo), by his simple presence of mind, compelled the regiment of Upland, then in a mutinous state of revolt, to take the oath of fidelity to the king, Gustavus III. (Tooke's *Catherine II.*)

Few names have a more honourable place in Sweden during the middle of the last century than that of Count Cromartie, knight commander of the Tower and Sword. He was Lord Macleod, who had been "out in the '45," and, after being in the Tower of London, entered the Swedish service, where he rose to the rank of lieutenant-general. Returning in 1777, he raised the old 73rd Highlanders, latterly known as the equally gallant 71st Highland Light Infantry. He died at Edinburgh in 1789, a major-general in the British service.

So lately as 1857 we find Count Hamilton, marshal of the kingdom of Sweden, and president *ex-officio* of the Assemblies of the Four Orders.

CHAPTER 23

The Scots in France

The long alliance and friendly intercourse between the kingdoms of Scotland and France forms one of the most interesting pictures in the national annals of the former, but dates in reality from the third year of the reign of William the Lion, though tradition and, in some instances, history take back the alliance to a remoter period, even to the days of Charlemagne; and, if we are to believe Boethius and Buchanan, the double tressure in our royal arms, *counter fleur-de-lysed or, armed azure*, was first assumed by King Achius, as the founder of the league. But this *bordure* could not have been put round the lion rampant, as that gallant symbol was first adopted by King William (according to Anderson's *Diplomata*) while heraldry and its laws were unknown in the ninth century.

Following tradition, first we may note that De Mezeray, in his *Histoire de France*, records that in 790 "began the indissoluble alliance between France and Scotland, Charlemagne having sent 4,000 men to the aid of King Achius, who sent in return two learned Scots, Clement and Alain," in whom originated the University of Paris. Next, Bishop Lesly states that so far back as 882 Charles III had twenty-four armed Scots, in whose fidelity and valour he reposed confidence, to attend his person—the first of the Scottish guard. Strange to say, Eginhardus, the secretary of Charlemagne, gives an account of the assistance the Scots gave that monarch in his wars; and Paulus Æmilius and Bellefoustus follow suit—the latter adding: "*Scotorum fideli opera non parum adjutas in bello Hispanico fuerat*"; while the prelate before quoted states that the King of Scotland sent 4,000 warriors under his brother William to assist Charles in his contest in Italy.

Following all this perhaps led Ariosto to enumerate among their alleged auxiliaries the Earls of Errol and Buchan, the Chief of the

174

Forbesses, and a Duke of Mar! (*Orlando Furioso, conte x.*)

In 1168 we come to more solid ground—the first authentic negotiation between Scotland and France—when William the Lion sent ambassadors to Louis the Young, to form an alliance against England. (Hailes' *Annals.*) It was renewed repeatedly, particularly in 1326 by Robert I, at Corbeil; in 1383 and 1390, during the reign of Robert II, when the ambassadors of Charles VI were royally entertained in the castle of Edinburgh; and at various intervals down to the reign of Mary and Francis.

In 1254, it is stated that the life of King Louis IX was twice preserved—once in France, and afterwards at Danicotta, in Egypt, in 1270, during the Holy War—by his faithful and valiant Scots sent to serve him by Alexander III. On this occasion the three commanders were Patrick Dunbar, Earl of March, Walter Stuart of Dundonald, and David Lindsay of Glenesk. This led to an increase in the number of Scots attending the King of France to 100 men, constituting them a *garde du corps* (*L'Escosse Française, par* A. Houston). "The practice of having armed Scots attendants appears to have been continued by the succeeding sovereigns of France, and Charles V is stated to have placed this corps on a regular establishment," says the War Office record of the 1st Royal Scots, which corps is alleged to represent the Archer Guard of immortal memory. Says Abercrombie, writing in 1711:

> The Garde Escossaise still enjoys, preferable to all those that ever did service in France, place and precedence. For example, the captain of the Scots guards is, by way of excellency, designed first captain of his Majesty's guards. He begins to attend on the first day of the year, and serves the first quarter. . . . When the king is crowned or anointed the captain of the Scots guards stands by him, and when the ceremony is performed takes the royal robe as his due. When the keys of a town or fortress are delivered up to the king he returns them that minute to the captain of the Scots guards.
>
> Twenty-five of this guard wear always, in testimony of their unspotted fidelity, white coats overlaid with silver lace; and six of these, in turns, stand next the king's person at all times and seasons in the palace, the church, in parliament, the courts of justice, and the reception of foreign ambassadors. It is the right of twenty-five of these gentlemen to carry the corpse of the deceased king to the royal sepulchre at St. Denis. To be short,

that troop of guards has, ever since the days of St. Louis, been in possession of all the honour and confidence the Kings of France can bestow upon their best friends and assured trustees; and it would look very strange in that country if they should see the *braves et fiers Escossois* (for so they characterise the nation) sit down contented with the sinister. (*Mart, Atch.*, vol. i.)

Among the guard in 1270 this author farther gives the names of the Earls of Garrick and Athole, John Stewart, Alexander Cumin, Robert Keith, William Gordon, George Durward, and John Quincy; and many of the Scots, including Adam Kilconcath, the Earl of Garrick, died of the plague on the coast of Africa, before Tunis. (Martin's *Genealog.*)

According to the memoirs of Philip de Commines, Louis IX had the Scots guard with him, "and very few besides," when in the war against the Count de Charolois he marched to the capture of Rouen; and again in the desperate sally at Liége the life of the king was saved by the Scots, "who behaved well, kept firm their ground, and shot their arrows freely, killing more of the Burgundians than the enemy."

In 1385 the Scots College at Paris was founded by David, Bishop of Moray, consecrated in 1299. It was built in the most ancient part of Paris, the Rue des Fosses St. Victor, as recorded on a brass plate in the chapel. On this plate were also the arms of the bishop and of the archbishop of Glasgow in 1588, and therein in later years were monuments to James VII and the Duke of Perth, the governor of his son and heir. That of the king was executed by Louis Gamier in 1703.

Of this college George Grout was rector in 1499, and John Grout rector in 1550 (*Rec. Scots Coll.*), and the celebrated Thomas Innes, who succeeded his brother Louis in that office, and died in 1744. The college was rebuilt by Robert Barclay in 1665.

The charters and historical documents prized here, above 400 in number, were of vast interest, but were all lost at the Revolution, when the body of the king was torn out of his coffin, "where he lay folded in black silk velvet," at the Benedictines, and flung into a lime pit. (*Scots Coll. MSS.*, 4to.) On the final demolition its funds were sunk in those of the Scots College at Douay.

In the chapel dedicated to St. Andrew were interred the *viscera* of Louisa Maria, daughter of King James; the heart of Mary Duchess of Perth; the *viscera* of James and Frances Jennings, Duchess of Tyrconnel, both of which were found so lately as 1883 in two leaden cases, and placed in the hands of Monsignor Rogerson, administrator of Scottish endowments.

In 1354, when the Black Prince won the Battle of Poitiers over the French, he found in the field against him 3,000 Scottish auxiliaries, led by William Earl of Douglas (a veteran of the battles of Durham and Halidonhill), who fought with remarkable bravery, was severely wounded, and narrowly escaped being taken prisoner with John King of France. (*Fordun,*) In this expedition he was accompanied by Sir William Baird of Evandale, who "with his family had been long in use to join the Douglases on every occasion." (*Surname of Baird.*)

In those days a set of freebooters, the result of the English invasions, infested France, They consisted chiefly of men who had been soldiers, and, forming themselves into bands or free companies, they pillaged on every hand and slew all who opposed them, destroying buildings, and paying no regard to Church or State, according to the Abbé de Choisi. Their chief leaders were the Chevalier de Vert of Auxerre, Hugues de Varennes, and one formidable adventurer, Robert the Scot, and they posted themselves in such places that attack was almost impossible.

These Malondrins, as they were named, chose their own leaders, observed discipline, and in the latter none was more exacting than Robert the Scot (*Hist. de Charles V, Dict. Militaire*, etc.). The English tolerated them as a species of allies, till Bertrand du Guesclin cleared the country of them and led them into Spain, ostensibly to fight the Moors, but in reality to crush Peter the Cruel.

In 1370 Charles V was still on the throne of France, and in that year there came to him three Scottish ambassadors, one of whom was Sir John Edmonstone of that ilk in Lothian, sent by David II to solicit the interposition of the Sacred College to procure a favourable decree in the suit prosecuted at the instance of Margaret Logic of Logic, queen-consort of Scotland, and in the following year it was specially stipulated that, "in case of a competition for the Scottish crown, the King of France should withstand any English influence and support the determination of the States of Scotland." (*Pinkerton.*)

By a treaty signed at Paris in August, 1383, the King of France engaged, when war began between Scotland and England, to send to the former 1,000 men at arms, with 1,000 suits of fine armour for Scottish gentlemen; but in this, as in many other instances, France proved false.

Under Charles VI and part of the reign of Charles VII Robert Patullo (or Pittillock), a native of Dundee, is stated to have been captain of the Scots guards, and to have distinguished himself, particularly during the expulsion of the English from Gascony. Prior to this, Henry V of England, having won the memorable Battle of Agincourt in 1415, and captured many of the principal towns in France, was actually acknowledged as heir to the throne by Charles VI, on which the Scots guard quitted his court in disgust, and marched to take part with the dauphin (afterwards Charles VII) in his resistance to this new arrangement, which would have deprived him of the succession to the throne. This brings us to the period referred to by Buchanan in his famous *Epithalamium* on the marriage of Francis of France and Mary of Scotland:—

When all the nations at one solemn call
Had sworn to whelm the dynasty of Gaul,
In that sad hour her liberty and laws
Had perished had not Scotland joined her cause,
No glorious fight her chieftains ever wan
Where Scotland flamed not foremost in the van.
Unless the Scots had bled, she ne'er had grown
To power, or seen her warlike foes o'erthrown.
Alone this nation Gallia's fortunes bore,
Her varied hazards in the war's uproar;
And often turned herself against the lance,
Destined to crush the rising power of France.

The fortunes of the latter were at the lowest ebb when Scotland sent her succour.

After the assembling of Parliament in 1420, it was resolved to send a force of auxiliaries to France, under Sir John Stuart of Coul, created Earl of Buchan, youngest son of Robert Duke of Albany, by Muriel Keith, of the house of Marischal, born sixty-six years after Bannockburn. These auxiliaries are stated by Buchanan at 7,000 men, by Balfour at 10,000, and were conveyed from Scotland by the fleet of Juan II of Castile from the west coast to France, where they landed at Rochelle, after a prosperous voyage. The following were some of the leaders in this expedition under the gallant Buchan:—

Sir Archibald Douglas, Earl of Wigton, afterwards Lord of Longueville and marshal of France; Sir John Stewart of Darnley, constable of the troops, afterwards slain at Orleans in 1429; Sir Robert Maxwell of Calderwood, who died of his wounds at

Chinon; Sir Robert Stewart of Railston; Sir William Crawford of Crawfordland, killed at the siege of Clonell in 1424; Sir Alexander Macauslon of the Lennox; Sir John Carmichael of that ilk; Sir John Swinton of that ilk, slain at Verneuil with Sir Alexander Buchanan of that ilk; Sir Hew Kennedy of Ardstinchar; Sir Robert Houston; Sir Henry Cunningham, third son of Kilmaurs; and Sir Alexander Stewart, great-grandson of Walter, the Lord High Steward.

It is stated (in Dalomoth's *Arms*, 1803) that in the presence of Charles VI Sir Alexander encountered a lion with his sword, which broke in the conflict, after which he slew it by a branch torn from a tree. To commemorate this the king augmented his arms by a "lion debruised, with a ragged staff in bend"—a story doubted in the English *Archæologia*,

All the knights and men-at-arms were accoutred and armed according to the Scots Acts of Parliament, vol. ii, and were under the regulations for the Scottish troops in the early part of the fifteenth century. By them pillage was forbidden under pain of death—which was also the punishment for any soldier who killed a comrade. "Any soldier striking a gentleman was to lose his ears, any gentleman defying another was to be put under arrest. If knights rioted they were to be deprived of their horses and armour; whoever unhorsed an Englishman was to have half his ransom, and every Scottish soldier was to have a white St. Andrew's Cross on his back and breast, which, if his *surcoat* was white, was to be broidered on a square or a circle of black cloth."

From Rochelle, Buchan marched his forces instantly to the aid of the *dauphin*, who was then endeavouring to rescue Languedoc, and by courier informed the earl that he had been deluded by the pretended reconciliation with the Duke of Burgundy at Pouilly-le-Fort; so to the former and his Scots was assigned the town and castle of Chatillon in Touraine, where they soon came to blows with the English and Burgundians; and there, in one of their first encounters, Sir Robert Maxwell was mortally wounded in 1420, and was interred in the church of the Friars Minors at Black Angers, after bequeathing his coat-of-mail to John Maxwell his page. (*Hist. of the Maxwells.*)

Before the arrival of Buchan, Walsingham and others record that a Scottish garrison in Fresnoi-le-Vicomte made a desperate resistance to the army of Henry of England, under Sir William Douglas of Drumlanrig, and the first of his house. In one sally 100 Scots were slain and the banner of Douglas taken. By Henry's orders it was hung as a trophy in the church of Notre-Dame de Rouen. The Scots defended themselves for eighteen months, till their countryman landed at Rochelle, which exasperated the King of England so much that in all treaties made by the Burgundians he declined to allow the Scots to be comprehended. Drumlanrig was afterwards killed in France in 1427. So barbarous was the King of England that he murdered in cold blood 30 Scottish men-at-arms whom he captured in the town of Meaux, on the Marne.

While to Tannequi de Chatel and other gallant French leaders was assigned the command of the French troops in Tours, to Buchan and his Scots was entrusted now the protection of the province of Anjou.

Of the English armies of those days we find but a sorry account in Brady's *History* and Dugdale's *Baronage*, etc., so far as pay went. From them, Hume (vol. iii) concludes that the numerous armies mentioned in these wars "consisted chiefly of ragamuffins who followed the corps and lived by plunder. Edward's army before Calais consisted of 30,094 men; yet its pay for sixteen months was only £127,201." Hence the savage outrages committed by such troops in Scotland and France.

Thomas Duke of Clarence, second son of Henry IV of England, who had recently been appointed governor of Normandy, was joined by Sir Thomas Freeport and two captains of Portuguese free lances on Easter Eve, 1421, after which he marched the English army towards Anjou to encounter the allied Scots under Buchan, and the Dauphinois under Maréchal de la Fayette, the Vicomte de Narbonne, and other leaders of high valour (Monstrelet's *Chron.*)

On the afternoon of the 22nd March he learned from certain Scottish foragers that the Earl of Buchan's force was encamped at Bougé, a little town twenty-two miles eastward of Angers.

"They are ours!" exclaimed Clarence, as he accoutred, "but let none follow me save the men-at-arms."

With the latter he set forth, "besides his gallant furniture and armour," says Buchanan, "wearing a royal diadem set with many jewels," leaving the Earl of Salisbury to follow with the archers and 4,000 infantry.

The Scots and Dauphinois held the ancient bridge of the Couanar, which was deep, narrow, and rapid at that point, and was the only means by which the adverse hosts could meet each other; and Clarence, we are told, was filled with fury to find that its passage was to be disputed by the Scots, and may perhaps have remembered the old English saying (introduced by Shakespeare in his *Henry V*):—

If that you would France win,
Then with Scotland first begin.

Sir John Stewart of Darnley and the Sieur de la Fontaine, who had been scouting with some cavalry, on seeing the advancing English fell back to report. "To your arms!" was the order of Buchan, who drew up the combined troops in front of the town.

Montacute, Earl of Salisbury, had orders to cross the stream by a ford and take the Scots in flank if he could, while Clarence with his men-at-arms, in their panoply of steel, was to assail the bridge in front Its defence was entrusted to Sir Robert Stewart of Railston, with thirty archers only; but, just as the skirmish began, Kennedy of Ardstinchar, who with a hundred Scots held a church dose by, in their hurry but half-armed, rushed forth, and by a shower of arrows drove the English back. Then Buchan pressed on at the head of 200 chosen Scottish men-at-arms, and in the narrow way between the parapets of the old bridge there ensued a close and dreadful *mêlée*, when, fired by the memories of a hundred years' war, the Scots and the English met in the shock of battle, as they alone could meet each other. The latter, says Buchanan, were exasperated to "be attacked by such implacable enemies, not only at home, but beyond the seas; so they fought stoutly, but none more so than Clarence himself, who was too well known by his armour."

On the other hand, the royal earl, a powerful warrior in his forty-second year, fought with all the heroism of his race; but Clarence, distinguished by his fatal coronet, was the mark of every Scottish sword and lance.

In the close *mêlée* he was quickly assailed by Sir John Carmichael (ancestor of the Earl of Hyndford), who spurred against him with lance in rest; the tough oak shaft was splintered on the corslet of Clarence, who was wounded in the face by Sir John Swinton of that ilk, and, just as he was falling from his saddle, had his brains dashed out by one blow from the Earl of Buchan's mace—"a steel hammer," Hume of Godscroft calls it, a weapon to which he had resorted after driving his lance through the prince's body.

His fall filled the English with blind fury. In crowds they pressed over the heaps of dead on the bridge to avenge him—knights, archers, and billmen intermingled, but jostling and impeding each other in such a manner that the Scots, by one furious charge, with helmets closed and lances in rest, drove them back, put them to flight, and cut them to pieces, the pursuit and flight being continued till night fell, with bridles loose, the victors scarcely pausing even to wipe their bloody blades upon their horses' manes. According to Bower, 1,700 English perished, while the Scots lost only two and the French twelve—a statement utterly incredible. The *Chronicle* of Monstrelet states that of the English there fell 3,000, and of the Dauphinois 11,000, including three good knights, Charles le Bouteiller, Gavin des Fontaines, and Sir John Grosin.

Among the English there fell the Lords of Tankerville and De Roos of Hamloke, Sir John Grey of Heton, and Gilbert de Umphreyille, titular Earl of Angus in Scotland. Two hundred knights and men-at-arms, with their battle-chargers and rich armour, fell into the hands of the Scots. Among the first were Henry Earl of Huntingdon, son of the half-sister of Richard II; and John, Earl of Somerset, whose sister Jane was afterwards queen of James I.

Buchan sent the body of Clarence to the Earl of Salisbury, and it was eventually interred in Canterbury Cathedral; but his coronet remained a trophy with the Scots. Sir John Stewart of Darnley purchased it from one of his soldiers for 1,000 angels; Sir Robert Houston afterwards lent him 5,000 upon it. Buchanan asserts that it was Macauslon from the Lennox who rent it from the duke's helmet. Sir John Carmichael, in memory of shivering his spear on the duke's corslet, added to his armorial coat a hand grasping a broken spear; but the honour of unhorsing him was claimed by Swinton and Sir Alexander Buchanan. To Hugh Kennedy, Charles VII of France gave, as an addition to his arms, *azure*, three *fleurs-de-lys or*, still borne by all his descendants.

On the Earl of Buchan was bestowed the office of Constable of France, last held by Charles of Lorraine—the first stranger who ever held such an honour—and with it he got princely domains, stretching over all the land between Chartres and Avranches. He was also made master of the horse.

After his victory he took possession of the castle of Chartres, on the Eure, and laid siege to the old fortress of Alençon (of which three battlemented towers yet remain), repulsing with the loss of 400 men the Earl of Salisbury, who attempted its relief. He then captured the town of Avranches, in Normandy, in the autumn of 1422, after which he returned to Scotland, in consequence of feuds which had broken out there, leaving his troops under the command of Sir John Stewart of Darnley, who was styled "Constable of the Scots in France." Charles VI died on the 21st of October that year, and the Duke of Bedford, whose name, was disgraced by his persecution of the Maid of Orleans, ordered Henry VI to be proclaimed King of France, while the *dauphin*, to whom Scotland adhered, was called in mockery "the King Bourges," as the English and Burgundians had all the best provinces of France, including Normandy, and the territory between the Loire and Schelat.

The Scots guards, of whom Darnley was now captain, were with Charles VII at the castle of Espailly, in Auvergne; and it is about this time that we first find the French mode of spelling the name of the Scottish royal family.

In the *Liste des Commandeurs des Gendarmes Escossais, etc.* (Père Daniel), under date 24th March, 1442, is *Jean Stuart*, Seigneur d'Arnelay et d'Aubigné.

Jean Stuart, fils du précédant, Seigneur d'Aubigné
Robert Stuart, cousin du précédant, Seigneur d'Aubigné fait Maréchal
de France en 1515.

To Charles VII all the princes of the blood and the best chivalry of France adhered, and his affairs were beginning to prosper, when there came to the castle of Espailly bad tidings of his Scottish auxiliaries at Crevant.

CHAPTER 24

The Scots in France—(Continued)

In the July of 1423 King Charles ordered a body of his allied French and Scottish forces to cross the Loire and invest the town of Crevant, then held by the enemy. It is in the district of Auxerre, and the river Yonne lay between the relieving force and the English and Burgundians, who were about 15,000 strong, drawn up in order of battle on a hill, with Crevant in their rear, the stream in front, with a stone bridge by which it was spanned.

The weather was so sultry that the attacking force suffered greatly on their march by the heat and the weight of their armour; thus many of the Scots men-at-arms proceeded on foot, leading their horses by the bridle. They were led by Sir John of Darnley; the French by the Maréchal de Senerac. The armour of the Scottish and French men-at-arms at this period differed somewhat from that of the English. They wore back and breast-plates, attached to which were various plates adapted to overlap the figure; and over the flanks on each side the soldier wore taces or plates attached to a small shield, covering the front of the thigh; and these taces were square, lozenge-shaped, or serrated, according to fancy. Gauntlets of steel were then recent French inventions, superseding long gloves of thick leather.

By the express orders of the Duchess of Burgundy, then at Dijon, the town was to he saved from the Scots particularly, whereupon the Marshal of Burgundy joined his forces to those of Salisbury, with whom were the Earl of Suffolk, Lord Willoughby of Eresby, and other heroes of Agincourt.

After solemn mass in Auxerre, and drinking a loving-cup together, 120 English and Burgundian horse, with as many archers, came boldly forward as scouts, as the old governor of Cambrai records, about 10 a. m. on a Saturday.

Under Darnley's orders were only 3,000 Scots and a few French, under Maréchal le Comte de Senerac, the Lords of Estissac and Ventadour. According to Monstrelet and others, with all their troops in glittering array, he and the other three leaders sat placidly in their saddles and saw the English and Burgundians cross the bridge of the Yonne and form in squares of foot and squadrons of horse when they ought to have held that bridge with cannon and cross-bow, forgetting the most simple rules of war; and terrible was the sequel.

The French, who had been demoralised since Agincourt, fell back under Senerac, leaving the whole brunt of battle to the Scots—a handful compared to the opposing force, which quickly overlapped them on both flanks, while a sortie from Crevant assailed their rear. Though fighting with their hereditary valour with spear, maul, and sword, the Scots fell into disorder. Desperately fought Stewart in the van to repair his first error, bat lost an eye by a sword-thrust through the bars of his visor, after which, blinded with blood, he surrendered himself to a Burgundian lord, Claude de Bevasir of Castillux; and there, too, was taken Sir William Crawford of Crawfordland, who remained a prisoner till the following year, but afterwards fell in France. De Ventadour also lost an eye and yielded himself to the Lord of Gamaches.

Of the Scots there fell 1,200, and among them, Monstrelet enumerates, a nephew of the absent Earl of Buchan; Sir William Hamilton and his son; Sir Thomas Swinton; Stephen and John Frasmeres (Ferrier?); while 400 Scots were made prisoners. In the wars of those days one successful campaign, with pay and plunder, with the ransom of a few prisoners, was supposed to be a small fortune to an English soldier. (Dugdale's *Baronage*.)

Solemn thanksgiving was offered up by the victors' in the churches of Crevant, and the first-fruits of it were the capture of two other towns on the Loire.

Sir John of Darnley was afterwards exchanged for the Lord Pole, brother of the Earl of Suffolk. He was made Lord of Aubigné, Concressault, and Evereux, with the right of quartering his arms with those of France. He arranged the marriage of the Princess Margaret of Scotland with the future, and infamous, Louis XI, and fell in his old age at the siege of Orleans in 1429.

The tidings of Crevant urged the return of the Constable Buchan to France from Scotland, whither came as envoys Renes of Chartres, chancellor of the former, and Juvenal des Ursins, Archbishop of Rheims, a celebrated prelate and historian; so another auxiliary force was equipped to take vengeance for the late defeat.

The Earl of Douglas—the same who lost an eye at Homildon, who fought at Shrewsbury, and defended the castle of Edinburgh in 1409—on being created Duke of Lorraine and Marshal of France, joined the constable with a body of horse and infantry. Hollinshed gives the new auxiliary force at 10,000 men. Among the leaders were Sir Alexander Home of that ilk; and Douglas, an aged Border-warrior who fought at Homildon; Adam Douglas, afterwards governor of Tours; Robert Hop-Pringle, the Laird of Smailholm, armour-bearer to the Earl of Douglas; two other Douglases of the lines of Queenbury and Lochleven; and Bernard Lindsay of the house of Glenesk.

In the spring of 1424 these forces landed at Rochelle and joined the other Scottish troops then in Poitou under Charles VII.

It is related by Godscroft that the aged Home of that ilk had resolved to send a younger kinsman in his place, but when he saw the Scottish troops departing his military spirit fired up anew.

"Ah, Sir Alexander," said the Earl of Douglas, "who would have thought that we should ever part?"

"Nor shall we now, my lord!" exclaimed the old knight; so he sailed with Douglas, and died in his armour on the field of Verneuil.

At this time the Duke of Bedford was besieging Ivri-la-Bataille, a Norman town, against the valiant Girault de la Pallière, who had agreed in his sore extremity to surrender, if not relieved by a certain day; so Charles marched to its relief with 9,000 Scots, under Buchan, Douglas, and Murray, according to Monstrelet, and the same number of French, under Ventadour, Narbonne, and de Tonnere; Buchan, as constable, commanding the whole, in conjunction with the Duke of Alençon.

Bedford led 26,000 men-at-arms and archers under Salisbury, Suffolk, and Willoughby; and when this relieving force came in sight of Ivri, St George's Cross was already flying on its walls, which still exist, together with a strong old tower into which the English garrison retired on the approach of Charles VII. When the force of the latter came in sight of Verneuil, "the Earl of Buchan," says Rapin, "was pleased to resign (the command) to the Earl of Douglas, his father-in-law, to whom the king sent for that purpose a patent constituting him lieutenant-general of the whole kingdom, otherwise the constable could not have acted under his orders." This was on the 17th August, 1424

Bedford, whom Douglas was wont to ridicule as "John with the leaden sword," resolved to wait the attack, and selected excellent ground, flanked by a hill on which he posted 2,000 archers with their protecting stakes; while Douglas drew up in order of battle before Verneuil, then a town of great strength, the ancient walls of which still remain, (as at time of first publication).

To the constable with his suite he assigned the centre; the wings he gave to Viscount Narbonne and Gilbert the Maréchal de la Fayette.

Each flank was covered by a thousand mounted *gendarmerie*, in complete mail, horse and man, with bow, mace, and battle-axe; and with the left flank were 900 Lombardy crossbowmen, sent by the Duke of Milan, mounted and in full armour.

Douglas held a council of war, before which he urged "that as the Duke of Bedford intended evidently to fight on strong ground, chosen by himself, battle should not be risked" But the French leaders, already jealous of the Scots, declared that "if battle were avoided the honour of France would suffer." Then the Viscount Narbonne ordered his bowmen to advance, and, in defiance of all authority, began his march, towards the English. Père Daniel and Hall record that "Douglas was infuriated by this disobedience; but that neither he nor the constable could avert the purpose of these rash French lords. Douglas was in a foreign land, and, afraid that his honour might suffer if the field was lost by only half his troops engaging, he issued orders for the whole to advance *uphill* and attack the English."

This was at three o'clock in the afternoon, and then began a conflict, of which every account is confused, but on the issue of which the fate of France and her king seemed to depend.

The English received the uphill charge of the Scots with a shout so hearty that it dismayed the French under Narbonne, who held back his column, leaving his allies to bear the brunt of all. Close, deadly, and terrible was the conflict, the Scots handling their long spears and heavy swords in close battle, choosing to die rather than surrender or give way. The French authorities admit that "the bravest leaders and most efficient troops who fought on their side that day were the Scots."

Yet it was a lost battle, and, choosing rather to die than surrender it, there fell the Constable Buchan; his father-in-law, the Earl of Douglas; two Sir James Douglases, Sir Walter Lindsay, Sir Alexander Home, Sir John Swinton of that ilk, Sir Robert Stewart, and Hop-Pringle of Smailholm, with many French knights and great lords of Dauphiny and Languedoc, with 4,000 men, the most of whom were Scots and

Italians. Hollinshed gives the slain at 9,700 of these, and 2,100 English. Many of the Italians had the hardihood to revisit the field, perhaps in search of plunder, but were shot down in the twilight and stripped of arms and clothing by the English archers.

Covered with wounds, the bodies of the Earls of Buchan and Douglas were borne from the field, and honourably interred by the English in the church of St. Gnetian, at Tours, where, and at Orleans, so lately as 1643, a daily mass was celebrated for the souls of the Scots who fell at Verneuil.

Buchan was succeeded as constable of France by Arthur, Duc de Bretagne, and left one daughter; who was married to George Lord Seton.

The power of Bedford grew weaker in France after the Battle of Verneuil, where more men fell on both sides than in any battle since Agincourt. Subsidies came grudgingly from London to aid the iniquitous war, and then Joan of Arc[1] came upon the scene when Charles VII was contemplating a flight to Scotland. In 1428 Bedford was ordered to cross the Loire and ravage those provinces which still adhered to the former, and, as a preparatory step, besieged Orleans, on which the eyes of all Europe were turned, for the numberless deeds of valour performed around the city. Cannon were extensively used, and by one of them the Earl of Salisbury was slain.

The siege had lasted four months, and, as the season was Lent, Bedford sent from Paris a vast quantity of salted herrings and other stores in 500 carts, with a train of artillery and 1,700 men, under Sir John Fastolffe, one of England's best generals, made Knight of the Garter by Henry VI. Under his orders were Sir Thomas Rampston and Sir Philip Hall, "with 1,000 followers," probably some of the unpaid "ragamuffins" referred to by Brady.

To cut off this force Charles VII despatched the Count of Clermont with 3,000 men, including the *cuirassiers* and archers of the Scottish guard under John Stewart, Count d'Aubigné, and the lancers of the Count Dunois. The glitter of their brilliant armour warned Fastolffe of their approach at seven in the morning of the 12th February, 1429. He made a barricade ("*lager*" it would now be called) of the herring waggons and carts, and posted his men in the rear thereof.

The French and Scottish men-at-arms dismounted and assailed the entrenchment with sword and battle-axe, while the archers plied their arrows; but the movement was begun too furiously by the Scots,

---

1. *Personal Recollections of Joan of Arc* by Mark Twain also published by Leonaur.

in their rancorous hate of the English and desire to avenge the day of Verneuil, though Clermont and Dunois had placed some guns in position which would soon have knocked the vehicles to pieces.

By lance, bill, and bow they were repulsed, and then Fastolffe, ordering some of the waggons to be withdrawn, issued forth and charged them furiously. Short and sharp was the conflict; but the Scots were rented and the French cannon taken. Stewart of Darnley and one of his sons were slain. Dunois was wounded, and, according to Monstrelet, there fell six-score great lords and 500 soldiers.

The conflict of Roverai was deemed of great importance in its time, as the convoy contained so much that was necessary for the English in Lent.

The Bastard of Orleans, who had sallied out to assist Clermont in cutting it off, preserved sufficient presence of mind to escape Fastolffe in the confusion, and to reach the city with 400 men. The successor of Darnley at the head of the Scottish guard was a native of Dundee (before referred to), named Robert Patullo, a soldier so famed for his success in many affairs in Guienne that he was called 'The Little King of Goscony'.

The Scoto-French alliance was supposed to be made closer when, in 1643, the Scottish Princess Margaret (daughter of James I), in her twelfth year, was united to the *dauphin*, afterwards the terrible Louis XI, then a year older. William Sinclair, third Earl of Orkney, the admiral of Scotland, and John Bishop of Brechin, with sixteen knights and esquires, 140 young gentlemen, and 1,000 men-at-arms in nine vessels, formed her train, to intercept which the English lawlessly sent out a piratical fleet, which was beaten by the Spaniards; thus the royal bride landed safely at Rochelle, and her marriage was solemnised on the 6th July. (*Pinkerton.*)

The unhappy bride had passed to a husband of famed malignity; and not all her prudence, wit, love of learning, taste for poetry, inherited from her princely father, nor her affability, could save her from the pangs of domestic distress.

The vague word of Jacques de Tilloy, a villainous courtier, accused her of conjugal infidelity, and destroyed her constitution, already enfeebled by harshness and neglect. The beautiful Margaret died in her twenty-first year, protesting her innocence, to the deep grief of her father-in-law, Charles VII.

Inspired by insular hate, Grafton, the Englishman, wrote of her brutally; but John Major calls her with more probability "*Virginum formosum et honestam*"; and his long residence as a doctor of the Sorbonne in Paris gave him opportunities for information, while his simplicity is a warrant for his veracity.

In 1440 the latter, in some manner, reconstituted the Scottish guard, and gave precedence to it over all the troops in France, designating it "*Le Garde-du-Corps Ecossais.*" The Scots *gendarmes* and *garde-du-corps* continued to form part of the French military force until about the year 1788 (War Office Record: 1st Foot). The dream of an English Empire in France ended in 1451.

The muster rolls of the Scottish *garde-du-corps* and the *gendarmerie*, extending from 1419 to 1791, have recently been published by Father Forbes-Leith, and are, the most interesting Scottish lists we possess.

In 1461 Charles VII died, and Louis XI succeeded him. In the vile conspiracies of the latter against his father he made many attempts without success to seduce the Scottish guard from its allegiance; and remembering this when he became king, he regarded them as his most trustworthy supporters in the course of those wars and intrigues by which he broke the power of the great feudal lords of France.

In 1465 they served in the conflict at Montlhéry—a bloody but indecisive battle fought between the troops of Louis XI and those of the *Ligue du Bien-Public*, commanded by the Comte de Charolois, afterwards Charles the Bold of Burgundy, where so many of his people fell that the field is still named the *Cimetière des Bourguinons*; and Louis was taken out of the field by the Scots, who fought in a circle round him, and conveyed to the old castle of Montlhéry, which still remains. (*De Mezeray.*) At this time Thomas Boyd, created Earl of Arran in 1468, was in the service of Charles the Bold, after the ruin of his family, and died in exile at Antwerp in 1471, according to Buchanan; though Ferreriers asserts that he was slain in Tuscany.

Some veterans of the Scottish guard would seem to have been at one time settled in the Département du Cher, according to a communication made by a French pastor to the Evangelical Alliance in June, 1863. The Duke of Henrichment, Constable of France, settled them on his lands, when for a time they turned their attention to iron-works and agriculture. "For four centuries," he continued, "they have kept distinct, without mingling with their neighbours, preserving their Scottish names with but slight variations, and also the tradition of their British origin."

Again, in 1878, the papers contained an account of "the Scottish colony of St. Martin d'Auxigny near Bourges," given by M. le Pasteur Vesson, of Dunkirk, to the effect "that Stuart of Aubigné had established them in the Royal forest of St. Martin d'Auxigny, where they numbered 3,000 persons, and had special privileges till 1789. A tall, strong race, they are quiet and shy, but very industrious and honest. Their names have been altered, but the Scottish original may be easily traced, as for instance Coen for Cowie; and in a contract one of them recently signed his name 'Opie de Perth.'" (*Times*, 1878.)

In 1483 Bernard Stewart of Aubigné, marshal of France, came to Scotland as ambassador from Charles VIII to renew the ancient league; and on returning he took back with him eighteen companies of Scottish infantry, "under the command of Donald Robertson, an expert and valiant commander," says Balfour, " who purchased much renown under the French king in the wars of Italy." (*Annales*, vol. i)

The Scottish auxiliaries certainly won much glory in the conquest of Naples and elsewhere in Italy in 1495.

Guichardin tells us in his history that when Charles VIII crossed the Alps the strength of his army was 40,000 men, with *four hundred* pieces of cannon, in that war which first revealed to Europe that France had risen to a place among the powers of the Continent; but Guichardin exaggerates. The army of Charles, who had pretensions to Naples as Thir of Anjou, consisted of 20,000 men, including the Scots under Stewart of Aubigné, whom he valued highly. "In Calabria," says Philip de Commines, "he left Monsieur d'Aubigny, a brave and honourable person, to command in chief. The king had made him constable of that kingdom, and given him the county of Aen and the *marquisat* of Iquillazzo." One of the chief causes of the French success, says De Mezeray, was their artillery drawn by horses, while those of the Italians were drawn by oxen.

Surrounded by the Scottish guard, Charles entered Florence in complete mail, with his lance resting on his thigh. They fought at Fornovo that battle at the foot of the Apennines, when a complete victory was won over the united states of Italy. After delivering Sienna and Pisa from the Tuscan yoke, Charles took possession of Rome as a conqueror, and Paulus Jovius and others have transmitted to us an interesting account of the French entry into the capital of Alexander VI.

First came the Swiss and Germans, keeping step to their drums, with banners displayed and parti-coloured dresses, their officers all distinguished by tall plumes in their helmets, and all armed with swords and pikes ten feet long. Every corps of 1,000 had 100 armed with arquebuses. Then came 5,000 Gascons, all archers; then the French cavalry, 2,500 of whom were heavily mailed , and twice that number more lightly armed, but all with fluted spears of great size, and the manes and ears of their horses cropped. Then came the king, guarded by the Scots, with 300 mounted archers and 200 French knights, armed with maces, and wearing gold and purple *surcoats* over their armour. The Scottish *Gardes de la Manche* are immediately next the king, and ride with white *hoquetons* over their mail, in token of their unspotted fidelity.

Philip de Commines specially mentions the Scottish archers at the Battle of Fornovo, in July, 1495, wherein, after a furious charge, the Italian Estradiots, whose favourite weapon was the *zagaye*, were driven in; yet only nine of the Scots were slain.

Charles VIII died in 1498, and was succeeded by Louis XII, under whom the Scots were again in Italy, serving against the Venetians in 1509, as the lists of the French army published at that time attest. In particular they fought at the Battle of Agnadel or Rivalta, when the Venetians were defeated with great loss in Lombardy; but of this war history is almost destitute of details.

CHAPTER 25

The Scots in France—(Continued)

According to the spirited work of Forbes-Leith and other authorities, the Scottish guard distinguished itself in the campaigns of Francis I, and bore itself nobly in the great Battle of Marignano and on the disastrous day of Pavia.

Francis I, who in 1615 succeeded to the throne of France, young, brave, and full of ambition, resolved that his first military enterprise should be the reconquest of Milan, and with this view marched towards the Alps a magnificent army on pretence of defending his frontier against the Swiss, who had taken up arms at the Papal instigation in order to protect Maximilian Sforza, the Duke of Milan, whom they deemed themselves bound in honour to support.

The armies came in sight of each other at Marignano on the Lambro, eleven miles south-east of Milan, where ensued one of the most obstinate battles of modern times, at four o'clock, on the 13th of October, 1515. Says Voltaire:

> An army of 26,000 Swiss, some with St. Peters's keys on their backs and breasts, some of them armed with pikes eighteen feet long, moved in close battalions, others with large two-handled swords, all advanced with loud shouts towards the king's camp in the neighbourhood of Marignano. Of all the battles in Italy this was the bloodiest and the longest. The French and Swiss, being mixed together in the obscurity of the night, were obliged to wait for daylight to renew the engagement.'

Surrounded by the Scottish guard, whose commander in that year was! Robert Stuart, son of the second Lord of Aubigné, the king at the first charge made on his vanguard repulsed it ere the darkness fell, and both armies halted amid the dead and wounded, "many of both," says De Mezeray, "lying down by each other all the night. The king, with his armour on, rested himself upon the carriage of a gun, when the great thirst his toil had brought upon him made him relish even a little water, mixed with dirt and blood, brought to him by a courteous soldier in his steel morion."

The moment day broke he attended to the disposition of his *arquebusiers*, gunners, and Genoese crossbowmen, and by cannon-shot, bullets, and arrows tore the dense Swiss battalions asunder, charging through them with his horse, himself at the head of the Garde-du-Corps Ecossais, and drove the enemy into a great wood, where numbers of them were out to pieces.

Of the Swiss, 10,000 fell; of the French, only 400! The former, though not routed, gave way, and so ended a strife which, says Voltaire, "the old Maréchal de Trivala used to call the Battle of Giants. Maximilian Sforza was carried into France, like Lewis the Moor, but upon milder conditions. He became a subject. The sovereign of the finest province in Italy was permitted to live in France on a moderate pension." The Chevalier Bayard, who had greatly contributed to the victory, was knighted on the field.

At the end of 1523 Francis I was joined by John Duke of Albany, previously regent of Scotland, where he had been aught but popular. Son of that infamous Alexander of Albany (who had been exiled for his intrigues with the English) and of his wife, a daughter of the Count de Boulogne, born in France, and the husband of a French wife, Anne de la Tour of Vendôme, he was more than half a Frenchman, and had disgusted many of the proud Scottish peers and chiefs; yet Francis, in virtue of his royal birth and rank as Count of Boulogne and Auvergne, gave him a high command in the French army, when he was encouraged by the Duke of Bouillon to make war upon the emperor and invade Luxembourg. Other favours were conferred on Albany when Francis led his army into Italy again in 1523, at that time when the constable of Bourbon formed a conspiracy against him, and, entering the Imperial service, endeavoured to thwart his designs upon the Italian peninsula.

Albany led a body of Scottish auxiliaries in this war, and to them Francis added 600 horse, 10,000 infantry, and a train of artillery; for to him, says De Mezeray, he assigned the complete conquest of Naples in 1524, the viceroy of which, Launoy, had succeeded Colonno in command there, Francis at the same time, to subdue the city of Milan, sent forward the Admiral Bonnivet and the Chevalier Bayard with 30,000 men.

While Lannoy continued to "amuse" the Duke of Albany in Tuscany the battle of Pavia was fought on the 24th of February, 1626. Previous to this Francis had laid siege to the city—"the city of a hundred towers"—in the October of the preceding year, and this led to the great contest in which the Scottish guard displayed the most unparalleled loyalty and devotion to duty.

Led by Pescara and Launoy, a united army advanced to the relief of Pavia, whence prudence would have dictated a retreat; but Francis despised to fall back, as his troops were strongly entrenched. Seldom have armies engaged with greater ardour, more national rivalry, and rancorous antipathy. The valour of the French made the Imperialists first give ground; but the fortunes of the day changed; The Swiss in the French service deserted *en masse*, while Pescara fell upon the *gendarmerie* in a fashion to which they were unaccustomed, a number of Spanish foot, says Guichordini; armed with heavy *arquebuses*, being chequered with the cavalry; while Leyra, sallying out of Pavia, made a dreadful assault on the French rear, and then the confusion and rout became general.

Surrounded by the Scottish guard and the flower of the nobles, Francis, whose horse was killed under him, fought with stern valour, and slew seven men with his own hand. Resisting desperately in a circle, man after man, *gendarme* and archer, knight and gentleman, the Scottish guard went down till, according to *L'écosse françoise* of A. Houston, only *four* remained alive, when Francis gave up his sword to Pomperant, a French gentleman, who followed the Constable de Bourbon, and ultimately it was handed to Lannoy. (*Brantome, Guichordin*, etc.) Before leaving as a prisoner for Pizzighettone he wrote to his mother the memorable letter containing the sublime laconism, "*Madame, tout est perdu fors l'honneur.*"

This event filled Europe with alarm; Milan was abandoned, and soon not a French soldier remained in Italy. The Duke of Albany was compelled, says, De Mezeray, to disband the Italian troops he had levied, and then to ship his French and Scots, the Spaniards "lending him some galleys for that purpose, those of the regent not being sufficient to transport them."

In October, 1633, we again hear of the Duke of Albany prominently, when he escorted to Marseilles Catharine de Nicolais, whose maternal aunt he had married. On the 10th of the same month the Pope, Clement VII, arrived at Marseilles in the king's galleys.

Three years after, Albany died in his own castle of Minfleur, nine miles from Clermont. Two relics of him still exist in France—his chapel and palace at Vic-le-Comte, in Auvergne.

On the 13th of August, 1548, our young Queen Mary, then in her girlhood, landed in France, the contracted bride of the *dauphin*; and two years afterwards we find a gentleman of the Scottish guard, Robert Stuart, supposed to be in the English or Protestant interest, accused of the desperate crime of attempting to poison her. What were the proofs of this seem vague; but he was arrested and executed publicly.

On the 14th of April, 1538, Mary was married to the *dauphin* with great pomp by the Cardinal Bourbon, in the cathedral church of Notre Dame—a ceremony attended by the King and Queen of France, four cardinals, the princes of the blood, and all the most august personages of the realm; and during the time that the sovereigns of Scotland and France were united in marriage their designation was:—*Francis et Maria de Gratia, Rex et Regina Scotia, Francia, Anglia et Hibernia.* The privileges of the Scots in France were most ample, and were in every way the same as those enjoyed by French subjects in Scotland by Act of Parliament.

These privileges were fully defined and confirmed by Henry, King of France, in a letter of naturalisation registered in the Parliament of Paris and Great Council of the Chamber of Accompts. Until the Revolution the effects of all strangers, *Scots excepted*, dying in France were liable to seizure by the law of that country, even though the heir was on the spot; and the reader may remember Sterne's indignant outburst on this subject in the introduction to his *Sentimental Journey*.

Three years before this auspicious royal marriage some of those concerned in the murder of Cardinal Beaton, and the subsequent defence of St. Andrews against the French fleet, took military service in France.

Henry IV having recalled from exile the Constable de Montmorencie—whom his father had warned him never to employ—in May, 1653, sent him with an army into Picardy, where the troops of the aged emperor, after seizing Lorraine and ravaging Flanders, were there levying war. With the army of the constable went Sir William Kirkcaldy of Grange, whom Henry had commissioned as a captain of light horse, whose armour covered only the upper part of the body, their trunk-hose being quilted and stuffed with bombast; their arms, petronels, swords, daggers, and demi-lances. Many of Kirkcaldy's friends and kinsmen now rode in their armour with the same host.

Among them we may enumerate Sir James Melville of Halhill, then in his 18th year; Archibald Mowbray of Barnhougal; and Norman Leslie, master of Rothes (one of the actual assassins of the cardinal), whom King Henry had appointed "colonel of the Scotts Lanciers"— says Balfour in his *Annales*—an appointment which he had won through the influence of "the Laird of Brunstone, another expatriated soldier of fortune who carried a lance in the Spanish wars." After various marches and movements, on reaching the neighbourhood of St. Quentin, the venerable constable, old in years and arms, "being in his grand climacterick," fell sick, and both armies went into winterquarters.

The spring of 1554 saw them in the field again. In attacking Dinant, a small but ancient city, the French were repulsed thrice by a tremendous arquebuse-fire, and no less than eleven standard-bearers were shot down in succession under their colours in the breach. At that crisis, Mowbray of Barnhougal (husband of Elizabeth Kirkcaldy of Grange), to set an example, rushed into the dangerous breach, sword in hand, but was compelled to retire, which he did untouched. (Melville's *Memoirs*.)

Eventually Dinant was taken, and afterwards a battle took place on the plain before Renti on the 31st of August 1554. On the preceding day, the constable, perceiving that the Spaniards meant to possess themselves of certain heights which commanded the French position, sent Norman Leslie's Scottish lancers and some other cavalry to drive the Imperialists back, and on this duty Melville thus describes him:— In view of the whole French army the master of Rothes, "with thirty Scotsmen, rode up the hill upon a fine grey gelding. He had above his coat of black velvet his coat of armour, with two broad white crosses, one before and the other behind, with sleeves of mail and a red bonnet upon his head, whereby he was known often by the constable, the Duke d'Enghien, and the Prince de Condé."

His party was diminished to only seven by the time he came within lance-length of the Imperialists, who were sixty in number; but he burst amid them like a thunderbolt, escaping the fire of the *arquebuses*, and struck five from their saddles with his long Scottish lance ere it broke to splinters. Then drawing his sword, he hewed among them again and again with the reckless valour for which he had ever been distinguished.

At the critical moment of this most unequal contest of seven Scottish knights against sixty Spaniards, a troop of Imperial spearmen were hastily idling along the hill to join in the encounter. By this time Leslie had received several bullets in his person, and finding himself unable to continue the conflict longer, he dashed spurs into his horse, galloped back to the constable, and fell faint and exhausted from his saddle, with the blood pouring through his burnished armour on the turf. (*Memoirs of Kirkcaldy of Grange.*)

By the king's desire he was borne to the royal tent, when the Prince de Condé remarked that "Hector of Troy had not behaved more valiantly than Norman Leslie." The royal surgeon dressed his wounds in vain, as he expired at Montreuil fifteen days after the battle, with his last breath deploring his share in the murder of Cardinal Beaton. (*Scot Chron.*, Hollinshed.) He was the son of George, fourth Earl of Rothes, by Margaret, daughter of Lord Crichton. On the day after his exploit the Battle of Renti ensued, and so furious was the charge of the Spanish vanguard that a portion of the army in which Sir William Kirkcaldy served, the *chevaux légers*, fell back, till the Spaniards were checked in turn by a column under the Vicomte de Tonannes and a knight of the house of Eglinton. Sir Gabriel de Montgomerie, styled Lord of Lorges in France (*Papers of the Archer Guard*), and ere long Renti was won.

So highly did King Henry value Norman Leslie's memory that the survivors of his Scottish troop of lancers were sent back to their own country under Crichton of Brunstone, says Hollinshed, laden with rewards and honours; and by his influence such as were exiles were restored to their estates, as a reward for their valour on the frontiers of Flanders.

At the Battle of St. Quentin, fought on St. Lawrence's Day, 1557, the old Constable de Montmorencie fought like a lion, but was unhorsed and captured alive by some Flemish knights. In that *mêlée* Sir James Melville of Halhill, who fought close by his side, was unhorsed by a blow on the helmet, but was remounted by his servant "upon a Scots gelding, which bore him right through the enemy," whose swords wore aimed at his defenceless head; but, leaping over several walls, he gained the barriers of La Fère, where he drew up at the booth of a barber-*chirurgeon* to have his wounds dressed, during which process his horse was kindly held, as he tells us, by Mr. Killigrew, an English gentleman who served in those wars. The defeat at St. Quentin nearly laid France at the foot of the emperor. Melville accompanied his friend the constable, a prisoner of war, to Cambray, where soon after a treaty of peace was concluded, and then Kirkcaldy of Grange returned home.

"I heard Henry II," Melville says, "point to him and say, 'Yonder is one of the most valiant men of our age!'"

Two years after St. Quentin he lost his friend and patron, Henry II, who was slain in a tournament when running a course with the Count de Montgomerie (captain of the Scottish guard). In tilting, the visor of the king's helmet flew up, and the lance of the Scot entered his eye. He died of the wound, and from that hour tournaments were abolished by law in France.

The new captain of the Scottish guard was James, third Earl of Arran. Queen Elizabeth, Coligni, and the Prior of St. Andrew's prevailed upon the earl—a weak man—to join with some of his archers in the conspiracy of Amboise in 1660, concocted by Condé against the Guises. It felled; he had to fly, and many of the guard perished in the catastrophe.

In 1559 Robert Stuart, Seigneur de Veziers, and designated as a kinsman of Queen Mary, was accused of being connected with the assassination of President Minard, who was pistolled in the streets at night, during the Huguenot turmoils. He was further accused of a design to fire Paris in several quarters, to achieve the liberation of all who were incarcerated for religion's sake. These accusations failed, but they rankled in the heart of Stuart—a bold, wild, and reckless spirit, who fought at the Battle of Dreux in 1662, when the Protestants, under Condé, were defeated, and their leader taken prisoner by the Duke de Guise, who shared his couch the night after with his mortal enemy and slept soundly by his side.

Stuart also fought at the Battle of St. Denis in 1567, where he slew with his own hand the veteran constable, the general of the Catholics, and where the Huguenots were defeated in consequence of their inferior numbers. The constable's death is thus recorded by Daulio in his *Civil Wars of France*, folio, 1646:—

The constable had received four wounds on the face and a great one from a battle-axe on the head, yet was endeavouring to rally his soldiers, when Robert Stuart rode up with his pistol, and "bent towards him"; whereupon the constable said, "Dost thou not know me? I am the constable!"

"Yes, I do," he replied; "and because I know thee I present thee this!" and shot him through the shoulder; but, as he was falling, Montmorencie hurled his broken sword with such force in Stuart's face that he beat out some of his teeth, broke his jawbone, and laid him on the field for dead. The constable was then abandoned and left to die by his soldiers. He was in his eightieth year. Stuart survived to fight again in the Battle of Brissar, on the 16th of March, 1669, but was taken prisoner and poniarded to death, probably by some friends of the constable. Another Robert Stuart would seem to have been about this time imprisoned on some charge in the castle of Vincennes, from which he escaped and fled.

Among the Scottish auxiliaries who served Henry III against the German and Swiss mercenaries who entered France in support of the King of Navarre was Mark Alexander Boyd, younger of Pinkhill, an extraordinary genius and scholar, author of *Eptstolæ Heroicum* and many other poetical and learned works, who was content to "trail a pike" as a poor private soldier till he was severely wounded in the ankle, and whose adventures, literary and otherwise, read like a romance. He died at Pinkhill in 1601; but a sketch of his life was written by Lord Hailes in 1783, and an excellent portrait of him was engraved by De Leu.

Among the Scots who fought at Coutras was William Duncan, younger of Airdrie; and Maynor, whose father had been taken prisoner at the Battle of Flodden.[1] In after years William had to fly from Scotland, as an enemy of Cardinal Beaton and a reformer. A wound in the bridle-arm at Coutras ended his soldiering as a Huguenot. Joining his kinsman, Mark Alexander Boyd, at Toulon, he engaged in poetry and controversial literature, and, with his second brother, Mark, took a high place among the learned of France. Some of his poems were inscribed to Henry IV, and one to his friend, the celebrated Balzac. Mark became physician to the royal household, and founded a branch of the Fifeshire Duncans in France, where his descendants still exist, (as at time of first publication). (*Old Scott. Reg.,* vol. 1114)

In 1853 we find William Baillie of Cormiston designed archer of the cross to Henry III King of France—a term of which it is difficult to define the meaning, though it is given him in the Scottish Privy Council Register in that year.

In the wars between Henry of Navarre and the Catholics the Scots in France bore their share. Thus, at the memorable Battle of Coutras, fought in 1587 on the plain near the confluence of the Dronne and

1. *The Battle of Flodden Field* by Robert Jones also published by Leonaur.

l'Isle, between these portions, when the squadrons of the Protestant chiefs, Tremouille and Turenne, were pierced by the charge of Lovardine, a slender company of Scottish gentlemen, who fought on the side of the former, attracted the attention of all the field, according to D'Aubigné and Mathieu.

Though formed up to support the reeling troops, and exposed to the whole shock of the victors, they would not yield a foot of ground, but fought shoulder to shoulder. They were without *cuirasses*, and had, we are told, only buff jerkins with thin plates of metal between the folds, and nearly every man of them was wounded. Henry of Navarre saw, with regret, their captain, called the Master of Wemyss (probably a mistake for Sir John, second son of Sir John Wemyss, twenty-first of that ilk), carried on the shoulders of David Herriot, one of his followers; and the king is said, "from observing the solicitude and care of the latter for his master's life, to have engaged him in his own service. What this Scottish troop suffered may be reckoned the hardest part of the loss sustained by the conquerors in this Battle of Coutras, as their whole loss is stated to have been only five gentlemen and thirty soldiers."

In 1588 Henry III was assassinated, and the succession to the throne of France was left open to the King of Navarre, who, early in the following year, was acknowledged as their master. Says the Duc de Sully in his memoirs:

Henry no longer doubted when he saw the Scots guards, who threw themselves at his feet, saying, 'Ah, sire! you are now our long and our master.' And some moments after Messires de Biron, de Dampierri, and several others did the same.

CHAPTER 26

The Scots in France—(Continued)

We have now reached that period when the 1st Royal Scots, first regiment of the British line, and the oldest in the world, makes its appearance in the military history of France.

Milner, a historian of the 18th century, designates the regiment "an old Scots corps" of uncertain date; but Sir John Hepburn (already referred to in our account of the Scots in Sweden) was commissioned as its colonel in France on the 26th January, 1683, the same date given in the British army lists. Says the War Office Record:

> This corps must have existed for some time as *independent companies* previously to its being constituted a regiment, as Père Daniel (*Histoire de la Milice Française*) states that it was sent from Scotland to France in the reign of James VI, and this monarch commenced his reign in 1567, when only a child, and died in 1625; hence it is evident that it had been in France some years before its formation as a regiment under Sir John Hepburn.

Père Daniel alludes to it in connection with Henry IV, associates its services with the wars of the League, and fixes the date of its arrival in France about 1590. The companies from which it was constituted are supposed to have been raised by men who served in the Scots Archer Guard; and as that force had ceased to exist, "the Royals," says the Record quoted, " may be considered as the representatives of that ancient body." It is certain that "the King of Scotland permitted his subjects to aid the Protestant cause, and several companies of Scottish foot were raised and sent to France in 1691."

The Duke de Sully refers to 4,000 Scots and English who came over about 1689, and refers to Scottish miners whom he employed at the siege of Dreux in 1593. (*Memoirs*, vol. i)

The English quitted France in 1696; but Henry IV, having discovered the value of these companies of hardy and valiant Scots, retained them in his service, (says the War Office Record.)

Birrel states in his diary that on the 12th July, 1606, the King of France's guard "mustered very bravely on the Links of Leith," were sworn, and thereafter received their pay; but this could only refer to recruits of the more ancient force—the Scots *garde-du-corps*, which was cavalry.

In 1610 Henry IV had been preparing for war with Austria, when he was murdered in the streets of Paris. After his death, his son, Louis XIII, being a minor, the intention was abandoned, and a part of the army was disbanded.

Ten years after, Louis XIII was uniting Bearn to the crown and restoring to the Catholics the churches appropriated by the Huguenots, who again prepared for war; and thus ere long the king found himself reduced to the necessity of besieging some of his other towns, among others St. Jean d'Angeli, on the Charente, one of the most vigorous defenders of which was the Rev. John Welch, of Nithsdale, formerly minister of Kirkcudbright, a distinguished divine (who, curiously enough, had begun life as a mosstrooper, but was banished by James VI for opposing episcopacy in 1606).

In St. Jean d'Angeli, which was strongly fortified, he had officiated as a clergyman for sixteen years when it was besieged by Louis XIII. The citizens were greatly encouraged in the defence by the fiery precepts and example of Mr. Welch, who took a place on the walls and served the cannon with his own hands, and when the town capitulated he boldly continued to preach as usual. On this Louis sent the Duke d'Epernon to bring him into his presence.

The duke appeared with a party of soldiers in the church and summoned Mr. Welch from the pulpit; but the latter coolly requested him to take a seat "and listen to the word of God." The duke did so, and heard the sermon to its close; but then took the preacher to the king, before whom Mr. Welch knelt and prayed for wisdom and assistance. Louis asked him sternly how he dared to preach on the verge of the court of France. He replied:

First I preach that you must be saved by the death and merits of Christ, and not your own; and I am sure conscience tells you that *your* own good works will never merit Heaven. Next, I preach that, as you are King of France, there is no man on earth above you; but those preachers whom you have, subject you to the Pope, which I will never do.

"Very well," replied Louis, whom the last remark gratified, "you shall be my minister," and dismissed him with an assurance of his protection.

When the town was besieged a second time, in 1621, "the king," says the *Atlas Geographicus*, 1711, "charged those who stormed it to take particular care that no hurt was done to Mr. Welch, or anyone belonging to him." He was sent under escort to Rochelle. He dared not then return to Loudon, but afterwards died there, under banishment, in his 53rd year. His widow, Elizabeth Knox, third daughter of the Reformer, died at Ayr in 1625.

In the paths of peace as well as those of war, other Scotsmen have distinguished themselves Among these we may mention David Home and the Strachans. "David Home," says Marchond, "was a Scotsman by birth, and of a very distinguished family, in which there have been frequently noblemen." He lived in the end of the 16th century, and was in succession minister of the reformed churches in Lower Guienne and Orleans—1603-20. He wrote against the Jesuits, and the assassination of Henry IV by the madman Ravaillac is said to have been occasioned greatly by his pen.

The Strachans were zealous Catholics—James and George, who enjoyed the protection of Cardinals Barberini and Dupenon. One of them was principal of the College of Loudon, where Verbon Grondier was tried and burned for sorcery, and where, in 1632, the *Supérieure* was examined on her possession by devils and her knowledge of Latin and requested the devil who possessed her to say "*aqua*" in the Scottish language."

By the year 1623 the Scottish guard in France would seem to have become somewhat decayed, as in that year, Balfour records, Lord Colville went to France to have it established according to its "first institution"; and the *History of the Earldom of Sutherland* states that in July, 1625, Lord Gordon made a muster of the corps on the Links of Leith, when his younger brother. Lord Melgum, was appointed lieutenant. The first gentleman of the company was Sir William Gordon, younger of Kindroch.

We have stated in its place how the result of the battle of Nordbrigen almost ruined the Protestant interests in Germany, but soon after the court of France agreed to support the declining cause; a

French army approached the Rhine, and several towns in Alsace received French garrisons.

In 1627 there was sent to France, by order of Charles I, a singular force—a strong band of archers under Alexander Macnaghton of that ilk, to serve in France, for whence they sailed with a number of the Mackinnon clan, accompanied by many pipers and harpers. (*Trans, Antiq. Soc. Scot.*)

In 1633 Sir John Hepburn obtained the command of the chief Scottish regiment, with the rank of *maréchal de camp*, according to Father Loguille, the Jesuit At this time (Sir Thomas Urquhart states) there were, among others, Scots who were colonels of horse and foot under Louis XIII—Sir Andrew Gray, Sir John Foulerton, Sir John Seton, Sir Patrick Murray, John Campbell, the future Earl of Irwin; Colonels Andrew Lindsay, Thomas Hume, John Forbess, John Leslie, Mowat, Morrison, and Livingstone. Sir John Seton was the oldest Scottish officer in the service, having been a captain in the guards in 1608. (*Mem. of the Somervilles.*) Andrew Rutherford of Hunthill also had a regiment, which he commanded till 1680, when he became a lieutenant-general. (*Douglas Peerage.*)

Among the privates in Hepburn's regiment in 1634 was a pikeman, John Middleton, who, after distinguishing himself on many occasions, rose in after years to be Earl of Middleton, general of Scottish cavalry, governor of Edinburgh Castle, and died in command of the combined English and Scottish troops at Tangiers in 1763.

In 1634 Jacques Nonpar, *maréchal de la force*, opened the new campaign, which was to spread the frontiers of France far beyond those of Champagne and Picardy; and on this expedition marched Sir John Hepburn with his regiment and several other Scottish commanders. The former had soon an opportunity of showing the skill he had won in besieging under the great Gustavus at the reduction of La Mothe, in March, which was entrusted to him and the regiments of Turenne and De Toneins, while La Force with the rest of the army penetrated into Lorraine.

The blockade lasted five months, during which Hepburn lost many of his best soldiers in assaults, against which the besiegers hurled enormous stones, which, says the Chevalier Andrew Ramsay, Knight of St. Lazare, "split into 1,000 pieces, killing and wounding all who dared to approach." (*Hist. de Turenne, par le Chev.* Ramsay, Paris, 1735.)

On the fall of La Mothe Hepburn received orders to rejoin the *maréchal de la force*, whom he joined with six regiments of pikes and musketeers, seven squadrons of horse, and a train of guns, after crossing the Rhine at Monninghein, and thus securing for his leader the safe passage of the great river of Germany. The famous Capuchin, Father Joseph du Tremblay, at this time accompanied the French army, and often thrust his advice upon its leaders. As the column of Hepburn approached Monninghein he pointed out on a map the various fortified towns which might be reduced with ease at other points. "Not so fast. Father Joseph," said Hepburn; "towns are not taken by a finger end," which reply was long a proverb in the French army.

The winter had come now, snow covered the mountains, and ice blocks were crashing in the narrow gorges through which the Neckar foamed towards the Rhine, while the troops, in half-armour and buffs, toiled on towards the high and heavy brow of the Juttenbuhl, where stood the "English Buildings," as they are misnamed—a palace erected by Elizabeth Stuart in imitation of a part of old Linlithgow Palace, her happy Scottish home. Here Hepburn broke the blockade of the Imperialists, relieved a Swedish garrison, and took possession of Heidelberg on the 23rd December.

The *maréchal de la force* and Hepburn now formed a junction with the Swedish army of the Duke of Saxe-Weimar at Loudon, consisting of 4,000 horse and 7,000 infantry—the latter of which were nearly all Scotsmen—the veterans of Gustavus. Among them was the remnant of the Green brigade, who hailed their old commander with joy, and beat the *Scottish March* at his approach, while one solitary piper—the last of Mackay's regiment—blew his notes of welcome, and all the survivors of the long career of Swedish glory were now incorporated in the *Régiment d'Hebron*, as it was named in the French service, and with it the Swedish regiment, whilom of Hepburn.

The strength of the latter was given in 1637 at the following:— The lieutenant-colonel, Munro; the major, Sir Patrick Monteith; 45 captains, one captain-lieutenant, 93 subalterns, 12 staff-officers, one piper, 664 non-commissioned officers, 96 drummers, and 48 companies of 150 pikes and muskets, making a grand total of 8,316 men, representing thus the Scoto-Bohemian bands of Sir Andrew Gray and all the Scotch corps of Gustavus Adolphus. By order of Louis XIII it was to take the right of all regiments then embodied.

Frequent quarrels now ensued between the regiment of Hepburn and that of Picardy, the oldest of the French line (raised in 1562), and commanded by the Duc de Charost, as they treated with ridicule the claims of Hepburn's corps to antiquity, and called them "Pontius Pilot's Guard," a *sobriquet* retained by the Royal Scots to this day. Thus, on one occasion, after a sharp dispute on some contested point of honour, an officer of Hepburn's said laughingly to one of the regiment of Picardy.

"We must be mistaken, *Monsieur*, for had *we* really been the guards of Monsieur Pontius Pilate, and done duty at the Sepulchre, the Holy Body had never left it," implying that Scottish soldiers would not have slept upon their posts, whereas those of the *Régiment de Picardy* did.

In the turns of the campaign at the village of Fresche, the enemy, under the Duke of Lorraine, fell unexpectedly upon the columns commanded by Hepburn and the famous Turenne, and a desperate conflict ensued. While each main body disputed the ground with the other, Hepburn—according to the folio *Histoire de Lorraine*—led 200 Scottish musketeers to the left flank of the foe, while the Chevalier Orthe, of Turenne's corps, led 100 French to the right, and both poured in a cross-ire, till Hepburn gave the order to "charge," and, with a rush downhill, all fell on with clubbed muskets—the bayonet was yet unknown—and the troops of Lorraine gave way; but famine compelled the French to retire.

At Bingen the Rhine was crossed again by a pontoon-bridge, while Hepburn and his Scots covered the sea. Says the memoir of the Duke d'Epernon, folio, 1670:

They fought for eight days, almost without intermission, leaving the ways by which they retreated more remarkable by the blood of their enemies than their own.

Not daring to halt, without food, encumbered by heavy armour and clumsy matchlocks, short of ammunition and all stores, the now dejected French troops traversed pathless woods and mountains, pursued by the Imperialists, who covered all the country; but Hepburn and Henri de la Tour d'Auvergne were conspicuous among the officers who encouraged the sick and the weary; and it was generally remarked that on this desperate retreat none suffered less than the hardy Scots of the *Régiment d'Hébron*.

In Paris the greatest alarm prevailed; Richelieu found himself on the brink of ruin, by ebb of that war he had undertaken for the glory of France, and the year 1635 closed in doubt and dread.

Louis XIII now ordered the diploma of a marshal of France to be expedited under his great seal at the court of Versailles for Sir John Hepburn, but the latter was fated not to receive it.

After the treaty of 1636 between the great cardinal and Duke Bernard of Saxe-Weimar against the emperor, Hepburn, with his Scottish regiment, above 8,000 strong, joined the duke, and the new campaign was opened with the siege of Taverne, which was obstinately defended, as the garrison daily expected to be relieved by Count Galas, who had given the governor. Colonel Mulheim, a promise to that effect; and Taverne was doomed to be the last scene of the gallant Hepburn's long and brilliant career.

Mulheim's garrison was numerous and resolute (*Hist. D'Alsace,* fol., 1727), and the town, situated among chestnut woods, then in all the foliage of May, was overlooked by beautiful scenery. The only approach to the citadel—whilom a castle of the Bishops of Strasburg—was a narrow pathway hewn out of the solid rock, steep, narrow, and swept by heavy cannon.

By the 9th June the breach in the walls was practicable, and the French, Scots, and German stormers advanced to the assault, pikes in front, musketry in rear, and colours flying over the helmets that glittered in the sun. Says an eye-witness:

> Nothing was heard for a time but the clash of swords and pikes, heavier blows of dubbed muskets and swung partisans as they struck fire from tempered corslets and morions, amid which the tall plumes of Hepburn, Turenne, and Count Jean of Hanau were seen floating in the foremost ranks, while the shouts of the victorious, the cries of the despairing and dying, the roar of muskets, arquebuses, and pistols, with the deeper boom of culverin and cannon-royal (48-pounder), seemed only to lend a greater fury to the stimulus of the assailants.'

Three hours the assault continued, but the stormers had to retire at last, leaving 400 men lying in the breach, the chief of whom, the Count of Hanau, was shot through the brain

A second and third assault were attempted with equally bad success, says the *Histoire de Turenne,* In an attempt to storm the postern Hepburn's regiment lost 60 men, and it was at this crisis their gallant leader fell. Rashly he had ventured to reconnoitre the great breach too closely, when a ball from the ramparts struck him in the neck, piercing his gorget. He fell from his horse, and was borne away by the Scots, to whom his fall was the signal for a fourth and furious assault. (*Mercure Français, tom.* xxi.)

It was led by Viscomte Turenne. The town was won, and the shouts

"A BALL FROM THE RAMPARTS STRUCK HIM
IN THE NECK."

of victory were the last sounds that reached the ears of the dying Hepburn as he lay with a crowd of his sorrowing comrades—the veterans of Bohemian, Swedish, and Bavarian wars—around him; and "his last words were touchingly expressive of regret that he should be buried so far from the secluded kirkyard where the bones of his forefathers lay," in Athelstaneford.

He was not quite in his 38th year. Wrote Cardinal Richelieu to Cardinal La Valette:

> I find it exceedingly difficult upon whom to bestow the colonel's regiment, because his eldest captain, who is related to him, is a Huguenot, and the Catholics earnestly petition to have it conferred upon one of their party, among whom we find the Lion Douglas, who is descended from one of the best families in Scotland.

Sir John Hepburn, who, as a contemporary writer, Lithgow, states, won the reputation of being "the best soldier in Christendom, and consequently in the world," was interred under a noble monument, which was erected to his memory by Louis XIV, in the left transept of the cathedral of Toul, but was destroyed by the Revolutionists in 1793.

By a letter from Père Georges, *curé* of the cathedral, the author was informed, in October, 1852, that during some repairs the coffin of the Scottish hero had been found and reinterred under a monument erected by the Emperor Napoleon III.

On the fall of Taverne Louis XIII conferred the command of the great Scottish regiment on Lieutenant-Colonel James Hepburn, who had borne that rank under Gustavus in 1632. He was of the ancient house of Waughton, whence sprang the Earls of Bothwell, and was soon after killed at the head of the corps when serving; but the circumstances connected with his fall are unknown.

At the close of 1637 he was succeeded by Lord James Douglas, son of the first Marquis of Douglas (who had won renown in the wars between Austria and the Protestant League), and in the following year the regiment joined the army under Maréchal de Chastillon to reduce Artois, then forming a portion of the Spanish Netherlands.

In that service, on the 12th July, at the siege of St. Omers, a strong force of the enemy attempted to scour the trenches held by Douglas's Scots, who repulsed them with a great loss in killed, wounded, and taken. (*Mercure Français.*)

At the siege of Hesdin, in 1639, the regiment was formed in brigade with that of Champagne; and in a conflict with the Spaniards, under the Marquis de Fuentes, lost four pieces of cannon. It was in 1648, when the Douglas regiment was under the orders of the Prince of Savoy at the siege of Turin in Piedmont, that the battalions of Scots guards before referred to, after serving at Runcroy and elsewhere under the Prince of Condé, were incorporated with the already numerous battalion of the Royal Scots regiment, and all formed the garrison of Turin after the surrender of the city on the 27th September.

The officers of one of these Guard battalions (the Earl of Irwin, Lord Saltoun, and others) raised an action against the King of France in the Scots Courts for the expense of this corps. (See *Trans, Antiq. Soc.*, 1859.)

The years 1644 and 1645 saw them fighting in the Netherlands in the division of Marshal Meilleraie, like other Scottish regiments (those of Chambers, Proslin, etc.), covering themselves with glory, while England was torn by the great Civil War, and Scotland was involved with that of the Covenant; and in 1648 "a troop of Scots *cuirassiers* and the regiment of Scots guards had an opportunity of distinguishing themselves at the battle of Lens, in Artois, under the Prince of Condé. The Spanish army, commanded by the Archduke Leopold, suffered a complete overthrow, lost 38 pieces of cannon, 100 standards, and colours." (W. O. Records.) In 1647 all the soldiers of Colonel Macdonald taken in Jura were given to Colonel Sir Henry Sinclair for his regiment, then in the French service.

In 1648 a treaty, concluded at Munster, gave peace to the most of Europe; but the war went on between France and Spain; and on the 6th May, 1649, 300 veteran Scots, who had been left to defend Ypres, in Flanders, after a fierce and desperate resistance, surrendered, but marched out with the honours of war, with drums beating and St. Andrew's Cross flying.

CHAPTER 27

The Scots in France—(Continued)

Charles II, when in exile, curiously enough prevailed upon Andrew Lord Gray of Kinfauns, when lieutenant of the Gendarmes Ecossais (under the captainship of the Duke of Albany), to resign that post in favour of the Marshal Schomberg, and, according to Douglas in his *Peerage*, no Scotsman ever possessed it again; but this is doubtful.

It is a little after this period that we find the Cuthberts—the Scoto-French family of Castlehill—coming into prominence, when Jean Baptiste Cuthbert, born at Rheims in 1619, in a house in the Rue de Ceres, was recommended to King Louis by Cardinal Mazarin in 1662-3, and made comptroller-general of France, and as such made the riches of the kingdom consist "in commerce," says Anquetil in his *Memoirs*, He died in 1683, full of fame as a minister of finance and marine, leaving a son behind, Marquis of Signaley, who was proved to claim his descent from the Cuthberts of Castlehill.

In a certificate lately furnished, under the seal of the Lord Lyon, of the descent of John Cuthbert, Baron of Castlehill, and of Jean Hay of Dalgetty, his spouse, the family seem to have been settled in Inverness "about the year 950," a little after the accession of Kenneth II. Their residence was the Auld Castlehill, once royal, now in ruins. Lord Lyon cites an Act of 1687, certifying the descent of Jean Baptiste Colbert, Marquis of Signaley, from this family through Edward Colbert, a son thereof, who went to France with Mary Lindsay of Edzell, his spouse, in 1280, accompanying Christian de Baliol (niece of Alexander III) when the latter went to marry Enguerrond de Guines, Lord of Coucy.

The Cuthberts held the lands of Castlehill and others for centuries; were frequently high sheriffs of Inverness; one fought at Harlaw in 1411 and captured the standard of the Lord of the Isles, and one, a hundred years later on, was styled "Alderman of Inverness." (Spot's *Miscel.*, vol. iv.) The family passed away in Scotland about the close of the 18th century; but in 1789 we find one of the French branch speaking in the National Assembly, on the abolition of tithes. In the *Edinburgh Advertiser* for that year he is called "a native of Scotland—Bishop of Rhodes. His name is Cuthbert; but, for what reason we know not, the prelate calls himself Colbert." His brother Lewis was provost-marshal of Jamaica (*Stat. Account.*) But the name is still found in France. Thus, in the *Annuaire Militaire*, 1805, Pierre E. Colbert appears as lieutenant of lancers in the Imperial guard; and in 1887 the wife of Count de Chabot was a Mademoiselle Colbert, for whom Lord Lyon prepared the document above quoted.

In 1650, when the revenues of Louis XIY became impaired, the Douglas regiment, like the most of the French troops, found a difficulty in procuring their pay; and King Charles II, having signed the Covenant, requested the return of the Scottish troops to Scotland; but Louis declined to permit this, and sent them to garrison the barrier towns of Picardy and Flanders; but the summer of 1652 saw them in the vicinity of Paris, under Marshal Turenne, against the insurgents, under Condé fighting at the barricades in the Faubourg St. Antoine, when Douglas's Scots, with whom the Duke of Abory was serving, stormed one of their works near the Seine, sword in hand, with irresistible valour, after which they retired to St. Denis with the king and court. (Clarke's *Hist, James II.*)

Condé now held Paris; the Spanish army entered France, and in the conflicts which ensued at Ablon, seven miles from Paris, Douglas's Scots bore a conspicuous part.

On one of these occasions a captain of his regiment was taken prisoner, but escaped, and brought information that the Prince of Condé had left the Spanish army through indisposition.

The king's army, being in want of provisions, sought winter quarters in Champagne, while the regiment of Douglas pressed the siege of Bar-le-Duc, and captured an Irish regiment in the Spanish service.

Château Portieu, in the Ardennes, was their next scene of service. On the march thither the weather was so severe that many of Douglas's soldiers were frozen to death, but the survivors stormed the town on the 10th of January, 1653.

In 1654 the still powerful regiment was employed in the Netherlands; and in 1655 its colonel, Lieutenant-General Lord James Douglas, commanded the flying camp between Douay and Arras. Many fierce skirmishes ensued, and in one of these he was killed, in October, in the twenty-eighth year of his age. A magnificent monument was erected to his memory in the church of St. Germain des Prés, where it still remains.

Near it is another monument to his grandfather, William, tenth Earl of Angus, one of the leaders of the Catholics in Scotland in 1592. He assumed a religious life, and dying at Paris in 1611, was interred in St. Germain des Prés. Copies of the long and elaborate Latin inscriptions on these two tombs are given in the *Scots Magazine* for 1767.

Lord James was succeeded in the colonelcy by his brother, Lord George, afterwards Earl of Dumbarton, referred to in the well-known song of "Dumbarton's drums beat bonnie, O!" In his youth he had been page of honour to Louis XIV, and made the profession of arms his choice.

In 1660 the French army was greatly reduced in strength, and Dumbarton's regiment of eight battalions was disbanded, all but eight companies, when in garrison at Avenues; and when—after the Restoration—Scotland and England began to form separate armies of guards, horse and foot, the Duke of Albany's troop of guards from Dunkirk and the regiment of Dumbarton from Flanders returned to Britain in 1661; but the latter returned to the French service in the following year.

At that time General Andrew Rutherford, afterwards Earl of Teviot, commander of a battalion of Scots guards in the French army, was governor of Dunkirk, and his corps was incorporated with that of Dumbarton, which in 1662 consisted of 23 companies of 100 files each, making a total of all ranks of above 2,500 men.

Three years after its return to France war broke out between Britain and Holland, and as Louis took part with the latter, the regiment of Dumbarton finally quitted the French service for that of its native country, and landed at Rye, in Sussex, on the 11th June, 1666, when reduced to 800 men. (Salmon's *Chron.*, *etc.*) All that follows may be stated briefly.

After being twelve months in Ireland, the regiment returned to the French service at the peace of Breda in 1668; and in an order issued by Louis XIY, 1670, respecting the rank of regiments, it appears as one of the first. (*Père Daniel.*)

In the war that broke out between France and the states-general in 1672, Dumbarton's regiment, now augmented to 16 companies, joined the division of Marshal Turenne, and under the Compte de Chomilly was at the siege and reduction of Grom in July. In 1674 the regiment, with the Scots battalion of Hamilton, served with Turenne's army on the Rhine, and in June was encamped at Philipsburg in Western Germany, with the brigade of Brigadier-General the Marquis of Douglas.

After an incredible deal of fighting, marching) and manoeuvring during' three years on the Rhine and in Alsace under the Marshals Luxembourg and de Gregin, the corps, in the spring of 1678, quitted the French service for ever; and since then, as the *First Royal Scots*, have been the premier regiment of the British army, and possesses a very long inheritance of history unequalled in the annals of war and glory.

At the Revolution the Earl of Dumbarton adhered to King James VII, whom he followed to France, where he died in 1692.

Among many others who followed the king into exile were David Viscount Dundee, K.T., who died in 1700; and James Galloway, third Lord Dunkeld, who had joined the brother of the former peer, and was with him at Killiecrankie, who fell in action a colonel in the French service, in which his son James attained the rank of a general officer, with a high reputation for valour and skill. His name appears in the French *Liste des Officiers Généraux* for May 10, 1748, as "my Lord Dunkell," and he was alive in 1764; but of him nothing more is known.

The period 1693-7 brings us to one of the most touching episodes in the story of our military exiles—the fate of the surviving officers of the army of Lord Dundee: men whose magnanimity was worthy of the most glorious ages of Athens and of Sparta. "It is delightful," wrote Robert Chambers, "to record the generous abandonment of all selfish considerations, and the utter devotion to a lofty and beautiful moral principle, which governed the actions of this noble band of gentlemen."

According to terms made, the surviving officers of Dundee's army were to have their work confined to France according to the tenor of their Scottish commissions; and so long as there was a hope of a successful landing on the British coast their pay was continued, till, on the paltry pretext of expedience, it was withdrawn, and they, only 150 in number, were reduced to penury, while Dutchmen were exalted to rank and power at home. Generously these Scottish officers made common stock of their jewellery, rings, and watches, and so forth, till starvation came upon them, and they obtained King James's permission to form themselves into a company of private soldiers for the service of King Louis. Previous to joining the army of Marshal Noailles, they took farewell of their native monarch at St. Germain—a last farewell it proved to most of them.

Of this most remarkable company Colonel Thomas Brown was captain; Colonels Andrew Scott and Alexander Gordon were lieutenants; Major James Buchan was ensign. The sergeants were three other officers, Jenner, Lyon, and Gordon; and in the rank-and-file men were three field-officers and forty-two captains. The rest were subalterns. One of the captains, John Ogilvie, afterwards killed on the banks of the Rhine, was author of the sweet song—

Adieu for evermore, my love,
Adieu for evermore.

King James VII chanced to be going forth to hunt on the morning when they paraded before the palace of his exile, in French uniform, with their fixed bayonets shining in the sun.

"What troops are these?" asked the king.

"Your Majesty's devoted Scottish subjects," replied an equerry; "but yesterday they all bore your Majesty's commission—*today* they are privates in the army of France."

Then James dismounted and approached them, nearly overcome with emotion. Said he:

Gentlemen, it grieves me beyond expression to see so many brave and loyal officers of my army reduced to the station of private sentinels. The sense of all you have undergone and lost has impressed me so deeply, and it ever please God to restore me to the throne of my ancestors, your services and your sufferings will be remembered? At your own desire you are going away far from me. Fear God; love one another; write your wants particularly to me, and you will ever find me your father and your king. (Dundas's *Officers*, 1714.)

With deep emotion they heard him; he received a list of their names, and, covering his face with his handkerchief sobbed heavily, while the whole line sank upon their knees, and bowed their heads. Then the word "march" was given, and they parted forever.

Perpignon in Rousillon was their first destination; then, after a journey of 900 miles in heavy marching order, they joined the army of Marshal Noailles.

"*Le gentilhomme est toujours gentilhomme,*" exclaimed that officer when he saw them.

The ladies of the city presented them with a purse of 200 *pistoles,* and bough tall their rings that remained—a *souvenir des officiers écossais;* and wherever they went the tears of the women and the acclamations of the men welcomed them.

On the 27th of May, 1693, this company, with some other Scottish companies, one entirely composed of deserters from the 1st Royal Scots, and two of Irish, mounted the trenches, at the siege of Rozas, on the coast of Catalonia. Major Rutherford led the Scottish grenadiers, and Colonel Brown commanded the whole; and so furious was the assault, that the governor beat a *chômage* and capitulated.

"*Ces sont mes enfants!*" cried Marshal Noailles, as he saw them storming the breach.

"By St. Iago, they alone have made us surrender!" cried the Spanish governor afterwards.

From thence they marched to Piscador, in the plain of the Fluvia, in that awful snow, when 16,000 men perished out of an army of 23,000, by starvation chiefly. Famine and the bullet slew many, but three-halfpence *per diem* sufficed to feed the Scottish officers, who were fain to eat horse-beans and garlic.

At Silistadt their sufferings increased, in that they had to part with their wigs and stockings for food. Bread they were unable to buy. In 1693 they marched to old Brissac, and 1697 saw them on the Rhine, where they performed one of the greatest military exploits of the age.

Chapter 28

The Scots in France—(Continued)

M. Necker de Saussure, in his *Voyage en Ecosse et aux Iles Hébrides*, 1806-8, refers pleasantly to the influence which he thought the ancient French alliance had on Scotland and her people. He wrote:

It is above all that, in relation to *strangers*, that the Scottish character is displayed to the greatest advantage. Hospitality in all its finest shades and under every form is the national virtue of Scotland. The inhabitants do not partake in the least of the coldness and prejudice towards foreigners, which is so justly the reproach of the best society in England. . . . In looking for the causes of this remarkable difference, we shall find them in the intimate relations which formerly existed between the kingdom of Scotland and continental governments, in particular the French nation.

This country (France) has always been the bitterest enemy and rival of England, and was, on the contrary, the closest ally of Scotland. The Scots ever enjoyed in France, up to the time of the Revolution, privileges from which other nations were excluded. They were exempt from the taxes on foreigners; they had at Paris a college consecrated to the Scottish Catholics and regulated by Scottish professors. Scotland also famished to the kings of France a company of bodyguards. So many privileges encouraged the nobles and gentlemen to travel in France, to educate their children there, and frequently to establish themselves in that country. They learned the French language, spoke it with facility, and on their return to their own country they introduced the tone and manners of the court of Versailles.

Towards the end of the 18th century, one of the most remarkable

Scots in the French army was John Oswald, a native of Edinburgh, who, in 1792, became a *chef de battalion* of that ferocious Republican army which marched against La Vendee.

His parents kept a coffee-house in the Parliament Close, celebrated in its day as John's Coffee-house, and there he is supposed to have been born about the year 1760. He served an apprenticeship to a jeweller, and in a frolic enlisted in the 18th Royal Irish, but, on succeeding to a good legacy, purchased an ensigncy in the 42nd Highlanders, to which corps he was gazetted on the 25th August, 1778.

On the 22nd March, 1780, he became lieutenant in the 2nd battalion, with which, in the January of the following year, he embarked at Portsmouth, under Colonel Norman Macleod of that ilk, for the West Indies, where he served for three years, and quickly made himself master of Latin and Creek. In 1783 he appeared in London, where he speedily distinguished himself as a violent Radical and pamphleteer, whose writings were "full of crude notions, absurd principles, and dangerous speculations." He also affected to imitate the Brahmins, and abstained from animal food. His verses won him the approbation of Robert Burns; and for the press he adopted the *nom de plume* of Sylvester Otway. His last work in London was *The Cry of Nature*, published in 1791.

The next year found him in Paris, when the fury of the Revolution was at its height, and when a new edition of his first pamphlet, *A Review of the Constitution of Great Britain*, with several addenda, soon won him admittance to the Jacobin Club, in which he gained such influence as to take a leading part in all its bloodthirsty projects. Eventually he was nominated by the Revolutionary government to the command of a regiment of infantry, "*sans culottes*," raised from the scum of Paris and the departments.

On being joined by his two sons, in the true spirit of equality he made them drummers! His adherence to discipline—won no doubt, in the old "Black Watch"—soon made him unpopular with the lawless scoundrels he led; and on attempting, it is said, to substitute an efficient pike for the wretched muskets with which they were armed, they mutinied against him.

His corps was one of the first employed in La Vendée, in that war which, for a time, the Royalists prosecuted with success from 1793 to 1795—a resistance singularly favoured by the woods, wilds, and thickets of the country; and then he was reported to be killed in battle; but the real story of his fate was that his own men took the opportunity of shooting him, his two sons, and an Englishman who held a commission in the regiment.

A few years after, a clergyman of Edinburgh published a work proving, to his own satisfaction at least, that Oswald was *not* shot in La Vendée; but, escaping, appeared in time as Napoleon Bonaparte! (Stuart's *Sketches*, etc.)

Under the First Empire there rose to the highest rank, civil and military, two men of old Scottish families—Law, who became Marquis of Lauriston and marshal of France; and Macdonald, who became Duke of Tarentum and also a marshal of France. The family of the former have taken deep root there, though the antecedents of their name were against them; for the first of them, in the land of their adoption, was the famous financial projector, John Law, who nearly brought ruin upon it in the reign of Louis XV; and whose varied adventures seem to pertain to romance rather than to solid history.

Descended from the Laws of Lithrie in Fifeshire, John Law was the only son of William Law, a goldsmith in Edinburgh, where he was born in April, 1671, probably in the Parliament Close, though some have averred, in the Tower of Lauriston. Though bred to no profession, early in life he exhibited a singular capacity for calculation. On the death of his father, he succeeded to the estate and Tower of Lauriston, an ancient mansion of the Merchiston Napiers, beautifully situated near the Firth of Forth, an edifice greatly embellished in recent years by Andrew Rutherford, Lord Advocate of Scotland. Gambling debts soon involved Law deeply, but his estate being entailed, it was saved. Tall, handsome, and much addicted to gallantry, he went to London, where he soon became well-known as Beau Law, and where he had a mortal quarrel with another young man known as Beau Wilson, an aspirant for fashionable fame about the end of the reign of William of Orange.

The dispute began between them on the 9th April, 1694, at the Fountain Inn, in the Strand, and a meeting was arranged for them by a Captain Wightmore, at a place then remote from streets, Bloomsbury, where the gallants of the period settled affairs of honour; and there, after one pass, Law ran Wilson through the body and killed him on the spot. "The cause of the quarrel arose from his (Wilson) taking away his own sister," says Evelyn, "from a lodging in a house where Law had a mistress, which the mistress of the house thinking a disparagement to it, and losing by it, instigated Law to this duel."

Law declared the meeting to be accidental A Scotsman was little likely to get justice in London then, so a jury found him guilty of murder; but, pending a commutation of sentence. Law escaped from the King's Bench, reached the Continent in safety, and was afterwards pardoned in 1717. Prior to this he had revisited Scotland, where, in 1701, he published, at Glasgow, "Proposals for Constituting a Council of Trade in Scotland;" but these, and other schemes, found no favour with the Scottish Parliament. Proceeding to France, he had recourse to gaming for his subsistence, and won enormous sums at play.

On obtaining an introduction to the Duke of Orleans, he offered his monetary scheme to Chomillart, the Minister of Finance, who deemed it so perilous that he ordered him to quit Paris in four-and-twenty hours; and in a similar manner it procured his expulsion from Genoa and Venice; but such was his success in play, that, on returning to Paris after the succession of Orleans to the Regency, he was in possession of fully £100,000 sterling; and having been fortunate enough to secure the patronage of the Regent, by letters patent, 2nd March, 1716, his bank was established, with a capital of 1,200 shares of 5,000 *livres* each, which soon bore a premium.

His bank became the office for all public receipts, and in 1717 there was annexed to it the famous Mississippi scheme, in which immense fortunes were realised, and the stock of which rose from 500 *livres* to 10,000 by the time the mania reached its zenith, and a frenzy seemed to possess the public mind.

Law's house in the Rue Quinquinpoix was hourly beset with applicants, who blocked up the street and rendered all progress impossible; for all ranks—peers, prelates, citizens, and mechanics, learned and unlearned, and even ladies of the highest rank, flocked to that Temple of Plutus, till Law was compelled to transfer his place for business to the Place Vendôme, where the tumult and noise became so great that he was again obliged to move, and purchased, at an enormous price, from the Prince de Carigna, the Hôtel Soissons, in the beautiful gardens of which he held his levies, and allotted stock to his clamorous clients.

Amid all this whirl Law retained a strong affection for his patrimonial home, "and a story in reference to this is told of a visit paid to him by the Duke of Argyll in Paris, at the time when his splendour and magnificence were at the highest. As an old friend, the duke was admitted directly to Mr. Law, whom he found busily engaged writing. The duke entertained no doubt that the great financier was busied with a subject of the highest importance, as crowds of the most distinguished individuals were waiting in the anterooms for an audience. Great was his Grace's astonishment when he learned that Mr. Law was merely writing to his gardener at Lauriston regarding the planting of cabbages at a particular spot!"

When the crash came, the amount of notes issued from Law's bank more than doubled all specie in France, and great difficulties arose from the scarcity of the latter, which was hoarded up and sent out of the country in large sums; thus tyrannical edicts were promulgated against all persons having more than 500 *livres* in specie, and Law's notes were declared valueless after the 1st November, 1720. The 10th of the following month saw John Law, the comptroller-general of French finance, flying from Paris to his country seat of Guermonde, with only 800 *louis* in his purse, and thence from France, never to return!

After residing in England, he returned to the Continent in 1725, and fixed his residence at Venice, where he died on the 21st March, 1729, in a state of poverty, yet occupied to the last in vast schemes of finance.

He married Lady Catherine Knollys, daughter of the third Earl of Banbury, by whom he had a son, William, and a daughter, who espoused her cousin, Viscount Wallingford, afterwards created Lord Althorpe.

His son, who had been born at Edinburgh in 1675, was protected by the Duchess of Bourbon. He rose to be a *maréchal de camp*, and remained in France. His cousin, James Francis Law, was created Comte de Tancarville receiving the venerable stronghold of that name in Quillebœuf, once the abode of the chamberlains of the Dukes of Burgundy, a grand edifice, stormed and demolished at the Revolution. Charles Grant (Vicomte de Vaux) records that among his brilliant services in India, the Comte de Tancarville, at the head of only 200 Frenchmen, persuaded Shah Zadol with 80,000 to march against the British in Bengal, when the *Shah* was defeated, and, with M. Law, "made prisoner on the same day that Pondicherrry surrendered."

This was on the 15th January, 1761, when the unfortunate Comte de Lally capitulated to Sir Eyre Coote. This was about the same time when a Scottish officer of Lally's, Colonel D. MacGregor, with 600 *sepoys*, 160 Frenchmen, and 1,000 *coolies*, so vigorously defended the ports of Gingce and Thiagur, that he was permitted to march out with all the honours of war.

In 1763, at the peace, Pondicherry was restored to France and Law, the Comte de Tancarville, was appointed governor and commander-in-chief of all the French settlements in the East Indies, where he amassed enormous wealth, most of which was swept away amid the future troubles of the French Indian campaign. His departure for India is thus announced in the London papers of April, 1764:—"Col. Law de Lauriston, appointed governor and commander-in-chief of the French establishments in the East Indies, is to go on board the *Duc de Praslin*, 50 guns, which, in company with the *Chameau* frigate, sails for Pondicherry at the latter end of this month." By his wife, Jeanne Carvalhoo, a lady of the Mauritius, he had six sons and four daughters.

Two of his sons he destined for the French army the eldest, who became marshal of France, was one of these; two others he resolved should be sailors, and the fates of both were miserable. One sailed with the gallant D'Entrecosteon in his voyage round the world, and was heard of no more; the other became an officer in the regiment of Hector, one of the seven battalions of loyal emigrants taken into British pay, and which, in 1796, embarked at Southampton on board of Admiral Warren's fleet for the ill-fated expedition to Cape Quiberon, under the Comtes D'Hervilly and De Pusaye. This little army, consisting chiefly of the regiments of Hector, Hervilly, Dudendrenne, 44th, or Royale-Marine, Royal-Louis, emigrant and artillery, were cut to pieces on the coast, the regiments of Hervilly and Dudendrenne massacring their own officers, according to the last dispatch of the Comte de Sombreuil; and all the prisoners, including young Law, were shot to death, by order of General Hoche.

The fourth son entered the British service in the West Indies, and rose to wealth afterwards as a merchant in the city of London; while the eldest, James Alexander Bernard Law, adhered to the fortunes of the monarchy. He was born at Pondicherry, on the 1st February, 1768, during the governorship of his father, the Comte de Tancarville, and in 1784 was at the Royal Military School of Paris, where, fortunately for himself, he was the fellow-student and friend of another student, Napoleon Bonaparte; and together they quitted the seminary as second lieutenants of artillery. Soon afterwards, Law married the daughter of M. le Duc, Maréchal de Camp and Inspector-General of Artillery, of which there was always a school at La Fère, and there their eldest son was born.

When the political storm of 1792 broke out, James Law with his family fled to Austria, where he accepted a commission under the emperor, and, as A.D.O. to General Beauvoir, served in the futile and severe campaigns against the armies of the Republic. In 1794 he greatly distinguished himself at the siege of Maestricht, when it fell into the hands of the French; and at the investment of Valenciennes, till the conquest of Holland by Pichegru.

Afterwards, in Italy, by a turn of fortune, he was among a party of captured emigrants and Austrians, who were brought before his old brother-student of La Fère, Bonaparte, whose protection he claimed, and who, assured him that there was but one way of escaping the penalty of death, to enter the French service as a private soldier. He did so, and the 6th April, 1796, saw him commanding as *chef de brigade* of horse artillery, and leading that force at Cortiglioniedelle-Stevione, where Bonaparte was defeated in June, and at Arcola, where, in November, the latter was victorious, and compelled the Austrians to raise the siege of Mantua.

Marengo was fought on the 4th June, 1800, and after the victory there, in which the Austrians, though supported by 100 guns loaded with grape, failed signally. Law—or Lauriston, as he was named—was ordered by Bonaparte to organise the 1st Regiment of Artillery on the system of their old 35th Regiment of La Fère; he also appointed him his premier A.D.C., in which capacity he served the campaign of Egypt; and, according to General Bourrienne, he was the most intelligent officer on the staff of the First Consul.

In 1801 he was sent to Denmark to urge that country in its resistance to Britain, and was engaged in many diplomatic missions "which, by the treaty of Amiens in October, 1801, gave to the powers of Europe a brief respite from the bloody occupations of recent years. On the 10th October, "Colonel Lauriston," as he was named in the English papers, arrived in London with the notification of the treaty, and, accompanied by the French plenipotentiary, had the horses taken from his carriage, which was dragged by the joyous populace, with incessant cheers, to their hotel in St. James's Street; when the A.D.C. of the First Consul came frequently to a window and bowed to the masses below, among whom he scattered gold.

He was seen to be tall, handsome, and young, wearing a blue uniform laced with gold, a white vest, and large black stock.

On the 15th he embarked at Dover, and was at Ratisbon, with the rank of brigadier-general, when, so early as September, 1802, the political horizon began to darken again, and he had to threaten the Diet, that unless the war losses were settled in two months, the Republic would send 100,000 bayonets into Germany; and when war was declared, to James Law was assigned the command of the troops ordered against Bavaria, in conjunction with Villeneuve—an expedition never carried out.

In February, 1805, he was appointed general of division, with the diploma of Count Lauriston, taking the title from his old hereditary tower in Linlithgowshire—one in which all his descendants still seem to take a pride.

On the 30th March following he sailed in the fleet of Admiral Villeneuve, with 9,000 men under his orders, to retake Surinam and St. Helena, after ravaging all our settlements on the coast of Guinea. The Count de Dumas, in writing of these things, says, "Singular that Bonaparte, on the eve of his coronation, should have been so intent on the capture of *St Helena!*"

The 13th May saw this expedition running along the beautiful coast of Martinique, where they bombarded the Diamond Rock, "which," says Brenton, "is in form very much resembling a round haystack, one side overhanging its base, but having deep moats all round it." Yet on its crumbling sides, never before trodden by man, our fearless sailors had skilfully formed a battery, after first carrying a cable over it by the string of a kite. Lauriston won the Rock by assault, with the loss of 800 men, and, but for the appearance of Nelson's fleet, might have retaken Martinique. On the 19th his expedition sailed for Europe, when final defeat awaited Villeneuve at Trafalgar, before which Lauriston rejoined the staff of the Emperor at Versailles.

The year 1805 saw him serving in the Austrian campaign, the victory of Austerlitz, and the capture of Vienna; after which he presided, in Presburg, at the execution of that treaty of peace which ended in the removal of all the Imperial arsenals from Venice, of which he was appointed governor in 1807; "and one of his first public acts, after entering the city, was to erect a splendid tomb above the hitherto obscure resting-place of his grand-uncle, John Law, the great financier."

The city and territory of Venice were then annexed to the French kingdom of Italy, and remained so till 1814.

The autumn of 1808 saw Count Lauriston, after attending the emperor at the great conference of Erfurt in Saxony, take his departure for Madrid, then possessed by the French army, with which he shared in some of the fierce encounters with guerillas and other patriots in the suburbs of that city; and when war was again declared against Austria, in 1809, Lauriston was on the staff of Eugene Beauharnais, who was then viceroy of Italy for the emperor, now, in fact supreme in Europe.

With Beauharnais he marched for the banks of the Danube. Deep then was the hatred cherished by Austria for France; thus she suffered herself to be hurried prematurely into a renewal of strife, which ended in swift and terrible disasters, for her finances were confused and her warlike preparations defective.

Lauriston marched through Hungary with Beauharnais, and, before Wagram had been won, on the 14th of June, 1809, Lauriston led more than one brilliant charge in the other battle which took place on the plain near the Raab, between the army of the Archduke John, who had retreated from Italy, supported by the Archduke Palatine with 25,000 Hungarian insurgents, and the French under Beauharnais and Marshal Marmont, each mustering about 50,000 men.

On the 12th and 13th the attacks of the French were repulsed with heavy loss; but, on being reinforced by a strong column under Marshal Davoust, the conflict was resumed on the morning of the 14th, when, after a noble resistance, the gallant but raw Hungarian lines were unable to withstand the well-trained troops of France, and by sunset the two archdukes were compelled to retreat, with the loss of 2,000 men. Beauharnais claimed a great victory; but the Austrians were in such strength at Comorn for some weeks afterwards as to show that the losses of the French rendered them unable to pursue; though the indefatigable Lauriston, pushing on with a column, on the 24th seized Raab, (or Nagy-Gyor), the capital of Buda, a place fortified by nature and art, capturing therein 1,500 men, who surrendered prisoners of war.

The great victory of Wagram followed on the 6th of July. Then Lauriston commanded the artillery of the Imperial guard; and when, in the second day's carnage. Napoleon's left wing fell into disorder, the count, with one hundred guns drawn at full speed, took an able position, opened fire, and swept away the Austrian left and centre by grape and canister, thus deciding the fate of the day! Ever memorable, perhaps, will this three days' battle be, in which some 400,000 men, with 1,600 guns, contended for mighty interests. "Ten pairs of colours, forty pieces of cannon, and 20,000 prisoners, including about 400 officers and a considerable number of generals, colonels, and majors, are the trophies of this victory," says the French bulletin. "The fields of battle are covered with the slain, among whom are the bodies of several generals."

In gratitude to Lauriston for his share in winning this crowning victory, the emperor with his own hands decorated him with the Grand Gordon of the Iron Crown of Lombardy, which the former had instituted on his coronation at Milan as King of Italy.

The peace, signed at Schönbrunn in October, followed—the peace to win which the Archduchess Maria Louisa was sacrificed to the ambition of the conqueror; and among those who escorted her from Vienna to Paris was Count Lauriston, now colonel-general of the Imperial guard.

Two important missions now devolved in succession upon this trusted officer. The first was one to Holland, to convey to Paris the children of Louis Napoleon, king of that country, who, beginning to doubt his brother's power, placed himself under the protection of Great Britain. The second was as ambassador to Russia, to demand the return of French garrisons into Riga and Revel, with the total exclusion of the British from the Baltic Sea.

Lauriston failed; the stupendous invasion of Russia followed, by an army such as had never been seen before—so perfect in equipment, so vast in numbers, and so gloriously led; but ruin came, and, amid the horrors of the retreat from Moscow, as a staff and artillery officer, multi-farious and brilliant were the services he performed in the cause of his leader. He held conferences with Count Kutusof to save Moscow and secure a peaceful retreat for the united armies of France, but in vain; and when that awful retrograde movement began—a retreat marked by miles upon miles of dead men and horses, abandoned guns, and other *débris*—to him it was that the emperor gave the onerous task of commanding the rearguard upon that darkened, desperate route, in which discipline passed away, and scarcely even courage remained, as Ségur records in his terrible narration.

After reaching Saxony, Lauriston picked out of the ruins of the famished, tattered, and bloodstained mobs of soldiery—the 5th corps of the Grand Army, and led it valiantly to battle at Lutzen, at Boutzen, and elsewhere, and at Leipzig, the results of which decided the retreat of the shattered French army across the Rhine, whither the allies followed them. But there was one mystery in the details of Leipzig. There, the bridge of the Elster was unexpectedly blown up—by an error, some allege; by the treachery of Napoleon, say others, to secure his safe flight, abandoning to the enemy the relics of a column, with which were Count Lauriston, Prince Poniatowski, and Marshal Macdonald.

The latter, a fiery and impetuous Celt, leaped his horse into the river and escaped; but the prince was drowned, with thousands more; and Lauriston, after a long and futile, but most gallant resistance, amid the blazing suburbs of Leipzig, was taken prisoner and sent to Berlin by the Prussians.

The sun of Napoleon was setting now!

On the south-east, Wellington, with 100,000 veterans of the Peninsular war—men who had never failed in battle-menaced France. On the north-east, the allied monarchs, with a million more, soon found their way to Paris, and Napoleon abdicated to Elba, with 400 chosen old soldiers as a bodyguard.

Meantime, Louis XVIII was on the throne of France, and, with enthusiastic loyalty, the fickle Parisians hailed the restoration of the Bourbons, and seemed eager to have the blood of him who had so long been their idol.

Lauriston came to Paris at this crisis. Louis XVIII reconstituted the old Mousquetaires Gris (that famous company of guards, of which Dumas' hero, Claude de Botz d'Artagnan, was commander from 1667 to 1673), and he gave the captaincy to Lauriston, who, true to the old spirit which led him first to serve the monarchy, when Bonaparte landed from Elba, accompanied Louis in his flight, and retired to his *château* near La Fère.

While the avaricious monarchs of Northern Europe were wrangling over the distribution of their spoils, the vast territories won by Napoleon, the latter suddenly left Elba, appeared in France, and the new rule of the Bourbons melted away before the figure of the returning emperor; but Waterloo was soon won, boastful Paris fell again, and, on the second restoration of Louis, Count Lauriston appeared at his court, then held at Cambrai, in the citadel which is deemed one of the strongest in Europe; and on the 17th of August, 1815, the king created him a peer of France, with the command of the infantry of the Garde Royale, when one of the first cares of the Bourbons was to remodel their army and place it on a footing adapted to the new order of things; but when 1830 came, the Royal guard was fated to be dissolved, and the Swiss guard was discharged the service.

In the year 1817 the count was created Marquis of Lauriston, and in the June of 1821 received his *bâton* as Marshal of France, in succession to his veteran comrade, Louis Davoust, Prince of Eckmühl—"the terrible Davoust," a title some of his actions procured him, for he was an excellent soldier but most unprincipled man. With his *bâton* Lauriston received command of the 2nd corps of the army of the Pyrenees, at a time when the whole Peninsula was in commotion, consequent on the embroilment of Ferdinand VII with his people and their new constitution. A French invasion followed; Madrid was occupied; Spain crashed; and Lauriston with his corps laid siege to Pompeluna, which was vigorously defended by Don Raymond de Salvador. It was a case of "war to the knife." The inhabitants barricaded their houses and fought to the death against the troops of Marshal Lauriston, whose dispatch in the *Moniteur* of 16th September gives a graphic account of his successful attack on the suburbs of that great stronghold of Northern Spain, which Salvador soon after surrendered to him.

This was the last scene of his military glory. After being a short time in the ministry, broken down by past campaigns and sufferings undergone in war, he died at Paris, somewhat suddenly, on the 10th June, 1828, with many of his old comrades around his bed, among them the Marshal Dukes of Ragusa and Reggio.

His eldest son, who bore for a time the title of Baron Clapperknowes, from a portion of the Lauriston estate in Lothian, was Gentleman du Roi to Charles X; his second son, Napoleon Law de Lauriston, was author of several historical works and essays; and the family name is still one of importance.

In the time of the Crimean war, Major-General Q. H. Law de Lauriston commanded a brigade of cavalry at Lyon; George Charles Law de Lauriston was *sous*-lieutenant of the 20th Foot Chasseurs; and Arthur Louis Law, his brother, was lieutenant of the 6th Chasseurs, *Cavalerie Légère*, in China. (*Annuaire Militaire*.)

"In the list of promotions," says a correspondent in the *Scotsman*, for September, 1875, "I see Law de Lauriston gets his squadron. He is descended from Mississippi Law, whose renown was once so great in the Rue de Quinquinpoix. The captain's grandfather rose to be marshal, having served under Napoleon in Spain, Germany, and Russia. His marshal's *bâton* is, strange to say, in the collection of a gentleman who is also in possession of the *bâton* of Marshal Saxe."

CHAPTER 29

The Scots in France—(Continued)

In 1784 there was gazetted to the regiment of Dillon, in France, Stephen James Joseph Macdonald, then in his nineteenth year, having been born on the 17th November, 1766.

The regiment of Lord Dillon was the 94th of the old French line, and 3rd of the Irish brigade, placed on the strength of the former in 1690, and, like all the rest of that brigade, wore scarlet uniform, and carried the British crown upon its colours. (*Liste Hist. des Troupes de France.*)

The young *sous*-lieutenant—who had previously been a cadet in the legion of Maillebois—was the son of Neil MacHector Macdonald, a gentleman of the Clan Ronald in Uist, who had been educated at the Scots College in Paris, and had received a lieutenancy in the regiment of Ogilvie, through the recommendation of Prince Charles, as he was one of the hundred and thirty fugitives who, after the horrors of Culloden, had embarked with him on the shore of Loch Nan-Namh in Moidart, near the wild hills amid which he had landed, so full of hope and high enterprise, but the year before!

Macdonald was a subaltern in the regiment of Colonel Dillon till 1792, when the latter was barbarously murdered by the Revolutionists at Lisle, and his soldiery, with all other foreign troops, were turned out of the French army.

A love affair—his engagement to his future wife, the beautiful Mademoiselle Jacob, whose father had joined the Revolutionists—kept Macdonald in France, where he made the first campaign of the new war as a staff-major, and on the 1st March, 1793, was appointed colonel of the ancient regiment of Picardy, and then general of brigade; and as such he served under Pichegru against the allied troops of Britain and Austria, winning high honour by his signal bravery at Comines, in West Flanders, and elsewhere; and on the retreat of the former, after the Austrian Netherlands were overrun, he pressed them hard and followed them into Holland. In that moment, says the *Edinburgh Herald* for 10th January, 1799, discovering a clansman in command of a harassed British brigade, he supplied him with every comfort that circumstances enabled him to afford; till the passage of the Waal on the ice, one of his most remarkable achievements.

The Directory had a dislike of Macdonald and his Scottish surname. For a time they deprived him of his command; the coarse deputy, St. Just, saying to Pichegru, "We like neither his face nor his name—they are not Republican." Yet Pichegru stood his friend; and for his services in Flanders and Holland, he was appointed a general of division, and as such appeared in Italy, but too late to have any part in that aggressive campaign of 1797, when the armies of republican France sought to spread their new and startling principles throughout the Italian states; but in 1798 he was in the army which, under Massena and Berthur, proclaimed the Republic in Rome, and grotesquely sent a tri-coloured cockade to the Pope, who retired to Florence.

Macdonald with his column was left to overawe the states of the Church, and suppress those risings which occurred among the peasantry—risings suppressed with great severity; and towards the end of 1798, as commander-in-chief of the Roman states, he ordered the levy of two regiments of cavalry and one of infantry in each department for the service of the Consulate.

After an incredible deal of toil, manoeuvring, fighting, and remarkable perils almost unequalled in war—through Naples, Calabria, and Sicily, when Cardinal Buffo, Fra Diavolo, Pronio, and other patriots, made savage by the course of events, led thousands from their fastnesses—all loyal and hardy mountaineers, seeking to free their native land from armies of Jacobin invaders, till 40,000 soldiers led by Mack dwindled down to 12,000; when Frenchmen were roasted alive, disembowelled, bound to trees, and left to be devoured by dogs and wolves— after facing horrors such as these, we say, Macdonald fought his way to Florence on the 5th of June, 1799, by forced marches.

Having collected the troops scattered throughout Tuscany, he found himself at the head of 38,000 men, all of whom—with the exception of the Polish legion—were French, and ready for the offensive. He detached Montrichard with his right wing to attack Klenau and raise the siege of Fort Urbino; while Olivier, after two encounters, overcame Hohenzollern, and not only obtained possession of Modena, but drove the Venetians beyond the Po. General Kray, alarmed by the successes of Macdonald's subalterns, drew off his artillery from before Mantua, and took ground in such a manner as, he hoped, to prevent the relief of the city.

But the exploits of Macdonald seemed only beginning. Although severely wounded in a recent action, he continued his march, and, on reaching Piacenza, formed a junction with General Victor, after which he attacked General Ott, on the same day, and compelled him to fall back upon the castle of San Giovanni.

Suwarrow, impatient of delay, and fired by the successes of Macdonald, threatened to storm the citadel of Turin and renew those scenes of carnage so dear to his savage nature; but Furella, who commanded then, defied him, and leaving General Klenau to push the siege, he collected at Alexandria seventeen battalions of Russians, twelve regiments of Austrian horse, three of Cossacks, and hurried on to support General Ott, after which ensued the three days' battle on the Trebur, an impetuous river of the Appenines which falls into the Po above Piacenza.

On the first day, 17th June, Suwarrow, having re-enforced the Imperial right wing, made a sudden attack, with the bayonet chiefly, on the French left, while their right was assailed with equal fury by the Russian Prince Gortchakoff. On this, Macdonald advanced with his centre against the already moving Austrians, but was compelled to fall back beyond the Tidone, covered by the fire of his artillery till nightfall

Early on the dawn of the 18th the allied Russians and Austrians crossed the slender Tidone, and in four great columns hurled their strength against him, as he drew up in order of battle again along the line of the Trebia. As the country was thickly intersected by hedges and ditches, the approach was tedious, the attack difficult; but the van-guard, under Prince Pangrazion, consisting of Cossacks, turned the flank with their bayonets. So dreadful was their charge that 500 Republicans perished there, while the adjutant-general, two colonels, and 600 of the Polish regiment of Dombroceski were taken prisoners; but Macdonald, undismayed and unvanquished, with 10,000 men crossed the river, and, sword in hand, led them up the opposite bank, till repelled by a dreadful cannon and musketry fire, which continued to flash out till eleven at night.

The battle of the third day, 19th June, did not begin till noon, as Macdonald waited for the Ligurians to come up under Lapoype; then, over ground strewn by the dead, the wounded, and the awful *débris* of the two days' previous fighting, the conflict began with freshened fury, when the column of Sweyskowski rushed into action, and, under cover of their batteries, the French forded the Trebia. Long and doubtful was the contest, horrible the carnage, till Melas, the Austrian, brought up his cannon at the critical moment, and Macdonald, with stern reluctance, began his retreat along the right bank of the river, leaving in possession of the enemy the field, where 12,000 of them lay dead, with 700 prisoners, three pairs of colours, and some artillery.

While the defeat of the Count Bellegarde and the surrender of Turin took place elsewhere, Macdonald, to whom we confine ourselves, pursued his march towards Tuscany, and, though still suffering from his wounds, personally directed all the movements of his troops; but finding it impossible to resist the joint attacks of the three great Austrian generals, Ott, Klenau, and Hohenzollern, he marched towards Lucca, to form a junction with Moreau, thus ending an expedition in which the French lost 12,000 men. Says Stephens:

> Yet Macdonald, derived no little glory from the retreat, effected without the surrender of a single battalion, though undertaken after the loss of a pitched battle and in the face of superior forces. (*Hist. of the Wars*, 1803.)

His health was now so impaired, though only in his 34th year, that he was fain to obtain the permission of Suwarrow to visit the baths of Pisa, and by that time the French had lost all their conquests in Naples and on the Adriatic coast.

When they seized on Tuscany, in October, 1800, Macdonald's column was stationed in the country of the Grisons, prepared to scale the Rhetian Alps and advance to succour their comrades in Italy. Crossing the Splügen—the usual way from the Grisons to Como—setting his soldiers the example, shovel in hand, to cut a passage through the snow, he was ready to turn the enemy's lines on the Mincio and Adige. Ere long he was in possession of the mountains of the Tyrol, hovering between Italy and Germany. He made himself master of Trent, and when the treaty of Treviso put an end to the war, he returned to Paris, in January, 1801.

There his opposition to certain measures of Napoleon caused him to be sent as minister to Denmark, and, notwithstanding all his bravery, loyalty, and endurance, *his Scottish name*, his sympathies for the banished Moreau, caused his omission from the list of the marshals of

MEETING OF NAPOLEON AND MACDONALD
AFTER WAGRAM

France created by Napoleon; and till 1809 he remained in retirement and forgotten.

In that year he received command of a division in the corps of Eugène Beauharnais, in the army of Italy, crossed the Isolo on the 15th of April, and defeated the Austrians at Goritz, in the Littorale, or coast-land, and without delay he joined the Grand Army of the emperor before the gates of Vienna. After fighting at Wagram, where 36,773 men of both armies bled on the field, and where corpses in every variety of uniform floated in hideous masses down the Danube, and when never was the headstrong valour of Macdonald[1] more conspicuous, he was embraced by Napoleon, who exclaimed, "Now, Macdonald, for life and death we are together!" He received his *bâton* of marshal. Says Bourrienne's editor:

> Among all the marshals of France, there is not one character so pure from every stain on a soldier's character, so daringly honest to Napoleon in his prosperity, so lastingly true to him in adversity, as this, his only Scottish officer.

After Wagram, he commanded in the Duchy of Grätz, in Lower Styria, when Napoleon became the husband of Maria Louisa, and was in the zenith of his power.

After serving with distinction in the Peninsular war, when he co-operated with Sachet at the siege of Tortosa, and possessed himself of Figueras, he marched at the head of the 10th Corps, of which the Prussian army formed only a part, on the terrible invasion of Russia, and, with orders to occupy the line of Riga and threaten St. Petersburg, he occupied the capital of Livonia in conjunction with a British naval force. The invasion part became a failure. On the 13th of December, 1812, he was abandoned by the Prussians in the face of the enemy, but by that time all was lost elsewhere, and the retreat from flaming Moscow began.

In 1813 Macdonald commanded an army in Saxony, when, at Mercebourg, he defeated the same Prussians who had abandoned him in the previous year; and the dreadful Battle of Leipzig soon followed—that three days' battle, when 340,000 men closed in the strife. France was defeated, a retreat to the Rhine became unavoidable, and the orders were issued for it at nightfall; but the execution was slow, and—whether by treachery or design will never now be known—the

---

1. *Recollections of Marshal Macdonald, Duke of Tarentum* by Jacques Macdonald also published by Leonaur.

bridge of the Elster was blown up while Macdonald and his corps were still defending Leipzig.

He threw himself into the river and escaped, to reach Napoleon, who continued his retreat to Mayence with the wretched relics of a shattered host, whose spirit was now dead, though a few under Macdonald, at the Battle of Hanau, made that last stand which was born of despair. Hope fled! The allies were closing on Paris, but Macdonald, true to the instincts of his loyal father, adhered to the fallen emperor, and the energy with which he espoused his cause at Fontainebleau embarrassed even the Emperor of Russia.

"I shall *never* forget the faithful services you have rendered me," said the Emperor Napoleon, who presented to him the magnificent robes he had received from Murad Bey at the battle of Mont Tabor in Egypt. (*Bourrienne*, etc.)

"Sire!" exclaimed Macdonald, "if ever I have a son this sabre shall be his noblest heritage."

He was now named Councillor of War and Chevalier of St. Louis; and, on the 6th June, peer of France by Louis XVIII; yet, when Napoleon landed from Elba, the first to join him was Macdonald, after seeing to the safe flight of the luckless king, whom he accompanied as far as Menin. The Imperial army crumbled into dust at Waterloo, and in 1818 Macdonald was one of the four marshals who had command of the Royal guard.

In 1825 he visited Scotland, and expressed to Scott, Jeffery, and Cockburn, in Edinburgh, "his pride that he had Scottish blood in his veins."

He visited the fields of Prestonpans, Bannockburn, and Culloden, and everywhere was welcomed with Highland ardour and hospitality, particularly at Armidale, where he was welcomed by the Macdonald clan in full tartan array, and saluted by fifteen pieces of cannon. At Castle Tiorin there was presented to him an aged clansman, Alaster Macdonald, who had fought by his father's side in the memorable '45.

After his return to France he lived a life of peace and seclusion, and died in his 75th year, on the 24th September, 1840, at his *château* near Courcelles.

The Duke of Tarentum was thrice married; first, as we have stated, to Mademoiselle Jacob, one of the most beautiful girls in France, by whom he had two daughters, one married to the Duke of Massa, in Italy, and one to the Comte de Perregoux. "He married, secondly,

Madame Joubert, formerly Mademoiselle Montholon, widow of his comrade, the brave General Joubert, who was slain in battle against Suwarrow at Novi, 16th August, 1799. By her he had one daughter, afterwards the Marchioness de Rochedragon. He married, thirdly, Madame de Bourgaing, widow of the ambassador, Baron de Bourgaing. They had two children; to the joy of the old marshal, one of them was a son, whom he named Alexander, who in October, 1824, was held at the baptismal font by H.M. Charles X and Madame the *Dauphinesse*, and who now inherits the dukedom of Tarentum and the sabre of Mont Tabor. Such was the career of Stephen Macdonald, the son of an obscure fugitive from the fatal field of Culloden." (*Biog. Universelle*, etc.)

We might think that the time had gone past when Scotsmen would enter the French service, but it is not quite so. Thus we find two at least in it—one during the Franco-Prussian war. Captain Ogilvie; and another in 1886, Baron Brown de Colstoun of Haddingtonshire, giving evidence as Rear-Admiral before the Budget Committee at Paris, on torpedoes.

The latter title is singular, as the only child and heiress of the last laird of the ancient line of Colstoun was married in 1805 to George, ninth Earl of Dalhousie, whose family represent it.

David Stuart Ogilvie, latterly staff captain of the French army, was the eldest son of Thomas Ogilvie of Corrimory, Inverness-shire. He had formerly been a lieutenant in the 20th Madras Native Infantry (or old 2nd Regiment), and in 1855 was captain of division in our Land Transport Corps in the Crimea. Subsequently he engaged in mercantile pursuits. These proving unfortunate, he joined the French army during the memorable war with Germany, but, though having only the nominal rank of captain, received, in the confusion consequent on military reverses, the important command of a battalion. He served with it at the defence of Paris, and led several brilliant sorties, in one of which he fell, mortally wounded.

Previous to this, "he had been attached to the army of the Loire, giving, it is said, M. Gambetta a plan of the campaign; but, as has been seen," adds the *Elgin Courant*, "he has died of his wounds, a brave and gallant soldier, which he had also showed himself to be in the Crimean war."

He was then in his 39th year, *and capitaine d'état* major of the 18th Corps d'Armée.

During the same strife Captain A. Duncan, a retired officer of

French cavalry, was elected commandant of the National Guard at Marseilles, in March, 1871.

Several Scottish names, some curiously misspelled, appear in the French *Annuaire Militaire*, during the Crimean war and about that period; such as Captain Pierre Macintosh, 63rd Regiment; Lieutenant Charles V. MacQueen, 66th Regiment; and L.V. MacQuienie, *chef de bataillon*, 12th Chasseurs à Pied; but these were, no doubt, only of Scottish descent, like Louis Nathaniel Russell, who in 1865 was lieutenant in the *Corps du Génie*, and in 1871 became Minister of War. A native of St. Brienne, in Brittany, his mother was a Scottish lady named Campbell, and he is described as possessing "the cold phlegm of an Englishman with the clever prudence of a Scotsman."

In many ways the French still remember kindly the old alliance, which placed the double tressure of *fleur-de-lys* round the Royal arms of Scotland.

"*Fier comme un Ecossais!*" (proud as a Scotsman) is still proverbial, with reference to the dashing men-at-arms of the Archer Guard, the fiery Highlanders and the stubborn ranks of Lowland pikemen and musketeers, who as Soldiers of Fortune upheld the glory of France— memories more particularly retained in the southern provinces, where Republicanism is less than elsewhere. Says General Stewart of Garth:

> The appearance of the Highland regiments revived these recollections, and when travelling through Gascony, Languedoc, and Provence, in 1814, I generally found that the mention of my name met with a desire to know if I was from Scotland, accompanied by many observations on the friendly connection which subsisted between France and Scotland, concluding with an expression of sincere regret at the interruption of that ancient intimacy.

Curiously enough, the French have never forgotten the predilection of their Scottish allies for the national haggis, which they still name *Pain bénit d'Ecosse*, or "the blessed bread of Scotland."

In Paris some relics of the ancient alliance still linger in the names of the thoroughfares; *viz*., the Rue d'Edimbourg, the Rue d'Ecosse, a street opening off the Rue St. Hillier; and the Rue Marie Stuart, now in New Paris, lying between the Rue Montorgueil and the Rue St. Denis.

In conclusion, we cannot do better than quote a French tribute to Scotland, taken from the *Temps* for 1887, when noticing a recent historical work by the well-known French scholar, M. Weisner. Says the *Temps:*

> When visiting Scotland, he was much struck by the friendly feeling for France still kept up in that noble country. Old ties between France and Scotland have never been forgotten in Edinburgh. The recollection of us is upheld there, through that of Mary Queen of Scots. Every spot which speaks of her speaks also of *us*. She was *our* Queen before she was Queen of the Scots. The fidelity of this sympathy is shown not only by the cordial welcome which all our compatriots receive, but by the tone of nearly all the Scottish press towards us. At times, when the London papers attack us most strenuously, when questions of foreign policy excite the national susceptibilities against us, the Scottish papers are absolutely free from a single word injurious to France! This reserve is so rare throughout *the rest of the world*, that it deserves our special gratitude and kindest recognition.

www.ingramcontent.com/pod-product-compliance
Lightning Source LLC
Chambersburg PA
CBHW032044080426
42733CB00006B/188